Dynamics of Caste, Religion, Culture and Politics: The Struggle of the Namasudras of Bengal, 1872-1971

Dynamics of Caste, Religion, Culture and Politics: The Struggle of the Namasudras of Bengal, 1872-1971

Rohidas Mondal

Foreword by
Prof. Chhanda Chatterjee

ABHIJEET PUBLICATIONS
NEW DELHI 110002

ABHIJEET PUBLICATIONS
4658-A, First Floor, Ambika Bhawan,
21 Ansari Road, New Delhi 110002
Phone: 011-23259444
E-mail: abhijeetpublication@gmail.com

DYNAMICS OF CASTE, CULTURE AND POLITICS: THE STRUGGLE OF THE NAMASUDRAS OF BENGAL, 1872-1971

First Published 2021

ISBN 978-81-953707-3-3

PRINTED IN INDIA

Published by J.K. Singh for Abhijeet Publications, New Delhi-110002, Lasertypeset by Abhijeet Typesetters, New Delhi and Printed at Milan Enterprises, New Delhi.

For my parents

who grew me up,

taught me to face challenges in society,

encouraged me enough in academic aspiration,

For Namasudras

who suffered a lot from social injustice.

Foreword

Dr. Rohidas Mondal's study of the Namasudras is a unique addition to the literature on the *Dalits* (depressed classes) in that it embodies the caste pride of this peasant caste, gives an insight into their cultural life and examines the privations suffered by this caste since the partition of their province. The treatment faced by them in the newly created East Pakistan immediately after the partition of Bengal demolishes the argument advanced by Joya Chatterji that the partition had been made inevitable by the unwillingness of the Bengali Hindu upper castes to accommodate the aspirations of the rising Muslim bourgeoisie. The agrarian caste of Namasudras, lying dispersed in several districts of East Pakistan, had huge chunks of cultivable land in their possession. They had always sided with the Muslims during the process of transfer of power and tied their fortunes with the Muslim League. They shared the same grievances against the superciliousness of the Hindu upper castes as the Muslims. Their leader Jogendranath Mandal had dreamt of a shared future of peace and progress in the newly created East Pakistan. But even before the ink was dry on the Partition Award, they had to confront brutal attacks on their lives, property and the honour of their women. The Nehru-Liaqat Agreement had left no room for the exchange of population. Thus it left them no option but to seek shelter on the Indian side of the border as refugees.

The Namasudra experience as refugees on the other side of the border was no less unpleasant. West Bengal was already choked with the problem of providing for the refugees and the economy of the province was approaching collapse. Bengal economy was still gasping under the impact of the man-made famine of 1943 and the scarcities and inflation following the Second World War. The refugees were therefore dispersed in Uttar Pradesh, Dandakaranya of Orissa and the Andaman and Nicobar Islands. The infrastructure and environment of Dandakaranya was so uncongenial that some of the refugees tried to escape to the Marichjhapi area of the Sundarbans only to be repulsed forcibly by the then CPI(M) led West Bengal government.

Today the Namasudras are a disgruntled lot. They are wooed by political parties on the eve of each election. But their main demand to integrate them in one place as a solid block in one province, so that they could wield more political influence for themselves has not yet been met. Namasudras also had their social aspirations expressed through the myth that they were the descendants of the sage Lomas or Namas, who had forgotten to usher them into brahminhood through *upanayana*, which resulted in their degradation into *Sudra* or low caste status. But their name still retains an indication of their high caste ranking in the prefix *namah*, which means worthy of respect. Upper caste unwillingness to take cognizance of this vital fact led them to evolve into a breakaway sect called *Matua* which was a new form of *Vaishnavism*, which taught absolute devotion to Lord Krishna and tolerance for all human beings. Dr. Mondal has provided certain insights into the workings of this society as an insider of this unique cult.

Dr. Mondal had started his work with me as a doctoral student of Visva-Bharati. But he had very clear cut views of his own from the very beginning and refused to toe the familiar line. He worked with an extraordinary love for the upliftment of his community and the presentation of its case before the literate world. I hope the publication of this work will fulfil his long-cherished dream.

Prof. Chhanda Chatterjee

Former Professor of History and
Director of Centre for Guru Nanak Studies
Visva-Bharati, Santiniketan

Acknowledgements

This book form of my thesis, *'The Evolution of a Peasant Caste: The Namasudra Community of Bengal 1872-1971'* has been submitted to Visva Bharati for the degree of PhD. under the supervision of Professor Chhanda Chatterjee. I am indebted to Professor Chhanda Chatterjee, my heartiest supporter and guide, without whose constant inspiration, rectification and verification of the typescripts, this book would not have been this book. Professor Rup Kumar Barman, the examiner and exacting critic of my study, whose comments, valuable suggestions and encouraging feedback inspired me to study this field of research. I cannot repay the debt of gratitude to my guide and my examiner and critic.

I am grateful to the Excellency of Prof. Sekhar Bandyopadhyay who has provided a wonderful study on Namasudras to inspire the scholars who have interest in studying this community. I am thankful to those Namasudras who supplied me with oral sources and shared their collective memories with me to enrich the source materials of this book. I also take this opportunity to convey my sincere thanks to my colleagues, at Dr Bhupendranath Dutta Smriti Mahavidyalaya, who extended their sincere co-operation for my study. The staff at Visva-Bharati Library, Kolkata National Library,

Burdwan Central Library, my college Library, and my friends for being helpful and supportive of my study. I am grateful to the UGC authority for financial support in the form of a Minor Research Project Grant. I am thankful to J.K. Singh of Abhijeet Publications for undertaking the burden of publication of this book.

I am proud of my Maa Golapi Rani Mondal and Baba Lt. Mukunda Mondal, who has taught me to face challenges and difficulties to lift with an academic aspiration in a miserable socio-economic background. I am thankful to my brothers, sisters and wife for their love and support for my academic work. And finally for my little daughter Anubha who always supplies me with a source of pleasant and refreshing pastime. I hope she will criticize my study during her higher education after going through this book. Despite having many supports, there must be many inaccuracies in this book for which I shall alone be responsible.

June 11, 2021
Burdwan

Dr Rohidas Mondal
Assistant Professor,
Department of History,
Dr. Bhupendra Nath Dutta Smriti Mahavidyalaya,
Hatgobindapur, Burdwan, W.B, PIN-713407
E-mail: rohidasmondal@gmail.com

Contents

Abbreviations

AASU	All Assam Student Union
ABDCA	All Bengal Depressed Castes Association
ABHPA	Agailjhara Bhegai Halder Public Academy
AISCF	All India Scheduled Caste Federation
AIDCA	All India Depressed Classes Association
AMPO	Authority of Andhra Pradesh, Chhattisgarh and Orissa
AANS	All Assam Namasudra Samiti
BPSCF	Bengal Provincial Scheduled Castes Federation
BDCA	Bengal Depressed Class Association
BNA	Bengal Namasudra Association
CPI (M)	Communist Party of India (Marxist)
DDA	Dandakaranya Development Authority
DCA	Depressed Castes Association
EIRC	East India Refugee Council
HM	Hindu Mahasabha
INC	Indian National Congress
KMP	Krishak Mazdoor Party

MM	Matua Mahasangha,
ML	Muslim League
MLA	Member of Legislative Assembly
NHS	Namasudra Hitaishini Samiti
SC	Scheduled Caste
SCF	Scheduled Caste Federation
ST	Scheduled Tribe
NVBKP	Nikhil Banga Bastuhara Karmi Parishad
SBBKP	Sara Bangla Bastuhara Karmi Parisad
SBBS	Sara Bangla Bastuhara Samiti
PBBS	Purba Bharat Bastuhara Sansad
UCRC	United Central Refugee Council

Introduction

Caste/*Varna* is about a three thousand years old phenomenon in India. With the rapid spread of education, modernization and urbanization, it is expected that the importance of caste should diminish. But it was again boosted up in post-independent India particularly after the publication of the Mandal Commission's report (1990). Caste discrimination has drawn the attention of modern researchers as the presence of social hierarchy and caste prejudice in Indian society led the minority upper castes to exploit and abuse the majority lower caste communities of India. But these majority caste communities can play a vital role in India's national progress if they can enjoy all the opportunities in society with freedom. The religious, social and political opportunities of the majority castes are controlled by the minority upper castes. The history of scheduled castes (SC), scheduled tribes (ST) and other backward castes (OBC) in India are not reflected with much more attention to the discourse of social scientists and historians of the privileged castes due to the presence of caste discrimination.

However, the caste conflict and the history of the lower castes communities of Bengal have drawn the attention of the current researchers, as these have flowed differently unlike deprived castes of other provinces of India. Even the caste classification of Bengal does not match with the caste system of other provinces. Moreover, the caste culture and caste conflict of Bengal had been different from the other parts of India. Those who were known as Chandals in Bengal were not Chandals, it was imposed on them for social jealousy. They were the Namashudras whose ethnic, social and religious characteristics never matched with those of the so-called Chandals of other provinces in India. The so-called historians left no explanation of ethnic, religious, cultural and social features of this community.

In other words, the majority of the deprived Hindu castes in Bengal were Namashudras.The anti-caste movement of Namasudras in Bengal is in many ways a part of the scheduled caste movement of India. Many also questioned whether this Namashudra community was Hindu or not. If they were not Hindus then what was their religion? What is the basis of their current religious, cultural and social features? Did the Sanskritization[1] take place in Bengal or not? The socio-cultural and anthropological features of the Namasudras are almost similar to the Hindu gentry but why are the Namasudras treated as lowest of the mankind?

The Namashudra community is distinctive in socio-religious and anthropological features among the scheduled caste communities in Bengal such as Rajbangshi, Shundi, Dom, Malo, Chamar, Karmakar, Dhopa, Methar, Muchi etc. Namasudras are the second largest community among the deprived Hindus of Bengal. Those who revolutionized the social, cultural and religious spheres of this community are not mentioned anywhere in Indian history. The common Indian researchers know about Periyar, Ambedkar but they know a little about the contribution of Harichand, Guruchand. But their contribution to the cultural and anti-caste movement of Bengal is undeniable. This community still plays an important role in the present socio-political and cultural spheres of Bengal but they are still considered as a neglected and hated caste in the privileged society. Therefore, the contemporary researchers among the deprived castes are curious about exactly what the Namasudras' original history was. So it deserves necessary research on this community.

This study looks at the origin of caste discrimination, the social awakening and the struggle of the Namasudras for socio-economic, educational, cultural and political rights as well as for the progress of the Indian nation. It examines the derivation of caste's name, the process of deprivation, the effort for assimilation and integration, the caste consciousness, and the progress of the Namasudras. The study is divided into five consecutive chapters besides the introduction and conclusion. A review of the pan-Indian caste system/the four-tier *Varna* classification and the foundation of the caste system in Bengal have been included in the introductory part of the study for understanding the social position of the Namasudras.

The Caste System in India

The institution of caste is not a religion, not a political organization but its scopes and influences have been infinitive in Indian society. The caste system had preserved the mastery of the privileged castes over the Shudras, Dalits and OBCs. It has been the basis of all discriminations and inequalities in Indian societies.[2] It has originated from the categorization of the Indo-Aryan society in about 1500 BCE and has extended, later, all over the Indian continent. Initially, the Aryans formed a four-tier *Varna* system for occupational classification and their separation from the Shudras. But it extends too many features over the years. The word *'Varna'* is used generally as *jati* and it is used habitually as an alternate of the English word caste. The word 'caste' has been derived from the Portuguese 'casta' and it has been used in Europe to designate different classes.[3]

Properly it is something not mixed, and it is used in the sense of race by the Spaniards and the Portuguese for the first time, and it has been applied to the people of India later (mid- 15th century).[4] The word *'Varna'* was published for the first time in *Purusha Sukta* in Rig-Veda. The literary meaning of *Varna* is colour. The four colours, white, red, yellow, and black, had been symbolized as the four castes Brahman, Kshatriya, Vaisya, and Shudra respectively for qualifying castes.[5]

There are many theories of caste origin in India. According to mythological theory, the Brahman, Kshatriya, Vaishya, and Shudra sprang from the mouth, arms, thigh, and feet of Brahma respectively.[6] The Hindus believed that the almighty Brahma himself created a four-tier Varna system based on the quality of the human.[7] According to *Purana* (Vayu and Markandeya), different qualities/ *gunas* have been the responsible factors for the creation of various castes. The qualities of *sattva, raja, tama* and its mixture make castes of Brahman, Kshatriya, Vaisya and Shudra. The Brahmin comes off with the quality of *sattva*/goodness, Kshatriyas with *raja* /passion, Vaisya with *raja/tama*/ passion/darkness, and Shudra with *tama* /darkness only.[8] According to age theory, all castes had been created based on *Satya/Krita, Tretâ, Dvapara,* and *Kali* and its' nature, where four ages symbolized the age of Brahman, Kshatriya, Vaisyas, and Shudras respectively. The *Upanishads, Smriti Shastras,* and Brahmin literature stated that the four Varnas had been categorized hierarchically based on occupational skill in the Rig-Vedic times (1800 BCE-1000 BCE). But the Aryans had changed the skill-oriented *Varna* system into birth-oriented in later Vedic times (1000 BCE-600 BCE), which has been continuing for centuries with the effort of the privileged castes.

The Brahman literature and scriptures have prescribed that the Kshatriyas/Rajanyas be responsible for the protection of the state and the Vaisyas for the work of cultivation and business. The Shudra had not provided the right to education and intellectual activities but to work manually and service to other *Varnas*. The fifth *Varna*/untouchable/*Asprisya* had been included in the caste system in medieval times with the idea of impureness and imperfection. The Hindus have accepted all the mythological, sociological and occupational theories as to the basis of social precedence, and it has been impossible to clarify all features of the caste system, as now existing, without reference to these theories.[9] According to the anthropological survey of India, 4635 separate caste communities and 635 tribes, with a diverse cultural feature, have been identified all over India.[10]

Caste has multidimensional aspects. It has been related to society, economics, politics, and cultural influences. A low caste is always considered as low on a social scale even after holding the highest position in an institution. It does not matter a person's economic, political and intellectual position because of the social mindset of the privileged castes of the Hindu society. All the Hindus except some liberal-minded persons believe in caste even today, so studies on caste have been going on over the centuries.

Origin of Caste Discrimination in India

Caste discrimination emerged from the legitimization of birth oriented caste system of later Vedic times in India. The mythological and sociological theory of the caste origin of the Aryans and its implementation to the *Varna* system of later Vedic times (1000BCE-600BCE) legitimized the caste discrimination in India. The Aryans/ Brahmins had apprehended the opportunities to have been as the supreme castes in Indian society for which they changed the skill-oriented caste system of early Vedic times into birth oriented in the later Vedic times. They reserved the highest opportunities for them forever.

Since Vedic times, they have been the most respectable caste having all good rights. They have been as the guru, masters of education, and conductor of rituals-ceremonies in Indian society, placing the other castes in the second, third, and fourth rank for Kshatriya, Vaisya, and Shudra, respectively based on *Varnas/jatis*, occupations, colours, etc. They classified the first three *Varnas/jatis* as twice-born /*dvija* and the last one, non-Aryans /aborigine demon/*das*/ *dasyu* /of India as many times born. Conquering the black aborigines/ fourth *Varna*, the fair Aryans had denoted the black aborigine as a slave.

The Brahmans had been as the priestly class and assigned the duties of officiating rituals, studying Veda, receiving gifts, drinking soma, teaching students, and giving alms. They had the rights to exclusive access to all higher religious, secular learning and knowledge'.[11] So their social position was higher than all the other castes. They could have been as the supreme caste in social hierarchy wearing matted locks as birth without perceiving the noble truths or true Brahmin.[12]

The castes who were a warrior in occupation had been categorized as Kshatriya and entrusted with administration and protection of the people, the duties of protecting people, kingdom, treasures, life and supporting the king and Brahmins won the rights to studying, sacrificing, giving alms, using weapons, and participating in rituals. Their responsibility was to assure good government and security of the nation. Their social position had been lower than that of the Brahman, but higher than that of the Vaisyas and Shudras. The Vaisyas and Shudras used to pay taxes to the king of Kshatriyas for the maintenance of the states. Their function was both executive and legislative. The lower castes, for some time, became elevated to the status of the Kshatriya through increasing political influence. The Gond had been a tribe, successfully asserted themselves as Kshatriya after gaining political power in a tract of central India, which proved the deficiency of *Varna* classification.[13]

The Vaishyas had been assigned the duties of looking after the trade, agriculture, and commerce of the state. They had been allowed for studying, sacrificing, giving alms, cultivating land, tending cattle, lending money and responsibility to ensure good production in the state. They had been allowed for *Upanayana*, which referred to them as *'Dvija'*. They had to pay taxes to the two upper castes, the landlords under which they had been as tenants. Their social position had been lower than the Brahman and the Kshatriya and superior to the Shudras.

Shudras had been prescribed to serve the upper three castes performing manual works in cultivation, scavenging, washing, artisanal work and leather dressing. They had been treated as serfs and placed lowest on the social scale. They had been divided into touchable and untouchable based on occupational statuses. The scavengers had been considered as untouchable, and as the 'fifth *Varna*' which has been abolished under article 17 of the Indian Constitution. They had not been allowed to study and listen to Vedic chants, eat with higher castes and perform duties in rituals with Brahmins, Kshatriyas, and Vaishyas. The fifth *Varna* / Untouchable /*Asprisya*/ *Achchut* had been included in caste features in the medieval period but it came from the very ancient idea of pollution.[14] It had been practised since time immemorial with the concept of impurity by privileged castes who initiated the practice of exploitation for the manual workers who had to engage in low-status works. The idea of untouchability had emerged from the continuation of eating cow flesh which was prohibited by the privileged castes. Someone of the Gupta kings (fourth century CE) banned the consumption of cow flesh and considered it a sin.[15] But the king did not ban the consumption of buffalo flesh as it was black.[16]

Various caste laws and orders grew amongst diverse castes/*jatis* in Indian society over years. Even many caste restrictions grew within a particular caste itself. For example, a leatherworker and a sweeper are both untouchable but a leatherworker would not degrade himself by eating or drinking with the sweeper nor would he consider marrying his daughter with a sweeper's son. The untouchables have been prohibited from eating, seating, marrying, even moving with other caste members. They were treated as impure in the body and imperfect in works. Even their shadow pollutes others in the consideration of privileged castes. All these caste discriminations influenced Indian society so much that the attempts of the government often failed to upset the established order of caste for allowing children from untouchables to attend school.[17]

The four-tier *Varna* system did not subsume all the occupational groups in India. The '*Varna* scheme' refers at best only to the broad categories of the society and not to its real and effective units'.[18] In place of four castes, thousands of castes and sub-castes grew in pre-colonial India. The four divisions of *Varnas/Jatis* led to germinate thousands of castes based on lineage, occupations, marriage, and social status of Indians. The Hindu scriptures/*Manusmriti* prescribed *Anulam* marriage (between highborn man and lowborn woman) as legal and *pratiloma* marriage (between a highborn woman and lowborn man) as illegal. It treated *pratilom* married couples and their children as outcastes, irreligious and low statuses. Over the years, *protilom* intermarriage has resulted in thousands of ill-legal hybrid people according to the marriage theory of *Manusmriti*. They all had been treated as out-castes and untouchables. These people accepted the caste laws and orders and habituated with the idea of caste restrictions due to their social belief and lack of social consciousness.

A caste, in this system, has generally distinguished with common laws and orders, name, *gotra,* origin, occupation, birth, ceremonies, tutelary deity, and exclusive commensality. The term *gotra* signifies clan/lineage/ a broader kin-unit tracing its descent from a real fictive progenitor, but it was not without significance that in the Rig Veda, the meaning of *gotra* was 'cow-pen 'and not lineage.[19] *Gotra* has been sub-divided into blood-related groups, kindred/ *banshas*. It has originated in the names of Sages/ *Risis,* like Kasyapa, Vasistha, Bhrigu, Goutama, Bharatdavaja, Atri, and Viswamitra *Muni*. Their number was seven/ eight. They all were Brahmin by caste. It is undoubtedly an all-India phenomenon in the sense that there is everywhere 'hereditary, endogamous groups which form a hierarchy, and that each of these groups has a traditional association with one or two occupations'.[20]

The Hindu caste laws and orders have been various in different parts of India and it has created various difficulties over the years. It has created a terrible burden before the development of the deprived castes. This burden has been most terrible on untouchables. The gradual stratification of caste, religion, social statuses, and economic activities are involved with the political issues in colonial and post-colonial times. The birth-oriented occupational reservation system and its continuation have led the Indians to be complex, discriminatory, and disintegrated. It has created many obstacles before the holistic development of the Indian people and nation.

The Foundation of Caste System in Bengal

A variety of castes and caste restrictions grew in all towns and villages of India with distinctive features by the effort of the privileged castes. India itself has been a land of diversity. Hence, to have varieties of castes and caste laws and orders in this country is relevant. Bengal had been a prosperous province of India having enough wealth, fertile lands, liberal folk culture and rich social practices which attracted all the invaders to India including Aryans. The indigenous people of ancient Bengal believed in various indigenous folk cultures, customs, and practices having no discrimination before the spread of Aryans' ritual culture. The indigenous people of Bengal had no communication with the four-tier *Varna* system in ancient times.[21] The people of Bengal had been influenced by the religious practice and cultures of Buddhism and Jainism which had an appeal to social equality. But the Brahmans/descendant of Aryans influenced the indigenous people of Bengal with their social system of caste discrimination. They led the indigenous people to be divided into many castes with discrimination after settled in Bengal.

They also were divided into many social gradations but these had been rarely expressed publicly.[22] In the pan Indian caste system, their sub-castes were *Utkal, Rarhi, Barendri, Kanya Kubja, Tamil, Tanjore,* etc. In Bengal, the Brahmans were divided broadly into *Kulin* and non-*Kulin* Brahman with distinctive features. The non-Kulin Brahmins/ *Srotriya* had been divided into *Siddha, Sadhya,* and the *Kashta* sub-castes. The pro-Brahman king Ballal Sen founded *kulinism* in Bengal for Brahmans. Though, Kulinism had not been confined only to Brahman castes but also other castes. In Bengal, *Kulinism* had been in practice amongst *Kayastha* and *Satgop* also.[23]

The *Kulin* Brahmins had been considered as higher than the Non-*Kulin* Brahmins. The marriage had been restricted between them. A *Kulin* Brahman could choose a bride from *Siddha, Srotriya,* and *Sadhya*. A *Siddha* Brahman had been prohibited to choose a bride from

Kashta. He could marry a bride from his sub-caste and *Sadhya*. A *Kashta* Brahman could marry the only bride from his sub-caste. A *Kulin* woman could marry only a *Kulin* man. A *Siddha* woman could marry a man of her sub-caste and *Kulin*.[24]

The Brahmans emigrated and settled in Bengal in early medieval times under the support of the Bengal kings.[25] According to *Tamrasasan* and some inscriptions, many Brahmans came to Bengal and settled in the villages, and lands that were provided by the Bengal kings/rich men and over the years the Brahman had been divided into *Radi, Barendra*, Vedic, *Sakdwipi*, etc.[26] The Brahmans had titled themselves in the name of their settlement places and villages. For example, their title Bandyopadhyay has originated from the village Bandyogati (in Birbhum) adding *Upadhyay*/pundit with it (Bandyo+upadhyay), Mukhopadhyay from the village Mukhoti (in Bankura), Chattopadhyay from the village Chatuti (in Barddhaman), Gangopadhyay from the village Gangory/Ganguli (in Barddhaman).[27] In the same way, their titles Pututunda, Pipolai, Bhattasali, Kusary Maschatak, Batbyal Ghoshal, Maitrya Lahiri, etc. originated from the name of their settlement places.[28] Many Brahmans settled in Bengal having no women with them. These Brahmans might marry the women of the indigenous people and led the formation of various castes and communities in Bengal. After the foundation of *kulinism* in Bengal, they could marry many times following the legitimization of polygamy. They could choose young girls from any castes/communities including Dom, Hadi, Muchi, and Chandal. The Muslims followed the *Kulin* Brahman as their rulers encouraged them to polygamy.[29] Their descendants had been categorized into many castes in Bengal.

The living style and ideology of the Brahmans had been appreciated by the Bengal kings but the Brahmans sometimes violated their ideal social laws and orders.[30] Their violation of endogamous laws might lead to the formation of more castes communities in Bengal. The five Brahmans, who were invited and supported by Bengal king Adisur, accompanied some servants whose descendants were categorized as *Karan/Kayastha/Uttam Sankar* and their titles had been Ghosh, Bose, Guha, Mitra, and Dutta.[31] *Brahma Vaivarta Purana* and *Manusanhita* illustrated that the *Vaidyas/Ambastha* had begotten from the womb of Kshatriya wife of Brahman and their descendants took the occupation of treatment and producing medicine, and they had been considered as Brahman caste in the four-tier Varna system, but they had not been considered as Brahman in Bengal for their practice of dissection of a dead body which was a work of impurity in the consideration of the Brahmans of Bengal.[32]

The people of Bengal are divided into four broad categories. The Brahmins, clean Shudras, unclean Shudras, and untouchables, and within these four categories, there were forty-one *jatis*.[33] The Shudras/ indigenous people had been divided into mainly three categories. (1) *Uttam sankar—Karan/Satsudra, Ambastha/Vaidya, Ugra, Gandhik, Banik, Magadh, Shankhik, Kanshakar, Kumbhakar, Tantubaya, Karmakar, Gop, Das/Chasi, Rajput, Napit, Modak, Barujibi, Sut/Sutradhar, Malakar, Tambuli and Toulik.* (2) *Madhyam Sankar—Takshak, Rajak, Swarnakar, Subarna Banik, Abhir, Tailakarak, Dhebar, Soundik, Nat, Sabak/Sabar, Shekhar and Jalik,* (3) *Adham Sankar—Malegrahi, Kudap, Chandal, Barur, Charmakar, Ghantajibi, Dolbahi, Malla and Taksha.* [34]

Raghunandan Bhattacharya, a traditional *smritikara* of Bengal (16th century CE) categorized the people of Bengal into Brahman, Vaidya, Kayastha, and Shudras with distinctive features. He divided the Shudras into touchable and untouchable and included numerous peasant communities in the category of Shudras. The

Shudras had further been divided into four groups based on restriction of taking food and water—(a)*Satshudra* and *Navasakh*, (b)*Jalacharaniya Shudras*, from whom Brahmans took water, (c)*Jalabyabaharya* Shudras, from whom the Brahmans did not take water, (d)*Asprisya*/ untouchables Sudras whose touch contaminated and polluted even the Ganges water, so the privileged castes avoided contact with these untouchables Shudras.[35]

The pro-Brahmin kings of Bengal encouraged the legitimization of caste discrimination in Bengal. They could degrade and upgrade the people of Bengal according to their self-interest.[36] The Brahmanical prescription legitimized the system of discrimination in the castes in Bengal. Under the legitimization of caste laws and orders, many castes and communities grew in ancient and medieval times in Bengal, including Bagdis, Baitis, Chamars, Chunaris, Chandals, Doms, Dhobis, Duley, Haris Kaibartyas, Shuri's, Poundras, Namasudras, etc. who suffered from social injustices, discriminations, parochialism, prejudice and untouchability for centuries.

The Namasudras had been included in the untouchables/ *Asprisya*/Chandal of Bengal but their anthropological features, traditional social customs, and rituals had not been analyzed in detail to justify their origin and social status. 'No evidence has ever been found for the determination of their identity as Chandal, rather their original customs and rituals determined their originality as higher in status among the people of Bengal.[37] The term 'Chandal' had been merely imposed on the Namasudras for degrading them on the social scale because of jealousy of the privileged castes. But they could not protest against this imposition and humiliation in pre-colonial times due to the deprivation of social rights, light of education, and wealth for centuries.

The Awakening of the Deprived Castes in India

Caste consciousness of the deprived castes emerged from the liberal activities of colonial rulers, missionaries and native reformers who brought the light of liberal social values and ideas in India. They spread the ideas of social equality and occupational liberty among the deprived castes. On the other hand, many leaders among the deprived castes had been influenced by the worldwide renaissance movements. The conscious leaders of Shudras, the untouchable and the other deprived castes dared to move against socio-economic exploitation and domination of the powerful and privileged Hindus who had the interest to continue traditional social laws and orders.

The deprived castes communities moved against the traditional caste laws and orders uniting themselves for claiming their socio-economic rights and respect receiving encouragement from the Europeans. They tried to unite under the platform of their traditional religions, in some areas under Hinduism in the name of a different sect. They faced huge barriers in that endeavour as India's economic and political power is involved in this process of movements. Very few of the untouchables could have reached the ideas of the Buddhist, Bhakti, Vedanta, Sanskritization, religious-secular, and conversion movements due to the social manipulation of the privileged castes. But many leaders and reformers had been enthusiastic to attract the untouchable and deprived castes to reform movements. Many non-Brahmins, anti-caste and anti-untouchability movements took place all over India in the last half of the nineteenth century and the first half of the twentieth century.

The Namasudras had no king power in medieval times when the process of categorization and legitimization of the caste ritual had been going on. They could realize that they had been socially marginalized and branded as untouchable by the Brahman pundits but they could not protest against the social humiliation due to the lack of socio-political power. The situation has been changed by the advent of Europeans in the power structure of India. The Namasudras began to be organized with the encouragement of the liberal colonial rulers in the middle of the 19th century and initiated protest movements against traditional social laws and orders while the Namasudra scholars have raised several questions on the socio-economic, cultural, religious, and political status of the Namasudras. They have realized their deprivation of socio-economic and educational rights due to the exploitation of the privileged castes and Zamindars. Harichand Thakur (1812-1878), belonging to a Namasudra family of the village Orakandi in Faridpur, organized Namasudra/Matua movements, for the first time in Bengal against the domination and exploitation of the Brahmans and Zamindars (1860s CE). His son Guruchand (1846-1937) continued the Namasudra movement being encouraged by his father's philosophical thoughts and liberal values of the European and Australian missionaries. Many Namasudra leaders and reformers including P.R. Thakur, Rasiklal Biswas, and Jogendra Nath Mandal, continued this movement in colonial and post-colonial times.

Not only Bengal but many parts of India witnessed the emergence of caste consciousness and protest movements in colonial times. In south India, Jyotirao Gobindarao Phule (1827-1890), belonging to an obscure backward family of fruit and vegetable growers of a village in Pune in Deccan, was inspired by the colonial rulers who established East India Company's power in Deccan shortly before his birth. He attacked the domination and exploitation of the Brahman religious authority, organizing an active movement against social injustices prevailing in the Hindu society. He organized a variety of social reform movements for their social rights, liberty of women, remarriage of widows, and prevention of infanticide as he noticed that the survival rate amongst children had been poor due to the existence of various social injustices and deprivation of economic rights. For economic prosperity of his people he 'did not simply demand jobs in the British administration but argued for the radical restructuring of that administrative itself, and the transfer of greater power into the hands of sympathetic British administrator, so that the lower castes might be re-educated to a set of Values more secular and egalitarian than those represented in Brahmanic religion as he regarded this as the prerequisite for all other forms of liberation for the lower castes'.[38]

Dr B.R. Ambedkar (1891-1956) initiated the 'Mahad Satyagraha Movement' against social injustices in Maharashtra and extended it all over India. He was born in a backward family of Mahad of Maharashtra but he was able to be one of the great educationists in the world studying MA (twice, 1915, 1916), M.Sc (1921), Barrister-at-law (1922), D.Sc. (1923), Ph.D (1927), LL.D. (1952), D.Lit (1953) abroad. He became a jurist, an economist, a social reformer, an anthropologist, a historian, a sociologist, a social scientist, an educationist, a freedom fighter, a journalist, a human rights activist, and a philosopher. He found that there was no exploitation in western countries based on caste. No one in western countries showed him disrespect for being a man of a lower caste. He was influenced greatly by western social values and ideas and comprehended that the quality of man does not depend on caste but on earning knowledge. This idea and concept inspired him to do something for his homeland. He believed that the caste discrimination is the main barrier before him so he determined to establish the theory 'everybody is equal on account of birth and earning knowledge' in the place of a theory of ancient Indian scriptures which prescribed birth-oriented caste discrimination.

Dr. Ambedkar's first attempt was to find out the fact behind the social injustices in India. He presented a paper on 'Caste in India: Their Mechanism, Genesis and Development' at an anthropology seminar at Columbia University (May 9, 1916). He introduced his movement in India founding the 'South Borough Committee' in 1919 for a universal adult franchise and one man one vote through which he argued that not a single person should be denied the opportunity of participating in the government. He founded *'Bahiskrita Hitakarini Sabha'* in March 1924 to get the socio-economic rights of the depressed castes. A mass movement was organized with gatherings of more than 3000 untouchables to get the right to drink the water of the Choudar tank/ pond in 1927.[39]

The situation of the lower castes in terms of caste discrimination made him worried about their position in free India. He attempted to influence the government for launching some laws of prevention for the depressed castes. He tried to establish before the government that the depressed caste in India is a section of people who are marginalized and victimized by privileged castes who enjoy all the opportunities. Organizing a meeting with the deprived castes in 1927 he burned a copy of the Manusrmiti openly before the public to protest the biased caste system which was prescribed in the scripture.[40] The Shudras were deprived of the sharing of wealth, education, job, and land due to this biased social system prevailing in the scriptures. The women also had been considered as a product of consumption of men on account of prescriptions of Manu.

The depressed castes needed the right to share the wealth and other opportunities for the entire development of the country. The Muslims as a minority group had been given a separate electorate for political rights. In the same way, Dr. Ambedkar demanded a separate electorate for the depressed caste Hindus. He claimed this to the government through different meetings and conferences. The demand for a separate electorate was granted in the British parliament in the round table conference but M.K. Gandhi vowed to keep the depressed people united with the Hindus. He was influenced greatly by the Hinduism of his devoutly religious parents who had been loyal to the Hinduism and *Varna* system. His devout mother was not devoid of the prejudices common among the *Vaishnava* Hindus.[41]

Gandhi ignored the political interest of the depressed castes due to his faith in Hinduism and the holding of a majority of Hindus. The demand for a separate electorate of the untouchable made him worried about the Indian politics and religion of Hinduism.[42] He applied the theory of nonviolence to move against the British but he did not take any step against caste discrimination and inequality, only his focus was on removing untouchability which was less important than political right and economic development of the untouchables. The demand for a separate electorate made him worried about the integration of the Hindus.

Dr. Ambedkar, the strong leader of the Shudras, demanded this separate electorate as he realized that Gandhi and the Congress leaders would never allow the Shudras in sharing political power. His experience showed disrespect to Hinduism. He was aware of the present system of the franchise of the Untouchables who would hardly have voting rights. Consequently, he demanded the removal of uniformity in the franchise because they had no mode of acquiring wealth.[43] The British rulers could not ignore his leadership for the Shudras in the roundtable conference as he already established himself as a lawyer, educational organizer, party builder, and a strong leader of the Shudras. So the demand of his separate electorate was granted in the conference.

Gandhi feared to be a minority of the Hindus to the Muslims and the scheduled castes which could lead to losing political power of the Hindus. Consequently, he started fast unto death to withdraw the recommendation of the separate electorate. On the other hand, Ambedkar was determined to get a separate electorate. He made out that the Sudras had no option to share the political power and the sake of their interest without a separate electorate. But his effort became in vain due to Gandhi's strong opposition. Gandhi made him compelled to compromise with his determined step. Consequently, offering their separate electorate in exchange for Gandhi's life and 151 reserve seats Dr. B.R. Ambedkar was compelled to sign in the Poona Pact in 1932.

The Congress leaders and Hindu gentries considered it as a great success of Gandhi in the question of integration among the Hindus.[44] It was granted in the Indian Act of 1935. The Hindu gentries considered that Gandhi was able to make a nationalist solution to the untouchable problem. On the other hand, the Shudras did not know the actual reason behind the policy of Gandhi and Congress leaders who desired to hold full power without sharing any political rights of the Shudras. The Congress leaders agreed to share the political power with the powerful Muslim community but did not admit the political right to the Shudras.

Many of the thinkers including Dr. B.R. Ambedkar at the time of transferring power were doubtful about the Congress leaders who were loyal to the ancient scriptures but going to take the responsibility of the country. In British Parliament, Churchill expressed his doubt on the ethics and policies of the future Indian rulers after freedom. He criticized the rulers of India as rascals, rogues, and free looters.[45] Ambedkar lamented saying 'It is sin to take birth in such a land whose people are so prejudiced'.[46]

Periyar E. V Ramasamy (1879-1973), father of the Dravidian movement, started the 'Self-Respect Movement'. He realized that the underlying interest of both nationalism and religion was Brahmanic privilege so he never worried about being branded as an antinationalist. Therefore, his call developed in time into a demand for an autonomous Dravida Nadu and establishment of a separate non-Brahmanic Dravidian Nation, as Pakistan[47]. Ambedkar supported Periyar as he believed that everywhere in the country some depressed castes were against Hindu nationalism. Hinduism was not against the interest of the depressed section of Indians but casteism, which was supported by it, was a curse to them. Therefore Hindu nationalism, which was supported by upper-caste Hindus, was an illusion to them. Hence, for Ambedkar, the idea of the Dravidistan of Periyar was suitable for all the deprived castes of India.

The deprived Sikhs initiated 'Adi-dharma Movement' in the 1920s in Punjab, with the consciousness of Gurbanta Singh belonging to a village of Jalandhar district and Mango Ram of a village in Hoshiarpur district in Punjab, who were influenced by the ideas of the British ethnographic classification and notions that the caste system originated through encounters between Dravidian and Aryan races.[48] It was against untouchability, social injustices, and exploitation. It had established a fact that 'the untouchable castes were capable of mobilizing for their benefits, and of organizing in a way that permitted them to compete under the condition that governs the socio-political areas at large'.[49] Thus, many movements against social injustice throughout the Indian continent created awareness among the backward castes in colonial times. But their movement could not draw much more attention from the Indian historical writers of privileged castes due to the presence of caste discrimination in Indian society.

Historical Writings on Namasudras of Bengal

The European scholars initiated historical and scientific studies on the caste and communities of Bengal from the beginning of the nineteenth century (1807-1814). It was started by Francis Buchanan Hamilton (1762-1829) under the supervision of the British East India Company. Many scholars contributed to this field of study. William Wilson Hunter[50] for the first time wrote the history of the lower castes of Bengal analyzing the status of all the lower castes including Namasudras but not in detail. In 1883, James Wise[51] had described the features of various castes and races of Bengal.

Thus, the colonial surveyors and ethnographers enumerated various caste communities of Bengal but they did not justify the social status and the ethnological features of the Namasudras. They enumerated whatever they collected from the words of the privileged/educated castes. James wise and H.H. Risley[52] had written many aspects of the Namasudras but they left no explanation for the social status and anthropological features of the community. Risley commented on the origin of Namasudra that the term Namah was either from *namas*/ adoration/deserving obeisance or *namate*/underneath / lower grade of Sudras.[53] He had done outstanding work (1891)[54] in which the history of almost all tribes and castes of Bengal including Namasudras in details including their origin, internal structure, marriage, birth customs, religion, occupations, social status, and many distributions in different districts of Bengal from the censuses of 1872 and 1881 but the nomenclature had to be rectified later for justification of caste statuses of some communities.

J.H. Hutton has compared the social status and anthropological features of the Namasudras with the other castes of India, which raised questions to Risley's survey. He suggested that the social position of the Namasudras did not coincide with their anthropological feature in Bengal as the Namasudras are longer headed, fair-skinned, and apt to be leptorrhine nose in some contrast to the bulk of the Muslim population of Bengal.[55] Niharranjan Ray has found a similarity between the anthropological features of Namasudras and the upper castes of Bengal.[56] Naresh Chandra Das has pointed out that the social degradation of Namasudras began in the time of Ballal Sen, who tried to dominate his opponents and made arrangements to be lowered in social position for the non-compromised groups of people.[57] He refers to the fact that the Namasudras were compelled to be inferior and to be deprived of exploitation and oppression by privileged castes and had been degraded to a lower status in the society.

The most well-known historian Sekhar Bandyopadhyay, among the Indian scholars who studied and pointed out many aspects of the 'Namasudras, believed that the Namasudras themselves had confusion about their origin and the term Namasudra which is not mentioned in any of the pre-nineteenth centuries medieval Bengali literature is extremely uncertain'. [58] But it seems that there are several legendaries in the collective memory of the Namasudras which they have been carrying generation after generation from time immemorial could justify their original identity. But it has been difficult for scholars of the deprived castes to justify the identification and contextualization of their real history based on legendaries and oral sources. Manosanta Biswas[59] has written a wonderful book in

Bengali on the Matua movement and pointed out many aspects of the Matuas, a great part of the Namasudras, including religion, education, culture and politics. Some writers such as Joya Chatterjee[60], Prafulla Kumar Chakroborty[61], Monika Mandal[62], Jagadish Chandra Mandal[63], Babul Kumar Pal[64] and Deep Halder[65] have pointed out many aspects of the Namasudras from the perspective of partition and its consequences on Namasudras. They did not cover all aspects of the history of the Namasudras.

Therefore, the Namasudras assume that their history has to be written in detail from all social perspectives by the social scientists with much more attention. Very few scholars have voluntarily contributed to finding out their missing history. Some writers depicted the religious activities and protest movements very well but they did not point out all aspects of the community. Historian Nihar Ranjan Ray and Sekhar Bandyopadhyay studied this community very well and pointed out many of the features of the community but it is essential to have sufficient parallel writings from different angles in justifying the real history of the struggle of the Namasudras. The existing writings on the community would be appropriately justified by available parallel narratives publishing from different perspectives following the experiences and agony of the dominated, humiliated, oppressed and exploited castes. The real history of the Namasudras could be revealed only by those historians who can feel the agony and struggle of the deprived castes who have been marginalized.

The Purpose of the Study

The Indian nation deserves the unity of all the castes and communities to face the challenges in the changing world. The majority of the Indian population consists of deprived castes who cannot contribute their best fruit of labour to the nation due to deprivation and exploitation. They even do not know their original history due to a lack of educational knowledge. Their history has not been reflected in the narratives of the social scientists and historians of the privileged castes. Very few of their scholars got the lights of education to write their history with scholarly thoughts to stimulate the deprived castes of India, to think about their historical contribution and future responsibility. Their presence in intellectual discourse is minimal and very few of them can write in English about the socio-economic and political concerns of the nation. It deserves parallel narratives on the struggle of the deprived caste-communities beside the discourses of the privileged castes.

This study is an attempt to collect the narratives of the Namasudras of Bengal to enrich the historical thought of the community. It aimed to explore the history of the community from the time when their socio-religious movement began in the 1870s to the time of the creation of Bangladesh in 1971 when their socio-political movement suffered a decline and almost disappeared. It looks at their struggle when they became a minority after the partition of the country with the movement against various kinds of socio-political injustice. It examines the controversy between the productive castes and the exploiter castes in the social history of Bengal.

It will show how the Namasudras originated in Bengal, organized as a unique community and progressed under the influence of liberal colonial rule and asserted against social injustice and inequality and how they became dispersed and disgruntled during and after the partition of India in 1947 and the creation of Bangladesh in 1971. The study has been divided into five consecutive chapters with an introduction and conclusion viz. Introduction, 1. The Namasudras in Caste, Conflict, and

Consciousness, 2. Socio-Cultural, Religious Practices and Beliefs of the Namasudras, 3. The Reform Movements and Progress, 4. Namasudras in Bengal Politics, 1901-1947, 5. The Partition and Struggle for Survival and Conclusion.

ENDNOTES AND REFERENCES

1. *M.N. Srinivas: The Oxford Srinivas,* With an Introduction by Ramchandra Guha, (New Delhi Oxford University Press, 2009).
2. Stanly Rice: *Origin of Hindu Customs,* (New Delhi, Universal Voice, 1937), p.29.
3. A.J.A. Dubois & H.K. Beauchamp: *Hindu Manners, Customs and Ceremonies: General View of Society in India and General Remarks on the Caste System,* 3rd edition, (Oxford University Press, 1906), p. 14.
4. L. Dumont: *Homo Hierarchicus: The Caste System and Its Implication,* (Oxford India Paperbacks: Delhi 1970/1998), p. 57.
5. A.J.A. Dubois & H.K. Beauchamp, *op.cit.,* p. 45.
6. *Brahmanahasy mukhamasid bahu rajanyah kritah,Uru tadasya yad vysya padmam shudra ajayat* (Purusa-Sukta, *Rig-Veda*).
7. *Chatuvarnang maya sristang guna karma vibhagasaha, Tasya kartaramapi mam biddhyakartarmabayam* (13th hymn in Bhagavad Gita).
8. John Muir: Original Sanskrit Text, Part 1: *Mythical and Legendary Account of the Origin of Caste, with an enquiry into its existence in the Vedic Age,* (Delhi, Oriental Publisher 1972), p. 140.
9. L.S.S. O'Malley: *India's Social Heritage.* (New Delhi, Bikash Publishing House Pvt. Ltd., 1934), p. 12.
10. *The Statesman,* 4.04.2015:16.
11. A.R. Desai: *Social Background of Indian Nationalism,* (Mumbai: Popular Prakashan, 1948), p. 228.
12. N.K. Bose: *The Structure of Hindu Society.* Translated with an introduction and notes by Andre Beteille (New Delhi, Orient Longman, 1975), p. 118.

13. M.N. Srinivas: *The Oxford Srinivas, With an Introduction by Ramchandra Guha,* (New Delhi, Oxford University Press, 2009), p. 168.
14. Irawati Karve: *Kinship Organization in India* (Bombay. Asia Publishing House, 1965), p. 7.
15. B.R. Ambedkar: *Annihilation of Caste: with an Introduction by Arundhuti Roy,* (Jaipur, Navayana Publishing Pvt. Ltd. 2014), p. 185.
16. K.I. Shepherd, & K.R. Karuppusamy (eds): *The Shudras Vision for a New Path* (Haryana, Penguin Random House India, 2021).
17. William Wiser & Charlotte: *Behind Mud Walls: 1930-1960,* (London, University of California Press, 1963), p. 39.
18. M.N. Srinivas: *op.cit.,* p. 168.
19. Suvira Jaiswal: *Caste: Origin, Function, and Dimensions of Change,* (New Delhi, Manohar Publishers, 1998), p.189.
20. M.N. Srinivas: *op. cit.,* p.3.
21. Rup Kumar Barman: *Caste Class and Culture: The Malos, Adwaita Malla Barman and History of India and Bangladesh,* (Abhijeet Publications, New Delhi, 2020), p. 22.
22. Irawati Karve: *op.cit.,* p. 7.
23. J.H. Hutton: *Caste in India,* 4th edition. (London, Oxford University Press, 1946/1963), p. 54.
24. *Ibid.,* p. 53.
25. R.C. Majumdar: *Bangladesher Itihas,* Vol. 1, (General Printer and Publishers, Kolkata, 1988), p. 220.
26. *Ibid.,* p. 217.
27. P.R. Sarkar: *Bangla o Bangali,* volume II, (Ananda Printers, Kolkata 1988), p. 291.
28. R.C. Majumdar: Bangladesher Itihas, Vol.1, (General Printer and Publishers, Kolkata), 1988, p. 217.
29. A.K. Brahma: *Bangali Jatir Utsa Sandhane,* (Jnanpith Publication, Kolkata, 2011), p. 26.
30. Majumdar, R.C., *op.cit.,* p. 220.
31. Brahma, A.K., *op.cit.,* p. 40.
32. Prabhat Ranjan Sarkar: Bangla o Bangali, volume II, (Kolkata, Ananda Printers, 1988), p. 292.

33. Dipankar Gupta (ed.): *Social Stratification*, (New Delhi, Oxford University Press, 1991), p. 178.

34. R.C. Majumdar: *op.cit.*, p. 214.

35. Ghanashyam Saha (ed.): *Caste and Democratic Politics in India*. (New Delhi, Permanent Black 2002): p. 44.

36. R.C. Majumdar: *op.cit.*, p. 215.

37. Jatin Bagchi: *Jati Dharma O Samaj Bibartan*, (Kolkata, Sanjib Prakashan, 1990), p. 152.

38. Rosalind O' Hanlon: *Caste, Conflict, and Ideology: Mahatma Jyotirao Phule and Caste Protest in Nineteenth-Century Western India*, (Permanent Black, originally Cambridge University Press, New Delhi, 1985), p. 138.

39. R. Mondal: *Ambedkar: Varna Vaisam yo o Asrisyatar Biruddhe Sangram*, in D. Ghosh (ed), *Samaj Biplabi Ambedkar: Jiban o Sadhona*, (in Bengali), Parul, 2016, Kolkata, p.14.

40. Debi Chatterjee: *Dr. Ambedkar Abodamita Jati Samuha o Bharatiyo Ganatantra*, in Prosenjit Deb Barman (ed), Vol.1, (*Uttaran Samayiki*, No.1, April 2007), Kolkata, p. 30.

41. B.R. Nanda: *Mahatma Gandhi: A Biography*, (Oxford University Press Calcutta, 1958), p. 346.

42. Yasmin Khan: *Harizan Andolon: Gandhi-Ambedkar Bitarka*, in Y. Khan (ed), *Dalit o Jatpat kotha*, (Education Forum, Kolkata, 2014), p. 347.

43. Sukhadeo Thorat & Narendra Kumar: *B.R. Ambedkar: Perspective on Social Exclusion and Inclusive Policies*, (Oxford University Press, New Delhi, 2008), p. 17.

44. *Ambedkar Rachana Sambhar*, Collected Works of Dr Ambedkar, (Dr. Ambedkar Foundation, New Delhi, 1999), p. 44.

45. Anil Ranjan Biswas: Dr. Ambedkarer Sambidhaner Karyakram Samikshak Jatio Commission, in Prosenjit Deb Barman (ed), *Uttaran Samayiki*, Vol. 1, No.1, (April, Kolkata 2007), p. 7.

46. Kant Biswas, *op. cit.*, p. 3.

47. Dirks, *op.cit.*, p. 263.

48. Nandini Goopta: Caste Deprivation and Politics: The Untouchables in U.P Towns in the early twentieth century,

in Peter Rob (ed.), *Dalit Movement and the Meanings of Labour in India,* (Oxford University Press, 1993).

49. Ghanshyam Shah: *Social Movement in India,* (Sage publication New Delhi, 2004), p. 121.

50. W.W. Hunter: *Annals of Rural Bengal,* (London, Smith, Elder and Co. 1868). *Statistical Account of Bengal,* 20 Vols. (London, Trubner & Co., 1875-77), Reprinted in India, (New Delhi, Concept Publishing Company, 1984).

51. James Wise: *Notes on the Races, Castes, and Trades of Eastern Bengal,* (London. Publisher not Known, 1883).

52. H.H. Risley: *Tribes and Castes of Bengal,* vol. 1, (Kolkata: Firma KLM Private Ltd., 1891), and James Wise: *Notes on the Races, Castes, and Trades of Eastern Bengal,* (London. Publisher not Known, 1883).

53. H.H. Risley: *Tribes and Castes of Bengal, vol. 1, (Kolkata: Firma KLM Private Ltd.,* 1891), and James Wise: *Notes on the Races, Castes, and Trades of Eastern Bengal,* (London. Publisher not Known, 1883).

54. H.H. Risley: *Tribes and Castes of Bengal,* vol. 1, (Kolkata: Firma KLM Private Ltd., 1891).

55. J.H. Hutton: *Caste in India,* 4th edition, (London, Oxford University Press, 1946), pp. 30-31.

56. Niharranjan Ray: *Bangalir Itihas: Adi parva,* vol. 1, (Kolkata, Dey's Publishing, 1949)

57. Naresh Chandra Das: *Namasudra Samproday o Bangladesh* (Kolkata, Dipali Book House, 1997), p. 125.

58. S. Bandyopadhyay: *Caste, Protest and Identity in Colonial India; The Namasudras of Bengal, 1872-1947,* (New Delhi: Oxford University Press, 2011), p. 11.

59. Manosanta Biswas: *Banglar Matua Andolan: Samaj Sanskriti Rajniti,* (Kolkata, Setu Prakashani, 2016).

60. Joya Chatterjee: *The spoils of Partition: Bengal and India, 1947-1967,* (New Delhi Cambridge University Press, 2007).

61. Prafulla Kumar Chakraborty: *The Marginal Men,* (Kolkata, Naya Udyog, 1999).

62. Monika Mandal: *Settling the Unsettled: A Study of Partition Refugees in West Bengal,* (New Delhi, Manohar, 2001).

63. Jagadish Chandra Mandal: *Mahapran Jogendranath,* Vol. I&II (Calcutta: Chaturtha Dunia, 1382 BS).
64. Babul Kumer Pal: *Barisal Theke Dandakaranya* (Kolkata, Mitram, 2010).
65. Deep Halder: *Blood Island: An Oral History of the Marichjhapi Massacre* (Noida, Harper Collins Publishers India, 2019).

1

The Namasudras in Caste, Conflict, and Consciousness

The Socio-economic Status

The Namasudras are the most numerous deprived caste amongst Hindus of Bengal. According to the census of 1872 and 1941, they constituted 8.30% and 10.72% of the total Hindu population respectively in united Bengal and 10.58% of the total scheduled caste population of West Bengal according to the 1961 Census. They concentrated mostly in the districts of Bakarganj, Faridpur, Khulna, Pabna, Jessore, Dhaka, Burdwan, Midnapur, Howrah, Twenty four Parganas, Murshidabad, Nadia and Cooch Behar. Occupationally they had divided into Dhani/Halua (land cultivator) Nunia (salt/nun producer/seller), Sefali (clean-tidy as *shefali* flower), Mougya (attacked by mag dasyu/bandit), Berua (a fish catcher with enclosure/byer), Jeeoni (alive fish seller), Chainya (caught fish using chani/small trap), Kadar/Karar (fish seller in the market by cutting), Ghasi (grass cutter), Baqqal(traders and hucksters) in pre-colonial times but they became united during their movements against social injustices in colonial times.

They were the 'second-largest Hindu caste in Bengal and the largest group among the Hindu agriculturalists of the eastern part of Bengal'.[1] The socio-economic position of the Namasudras in Bengal has caused controversy among sociologists and Historians. The original caste identity of the Namasudras is not documented in detail in any writings. Their complexion and anthropological features do not coincide with their social position which is claimed by the privileged Hindu gentries of Bengal. No document has justified their social status and physical features. The privileged castes[2] considered the Namasudras as the lowest of the mankind. Some scholars raised the question that they used to observe all the social customs including worshipping, first rice eating ceremony *(Annprasan)*, funeral ceremony *(Sraddha)*, the sacrament of offering food to the manes *(Pindi)*, etc., and their complexion had been same as the Hindu gentries of Bengal, so how can they consider them as the lowest of mankind based on their occupation? The Namasudras realized that the reason behind their low socio-economic status was an exploitation of the Brahmin and Zamindars who compelled the Namasudras to take low-status work for earning their bread. Nihar Ranjan Ray in his research did not find any argument behind their low social status, he found that their complexion, the physical structure had been the same as the Brahmans of North India but they had been treated as the lowest on the social scale.[3]

Nevertheless, the Namasudras had been a courageous community in Bengal.[4] They had to be dominated and exploited due to the lack of the king's power among them. But they had been surviving as a skilled peasant community of Bengal with a sound socio-religious and cultural spirit. They were included in the list of scheduled castes as they had been financially poor and identified as lower caste during colonial times. They had to be divided into various occupational groups as peasants, carpenters, fisherman, business, boat makers, etc. due to financial exploitation of the landlords and moneylenders. During colonial times they became united and constructed themselves as a separate socio-religious and cultural sect in Hinduism. Most of the Namasudras rejected the traditional biased caste laws and orders which made them marginalized from the main folk of the Hindus who have questioned the social identity of the Namasudras in Bengal.

The Caste Identity

The term 'Namasudra/Namahshudra' might have originated from a combined word of Namah and Shudra, in the consequence of social conflict in medieval times in Bengal. During the Pal reign, there was no social discrimination in Bengal, and the Namasudras were a noble community among the Hindus of Bengal.[5] The word Namah came from Namasha/ Lomasha Muni, the proverbial ancestor of the Namasudras or *Namasya* who deserve obeisance/*Namaskar* and Sudra came from the name of the fourth Varna of the Hindu four-tier Varna system. The controversy regarding the caste origin of the Namasudras emerged from the process of nomenclature during the first census of Bengal while the census authority had recorded their community's name as 'Chandal' in place of 'Namasudra'. The Namasudras believed that the census authority might be influenced by the educated privileged castes that had been treating the Namasuras as Chandal due to the low profession of some Namasudras who had been compelled to take some work of low status as cleaning of the jail due to the financial crisis. The term Chandals had been used as the identity of some tribes of Northern and southern India who were considered to be begotten from the illicit union of Brahman woman and Shudra man.

The Chandal had been anthropologically different from the upper castes of India. The colonial ethnographers and surveyors traced Chandal as a generic title of some tribal people of India.[6] The anthropological features and social status of the Chandal tribe were different from the Hindu gentries of India. The Namasudras of Bengal had no anthropological similarity with this Chandal tribe but they had been imposed the term based on their occupational status due to the consequence of social conflict in medieval times. Privileged castes called them 'Shudras' or low caste to justify their exploitation of the fruits of the labour of these people. But they are said to have originated from the union of Brahmin with a non-Brahmin woman. They, therefore, observe their funeral rites/*Shraddha* on the eleventh day of a person's death in the same manner as the Brahmins. They were, therefore, called 'Namasudras' since the social conflict between the king's power and the social authority during Sen's rule of Bengal.

There are mainly two groups of scholars on the clarification of the origin of the Namasudras of Bengal. One group of scholars argued on their Brahmin origin and the other group argued on their Chandal origin. This contradiction has been going on without proper clarification but with sentiment and caste conflicts. It needs proper historical clarification and authentication on the origin of the Namasudras to discontinue the social dishonour and conflicts. But there are very few historical and anthropological documents to prove their original identity. Some possible anthropological and social features are there to justify the origin, but that is avoided by the historians of the privileged castes.

The Namasudras scholars have argued on the Brahmin origin. They believed that the Namasudras originated from the descendants of Namasa Muni, son of Kashyapa Muni and they had been as dignified social group before the social conflict in medieval Bengal and this term had been imposed on the Namasudras by the jealousy of the privileged castes to lower the social position of the courageous Namasudras. Traditionally they utter Kasyapa as their clan/*gotra* name during rituals and ceremonies and anthropologically they are similar to the Brahman, Vaidya, and Kayasthas of Bengal.

Therefore, it is most possible that the Namasudras are originally Brahmin. The present anthropological feature and complexion of the Namasudras coincide with the Brahmans of north India. Nihar Ranjan Ray refers to the fact that the anthropological feature and socio-cultural practices of Namasudras had been similar to the Brahmans of north India and Brahman, Vaidya, and Kayastha of Bengal but they had been socially placed in the lower in Bengal, and no argument has ever been found in the history of Bengal for this unreasonable social status.[7]. The Namasudras scholars claimed them as descendants of five priest Brahmans, of Kanauj, who was invited by a feudal king during the decline of Pal rule for performing some Vedic sacrifices as there was no Brahman in Bengal due to the influence of Buddhism which had been patronized by pal kings.[8] These Brahmans were from five different clans /*gotra* (Bharadwaj, Sabarna, Shandilla, Kanwar, and Batsya), who lost their purity due to taking a gift from Adisur. These Brahmans invited some other eight/nine Brahmans from six clans (Bharadwaj, Shandilya, Sabarna, Batsya and Kasyapa) in Bengal for regaining the previsions purity associated with them. These Brahman came to know that the king had a Non-Brahmin prostitute-like wife, so they cursed the king for his dishonest instincts. After his death, Adisur's minister Samanta Sen established the Sen Dynasty in Bengal. The Sen King Ballal Sen married a non-Brahmin beautiful bride from Dom caste and he invited the Brahmans in his reception ceremony. But the Brahmans did not accept the invitation considering the marriage as illegal. Getting angry for this refusal and knowing the previous incidents, Ballal Sen punished all the invited Brahmans tearing their holy thread and degrading them socially. He made an arrangement for degrading them to Shudra but his minister suggested degrading them in the name Namah-Shudra for continuing the minimum Brahmanical tradition and ordered the public of Bengal that they could neglect and torture the degraded Brahman, as they wish.[9] Jatin Bagchi refers to the fact that the Namasudras used to wear holy thread but they left it due to the security of their lives from the cruelty of king Ballal Sen who attempted to kill all the Namasudras due to facing social protest from them.[10] When Ballal Sen ordered his men to punish the Namasudras, they tore their thread and introduced them as non-Brahmin and settled in some marshy lands of eastern Bengal.

Hence, the descendants of these Brahmans began to introduce them as Namahshudra and settled in some unknown and marshy land of Bengal. Over the years, for hiding their original identity and disrupting their caste, they discounted some of the social practices including their recitation of the Gayatri mantra and observation of Upanayana. But they continued most of the social customs including birth, *annaprasan*, marriage, and funeral ceremony, and uttering their gotra/clan's name during social customs and ceremonies. They continue uttering their best clan's name Kasyapa discarding the other clan's names (Bharadwaj, Sabarna, Shandilla, Kanwar, and Batsya), except the descendants Hari-Guruchand who remember their clan's name Batsya.[11] For becoming one single clan after their social degradation, they faced the problem of marriage within the same clan. According to social marriage laws marriage was prohibited within the same clan. In this case, they continued their marriage within the same clan but out of the same kinder/*bansha/ jnyati*, they remembered their fourteenth generation as the same kinder, and no marriage had been taking place within the same kinder.

A legend has been in the collective memory of the Namasudras and the book *Sakti sangama tantra* (written in the 16th century CE)[12] which clarifies their Brahmin origin. It urged that Maharshi Brahma had seven sons; their names were Marichi, Atri Angira, Pulasta, Pulaha, Krutu, and Basista. Kashyapa was the son of Marichi and Namas Muni was the son of Kashyapa. Namas Muni married Sulochana, the daughter of Ruchi. They lived in Mathura in north India. Namas Muni left the house to pursue his realization of God. He had two sons Kritiban and Urban. His wife Sulochona died when her twin sons were six months old. Namas Muni returned home when his sons crossed the age of fourteen years wearing a holy thread. According to social laws, wearing holy thread was prohibited after fourteen years old. Namas Muni worried and suddenly left the house again to find a solution. He, surrendering him to god, continued his pursuit of realization till meeting with Srihari. His sons also left home to search for their father. Rendering many areas they reached the kingdom of Srinmanta, a Shudra king, in Siliguri in north Bengal. King Srimanta sheltered them and he married his two daughters Lipika and Sapatrika with two sons of Namas Muni. Meanwhile, Namas Muni succeeds in his austerity and meets with Shrihari. Shrihari advised him not to be worried about the upanayana of his sons as the attaining of the knowledge of Brahma is the only criteria to be a true Brahman, not the upanayana and without upanayana, his descendant would be Brahman if they know the Brahma and his descendant would be named combined in the name of Namah and Shudra as his son married Shudra, daughter. Gradually, the descendants of Namas

Muni made a strong community throughout Bengal. Another legend of the Dacca Chandal elucidates that the son of the Brahman Vasishtha was humiliated by his father and turned into Chandal as punishment for killing a Brahman by misadventure while hunting.

Dr. Wise refers to the fact that some Namasudras consider Namasa / Lomasa Muni as their mythical ancestor, so the descendant of Namasa Muni might have been developed in the name Nama-Sudra.[13] The tradition of Dacca Chandal clarifies that their ancestor was Bamdeb(Brahman).[14] They were degraded from Brahman to Shudra due to their association with Shudras/Chandal. Risley wrote that they were formerly Brahmans and became degraded by eating with Shudras, as they celebrate *Shraddha* on the eleventh day as Brahmans do, and the Gayawal priests conduct the obsequies ceremonies of the Bengali Chandals without any compunction.[15] Mr. Wells refers to the fact that 'a tradition of Hindu invention, current among the Namasudras of Faridpur, to the effect that they were originally a complete Hindu community, consisting of persons of all castes, from the Brahman downwards, who, on having the misfortune to be cursed in a body by a vengeful Brahman of unutterable sanctity in Dacca, quitted their ancestral homes and emigrated bodily to the southern wastes of Faridpur, Jessore, and Bakarganj'.[16]

Rasbihari Ray refers to the fact that generally, people follow social customs and rituals of their ancestors, the traditional social customs and rituals of the Namasudras justified them as pure Brahman but unjustly deprived of social justice during Ballal Sen due to social conflicts.[17] He argued that Namah and Brahman have the same meaning; both deserve Namaskar. Their ancestor Kasyapa Muni, following the advice and wish of his grandfather Brahma, married many times and created new progeny, the Namasudras were descendants of one of his wives named Sandhya who was Brahmin in origin.[18] Raicharan Biswas writes the Namasudras were descendants of Brahmin sages as they traditionally observed customs and rituals like Brahman but their opponent had applied anger or envy on them for facing social protest. [19] N. K. Bose writes 'their livelihood of agriculture was exactly like the Aryans.[20] N. C Das regards them as descendants of Namasa Muni from whom their name Namah-Shudra originated and they were either superior among Shudras who deserved *namaskar* from others or higher than that of the Shudras.[21] Therefore, the Namasudra scholars believed that the zealously of the pro-Brahmin kings led to marginalize the Namasudra and abused the degraded name Chandal.[22] The word 'Namasudra may have originated from the distortion of the word Naba-Shudra to Namasudra or Namasudra. One group of Namasudras regarded themselves as Namah-Shudra which means the Shudras who deserve *namaskar* from others. But they had been treated as Chandal, the lowest of mankind by their opponent in Bengal'. [23]

The second group of scholars argued on the Chandal origin of the Namasudras. They argue that the Namasudras had been on a low social scale and the occupations were of low status and also their woman goes to market. So they are similar to the Chandal of northern and southern India, having iron ornaments, dresses of dead bodies, dogs, and monkeys as their wealth. But there is no authentic document that proves that the Namasudras used such wealth as Chandal. Chandals were outcastes, untouchable/ fifth Varna performing menial duties for Brahmin and living on the outskirts of the cities apart from the dwellings of the privileged and dominant castes.[24] This group of scholars, therefore, supports the caste theory of Manu. Manu's theory prescribed that the Chandals had been born into the womb of the Brahmin wife of a Shudra man, with forceful and unlawful pratiloma marriage.

But it is not justifiable for the Namasudras as their population in Bengal has been more than that of the total population of Brahman (population ratio of Brahman and Namasudras was 1100105:1620545/1:1.47) according to the 1872 Census, so how does it justify growing more population from the illicit union of Brahman wife and Sudra man than that of the legitimate marriage? It is possible that the derivation of the name 'Chandal' is uncertain and it is a plausible conjecture that it may have been like the Shudra, tribal name of one of the aboriginal races whom the Aryan found in the possession of the soil'.[25]

Nevertheless, the Namasudras have no respectable position in Bengal society. The Hindu privileged castes even today considered them Chandal due to the existence of caste discrimination in their mindset. But the Namasudras have been influenced by the revolutionary thoughts of the reformers and got the light of education due to the change in the socio-educational system after the advent of Europeans who established educational institutions for all castes and communities and provided liberal social value and ideas.

The Awakening

The British had brought opportunities in various aspects for the deprived castes of India. The weaker castes have got the light of knowledge to identify their socio-economic status and their needs to rectify and reform the socio-cultural system prevailing in the Hindu society. The movements for social identification and social reforms and unity had been initiated throughout the country. The Namasudras of Bengal moved for the first time for the determination of self-respect and identity and unity in the middle of the nineteenth century.

Harichand Thakur (1812-1878), for the first time, organized a socio-religious movement against social humiliation and injustice in the middle of the nineteenth century in Bengal. His confrontation was very significant at that time as they were then depressed and uneducated. He was able to initiate a religious reform movement founding a separate religious sect/Matuaism in Hinduism for religious and cultural freedom of the depressed castes. His endeavour encouraged his son Guruchand who organized several movements for social development and self-identity since the 1870s.

He organized a self-affirmation movement against educated Hindu gentries who influenced census authority to introduce Namasudras as *Chandal* in the census report (1872 CE). It was the same time when the Namasudras organized an incident in Amgram village of Faridpur district (March 1973). A rich man among Namasudras, Charan Sapa of Amgram village invited more than ten thousand people including Brahmans and Kayasthas in his father's funeral ceremony. All the invitees participated in the ceremony except the Kayasthas who declared Namasudras as lower castes. They refused the invitation pointing out that they were unable to participate in the ritual of a Chandal as they did works of low category and their women used to go to market which urged their low-social status and disgrace.

The Namasudras took it as an act of immense dishonour to them. Hence, they initiated a movement protesting the Kayasthas. They organized a big meeting in that village and decided not to participate in any work for the Kayasthas and other dominant castes. The Namasudras of Jessore and Bakarganj joined in this movement. Consequently, the dominant castes faced various difficulties due to this non-cooperation movement of the Namasudras. The Kayasthas and Muslim gentries drew the attention of the district administrator of Faridpur, W. S. Wales, to protest against it but when Wales came to know the fact he criticized the restricted social system where only the Namasudras had to be responsible for the scavenger's work and other manual activities. He remarked that all men should be equal according to social law and justice; if only the Namasudras alone are compelled to the work of scavengers then it would be a violation of social justice. He drew the attention of the Lieutenant Governor of Bengal Sir George Campbell who, after eight months of the strike, issued an order in which it was written that no one would be forced to do the work of scavenger. This order encouraged the Namasudras to move against social injustice prevailing in Hindu society.

They united themselves by getting inspiration from this social boycott movement.[26] Guruchand Thakur (1846-1937) arranged several meetings, for discussing the problems and their way out regarding caste discrimination and social injustice. In 1881, he arranged a big conference at village Dattadanga in the Mollarhat police station of Khulna district for discussing their plan against social injustice.[27] More than five thousand Namasudras from Faridpur, Barisal, Jessore, Khulna Dacca, and Mymensingh attended this conference. It was the first big conference among the Namasudras in which Guruchand in his presidential address encouraged the Namasudras to organize themselves for upliftment. He attached great importance to the education of their children for the holistic development of the community rather than direct protest against the Brahmans and Zamindar. A memorandum had been prepared in this meeting for plans and prospects. They sent a deputation to Lieutenant Governor of Bengal Sir Lancelot Hare for demanding equal rights in social activities and for government jobs (1906 CE). Mr. Hare later submitted a report to the Governor-General of India with this demand and consequently, a declaration was included in the Morley Minto Reform Act in 1909 for extending the facilities of education and government jobs to the backward castes of Bengal. Accordingly, Namasudras secured the right to education in government schools and government jobs. This movement led the colonial government to take reservation policy for the backward castes of India in education and government jobs, which was later passed in the Montagu Chelmsford Reform Act of 1919.

A new atmosphere emerged at that time, while the Namasudras constructed a strong self-image and identity, getting the support of the colonial rulers. The British rulers introduced the principles of equality before the law and took steps to remove the social barriers of the Namasudras by reforms. The Namasudras and other deprived castes got chances to mobilize socially. The socio-cultural practices of Namasudras had also been mobilized with socio-economic and ideological change.

ENDNOTES AND REFERENCES

1. S. Bandyopadhyay: *Caste, Protest, and Identity in Colonial India: The Namasudras of Bengal, 1872-1947,* (New Delhi: Oxford University Press, 2011), p. 5.
2. Rosalind O'Hanilon: Caste, Conflict, and Ideology: Mahatma Jyotirao Phule and Caste Protest in Nineteenth-Century Western India, (Permanent black, originally Cambridge University Press, Nẹw Delhi, 1985), p. 141.
3. Niharranjan Ray: *Bangalir Itihas: Adi Parba,* Part I, (Kolkata, Dey's Publishing 1949), p. 37.
4. S Bandyopadhyay, *op.cit.,* p.46.
5. Naresh Chandra Das: Namasudra Samproday o Bangladesh (Kolkata, Dipali Book House, 1997), p. 17.
6. H.H. Risley: *Tribes and Castes of Bengal,* vol. 1&II. (Kolkata: Firma KLM Private Ltd., 1891), p. 183 and Wise James: *Notes on the Races, Castes, and Trades of Eastern Bengal,* (London. Publisher not Known, 1883), p. 256.
7. Niharranjan Ray: *op.cit.,* p. 36.

8. Debendralal Biswas: *Oitihasik Mahakabi Marsi Tarak Sarkar,* (Biswas Printing House, Kolkata, 1995), p. 5. and also Kulajis/genealogical texts of early medieval times.
9. *Ibid.*
10. Jatin Bagchi: Jati Dharma O Samaj Bibartan, (Kolkata, Sanjib Prakashan, 1990), p. 152.
11. Debendralal Biswas, *op.cit.,* p. 5.
12. Sarat Chandra Biswas: *Namasudra Samprodaer atmakotha,* (Srimali Computers, Calcutta, 2005), p. 6.
13. H.H. Risley: *op.cit.,* p. 183.
14. *Ibid.,* p. 184.
15. *Ibid.*
16. Appendix of the Census of 1872, p. vi.
17. Ray Rasbehari: *Saral Namasudra Dvija Darpan,* (Khulna, Publisher not Known, 1321 BS), p. 36.
18. *Ibid.*
19. in *'Namasudra Shurid'* January 1908.
20. Bose N. K: *The Structure of Hindu Society,* translated with an introduction and notes by Andre Beteille (New Delhi, Orient Longman, 1975): p. 158.
21. Naresh Chandra Das: *op.cit.,* p. 15.
22. Jatin Bagchi: *op.cit.,* p. 152.
23. James Wise: *Notes on the Races, Castes and Trades of Eastern Bengal,* (London. Publisher not Known, 1883), p. 256.
24. H.H Risley: *Tribes and Castes of Bengal,* vol. 1&II. (Kolkata: Firma KLM Private Ltd., 1891), p. 183.
25. *Ibid.*
26. Manosanta Biswas: *Banglar Matua Andolan: Samaj Sanskriti Rajniti,* (Kolkata, Setu Prakashani, 2016), p. 233.
27. S. Bandyopadhyay, *op. cit.,* p. 51.

2

The Socio-Cultural, Religious Practices and Beliefs

The distinctive socio-cultural practices and beliefs of the Namasudras might have emerged from the cultural exclusion from the main folk of Bengal due to the social conflict in mediaeval times. The popular culture of Namasudra had been structured to protest the social injustices since the legitimization of caste discrimination, domination, and exploitation of privileged castes in Bengal. It had not been confined only to the backward caste communities but also influenced others all over the Bengal province. It affected the conservativeness and dominant mindset of the privileged castes of Bengal as the majority of the caste communities accepted and appreciated the popular culture of the Namasudras. But it could not reframe the radicalism and caste-discrimination theory of the Brahmanic culture.

The Namasudras believed in many traditional and non-traditional socio-religious customs, ceremonies, and festivals. They concentrated on agricultural works which led them to observe many agricultural-related ceremonies, festivals, worshipping, and vows in pre-colonial and colonial times. The exploitation and domination of the Brahmans and landlords led them to organize many literary and cultural activities including Matua religious movement, Matua religious assembly, Matua music/ *sangeet* folk songs/*Kabigan*, theatre, etc for both the purpose of cultural spiritual aspiration and social awakening of the backward. They have some common traditional socio-religious practices and some uncommon revolutionary activities. The dominant caste communities of Bengal played an important role in the socio-cultural changes of the Namasudras. This chapter of the study aimed to explore some selected socio-cultural practices, beliefs, customs, rituals, and ceremonies which played an important role in the socio-cultural and religious lives of the Namasudras.

I

The Practice and Belief in Cultivation

The Namasudras had been mainly a skilled peasant community in pre-colonial times. They were pious, devotional, and serious to their work of cultivation and other professions. They believed in many ceremonies and festivals related to cultivation for sustainable development and prosperity. They had habituated to commence their cultivation with a devotional ceremony/ worshipping. They had mainly two cultivation seasons due to having marshy lands in their areas. The cultivation in the winter season (mid-September to mid-November) begins after the water goes down from land and cultivation in the rainy season (April-May) starts before the rainy season begins. Both the season of cultivation commenced with worshipping eco-god/*Vastu debota*, plough, ploughed cows, by fasting, bathing cows, drawing a symbol of good energy by drawing with vermilion on the plough and eco-pillar/*vastu Kham* of house. After the completion of worshipping, a farmer starts ploughing cropland parallel the first time and cross parallel later. After completion of ploughing the farmers prepared seed for planting, keeping a handful of it with a glass of water in front of eco-pillar/*Vastu Kham* of house room, praying to eco-god for good production.

The commencement of cultivation was called *Mut-Mela*. The purpose of the ceremony was to expect plenty of production for the season from the crops-land. They believed that the proper beginning with devotion to the god of nature/crops-land at the right time would bring plenty of production without damaging the crops and without a chance of growing anger of the god / nature. They initiated the program by inviting some neighbouring farmers who cooperated with the host with their plough in beginning proper farming. After the farming, they celebrated a grant meal at the host's house. After commencement, they enjoy the entire process of farming/cultivation by singing various songs which releases their misery of social injustice and financial crisis. They are never frustrated for being victimized by exploitation and domination. Initially, after social degradation, they became habituated with the imposition of caste discrimination and theories of the privileged castes and had been in a non-protesting mood. They had tried to be peaceful with their main occupation of cultivation. Some of their traditional habitual cultural practices and popular culture led them to be satisfied in the hard labour through various occupations including cultivation. They used to sing glorification/kirtan, folklore / *Palli geeti*, poetry while farming, and enjoyed their lives. Thus they enjoyed their cultural spirit both formally and informally. They voluntarily used to sing songs during their cultivation to enjoy their farming without any feelings of suffering. The song below expresses their attitude in cultivation.

Amara chasi pallybasi mati bhalo basi,
Anandete sabai mile Jami chas kori,
Kachi hate matla mete, nitrate jai dhaner khete,

Kalar pathay bhat bere khai ailer pore bosi,
Amra chasi palli basi mati bhalo basi,
Mati moder anger bhushan,
Matir kole kori sayan, seser dine mudi nayan
Ei matite misi
Jana bhore bailam langal tabu nitya upabasi,
Chaitra mase lagai fasal jaista mase kati,
Ashar mase mahajan ese fasal korlo khali,
Amra chasi palli basi mati bhalo basi.[1]

It says 'We the peasants love the soil and cultivate the land together with joy. We go to paddy fields eagerly with a scythe to clean the weeds, sitting down to eat rice on banana leaves. The soil adorns our body's limbs, we sleep on the soil, on the last day we sleep joining with this soil. We have been ploughing all over our lives but we are always fasting. We planted the crop in April/*Chaitra* and picked it in June/*Jaistha* but in July/*Ashar* the moneylenders came and took away all the harvest'.

They used to harvest ripe crops systematically with a special ceremony of joy in the name *Nabanna/aagtola*. They could select a proper date/time/day for the collection of the ripened crops following the weather condition. The date of harvesting had to be decided by an experienced member of a family, as no difficulties would appear during the harvesting. Traditionally, on the first day of harvesting, a bunch/bundle of crops/*aag* had to be collected/*tola* on the selected day before the main harvesting. At the end of the harvesting they kept a few of the crops (*Daoabaarano*) looking forward to the opportunity for the next farming. After completion of harvesting, they had to organize a ceremony/*Nabanna* (the first rice-eating ceremony of the season) for enjoying the bountiful production of the season. They liked to invite neighbours for enjoyment at the grand meal of the ceremony.

Namasudras believed that crop-land is the deity of crops. This deity has to be satisfied by worshipping with devotion for getting sufficient crops from the land. For this purpose, the peasant Namasudras observed *Kshetra Pujâ* in the month of *Agrahâyan* (mid-November to mid-December). They arranged various kinds of necessary ingredients including new rice and cake made of the juice of date tree (Khejur gur) cooking them together. Fasting the whole day all the family members had to participate in this worshipping. They prayed the blessings of the deity, eating prasad kept on *Kula*. It was observed without a priest.

They observed the worship of not only *Kshetra Thakur* but also *Gopaalan Thakur*, or Manik Thakur, which were related to agriculture. The cows were essential for their cultivation. They believe in worshipping cows for bringing a good future for the family's cultivation and financial progress. They worshipped the cow, in the name of the *Gopâlan Thâkur / Mânik Thâkur*, once in a year in *Pous* (mid-December to mid-January). They, with fasting, took care of the cows bathing and feeding them well in the early morning beside an arrangement of the worshipping. A special kind of cooked food, a mixture of milk and raw rice (*atop chal*) was arranged for feeding cows. The cooked food had to be kept on a banana leaf during worshipping. On the other hand, another kind of food cooked with rice, milk, and sugar (*mistânna*) had to arrange for compliance (*Prasad*) for worshipping. The invited people took *prasad* after feeding cooked rice to cows and paying respect to cows. They believed that if they pay respect and devotion to cows the progress in cultivation and financial condition of the family would improve automatically with the blessing of cow-deity, *Mânik Thâkur*. They celebrate the ceremony saying a rhyme: O Manik Thakur, cheet cheet, cheet! Bring male and female calves every year.[2] They worshipped the same for the second time on the last day of the month (Pous *Sankrânti)* when they used to give stamps of paste made of un-boiled rice using the front side of the *Kalki* made of soil, used in Trinâth Thâkur's worshipping.

II

The Ceremonies:

Sack of Brothers, Tribute to Guru, Pous Sankranti, First Cow Milk, Trinath Thakurer Mela, and Horisobha

They had a tradition of putting Tilak drops on the forehead of Brothers (*Bhai-Chhaatu / Bhai-Fotaa*) in their social practices on a particular date of every year. The purpose of this ceremony was to pray for the safe life of brothers. It had to be organized in the month of *Chaitra* (March-April) while some diseases such as pox/ *Basanta* and cholera appeared. There was no arrangement for the treatment of such diseases at that time in the villages of the Namasudras. So, they had nothing to do without praying to God. They believed that dust from fried pigeon-pea/*Chhatu,* coconut water and some particular foods were nutritious for protection from diseases. Accordingly, they arranged the ceremony with this nutritious food at the house of a sister. Generally, married sisters invite their brothers and pre-married family members to participate in this ceremony at their in law's house. They pray for blessings for their brothers' safe lives and the prosperity of the pre-married family. After the completion of the ceremony, the elder sisters had to give some rupees to their brothers as blessings.

They had been faithful to Brahman Gurus / their

religious guides. The gurus guided them not only spiritually but also socio-economic and educationally. The Namasudras traditionally believed in the initiation of gurus who suggested that without initiation a man's meal is equal to excretion, water is equal to urine and his destination after death is hell.[3] Consequently, all the Namasudras accepted the guidelines of a guru as mandatory in their spiritual lives. After initiation, every disciple had to arrange ceremonies namely *Brahman-Bhojan* for grant meals regularly weekly, or monthly. Organizing Brahman-*Bhojan* they had to offer crops, dresses, and rupees to their gurus.[4] Their gurus taught them that only the fortunate could donate offerings to Brahman gurus. The offerings would bring opportunities for earning more in the future and give a prosperous life in the next birth. They believed in the teachings of their gurus and followed their guidelines both spiritually and materially. The donations were only for Varna-Brahman or Brahman Gurus selected for Namasudras.

The ceremony which was celebrated at the end of the month of *Pous* (mid-January) was called *Poush-Sankranti /Poush-Parbon.* The purpose of the ceremony was to initiate taking some food suitable for the winter season and to make preparation for the good health of their lives and their cattle in the severe winter. It was a season of some delicious food such as the juice of date tree (*Khejur-ras),* sugar cane, and others. They occasionally made a cake using these foods. They took these foods themselves and fed them to their cattle. It was not only delicious but also useful in strengthening health to face the severe winter. They had to live in miserable circumstances due to their poor financial condition and unhealthy living conditions. So they started to become conscious regarding their health at this time. They had their rooms made of bamboo, jute, and straw which were not enough for the protection of their lives from the severity of the winter. On the first day of this ceremony, some relatives were invited to take the food made for the ceremony with various types of food, particularly cakes made of milk, sweet, *khejur-ras*, sugar cane, and rice powder. A special kind of food was also cooked without sweets for their cattle. They had to feed it to their cattle for protection of their health from various types of diseases that appeared in the winter season.

Every cultivator had their milk cow. Milk was their imperative food to keep their health good and fit for cultivation. But they did not take cow's milk without arranging *Go-kher-Nadu* (ceremony for taking milk of cow for the first time). The ceremony was held on the 21st day of the birth of a calf for the first time and on the eleventh day for the second time and more. They believed that milk should not be taken before the selected time for the sake of the life of the calf as well as for the sake of their own lives from any kind of hazard.[5] The neighbours were invited to attend the ceremony held on the evening of the particular day and to take food made of cow's milk of the cow and sweet. A noticeable feature was their style of taking *Nadu*. The young men performed *bag nadu*, a special kind of gymnastics, to take the food. Some farmers arranged the ceremony of *Trinath Thakurer Mela* (fair of Trinath Thakur) on the same day of the ceremony.

The Namasudra peasants observed *Puja of Trinath Thakur* (a united form of Brahma, Vishnu, and Maheshwar) for the good health of their cattle and the peace and prosperity of their lives. The commencement of this worship is unknown. It might emerge from the idea of Brahma Vishnu and Maheshwar in time immemorial. They believed that observation of this *puja* would bring a good relationship with the family members as well as a peaceful atmosphere in the society. Sometimes the purpose of this worshipping became concentrated on their domestic animal. They mostly were worried about the health of their cattle and they became helpless when their cattle were afflicted by any disease, sometimes their cattle died because they rarely found any doctor for treatment of cattle in their villages. They believed that the kindness of *Trinath Thakur* could save their cattle if they were devoted to this god. Therefore this worship was more popular among the Namasudras than the other Hindus of Bengal.

Generally, on the seventh/eleventh/twenty-first day of a calf's birth, this worshipping was organized, arranging various types of food made of milk of the cow and items made of rice. The relatives and neighbours had to be invited to this ceremony. They gathered in the house of the invitee in the evening and observed this Puja with music and singing. The devotees performed music with their instruments. Their songs were related to *Trinath Thakur*. A noticeable feature of this ceremony was smoking cannabis/ *Gânjâ* which was a favourite one in the items arranged for this worshipping. The devotees enjoyed mostly smoking a little amount of cannabis. *Bâghnâdu,* a gymnastic style of taking *Nadu* had to be performed by the young boys at the beginning of the ceremony. *Nadu* had to be made with milk powder. After completion of this primary program the main ceremony had to introduce singing the following song:

(a) *Ây jâi sakale sakale Trinather Melây,*
Oki ahâre fuler dâl nâmaiâ de
Âmi Trinâth Thâkurer karibo pujâ
sâji bhariâ de.
Âmi Vishnu dever karibo pujâ
sâji bhariâ de.
Ây jâi sakole sakaley Trinâther Melâi.[6]

It says 'come everybody to the fair of Trinath, I will pray to Trinath with a full basket of flowers so, please pull down the branches of beautiful flowers to fill up the basket'. The following song narrated the nature of the worshipping'.

(b) *Tin paisâte hai jar melâ*

kalite trinather melâ,

Jethâi khoray nâche, kânâi dekhe,

bobây bale bhombolâ, kalite trinâther melâ.

Ek paisâr pân supâri tin khili bânâi,

Âr ek paisâr ganja diye tin kalki sâjâi,

Âr ek paisâr tel diye tin bâti jâlâi.[7]

This song says 'only three small coin/paisa are needed for worshipping *Trinâth Thakur*, where lame can dance, blind can see and dumb can tell *bhombolâ*. Betel-leaf and betel-nut of one *paisa* for making three *khili* of *the pan*, *Ganja* of one *paisa* for making three *Kalki* of smoking, oil of one *paisa* for lighting three lamps were only required in this worship'.

The Namasudras believed in a tradition of telling a legend during the ceremony. A particular legend story had to be narrated by a devotee to the audience. This tradition has been continuing generation after generation. They introduced every worship with a narration of the legend generally by an older member of the community beside the devotees. The legend[8] was that *Trinâth Thâkur* himself rescued a family from an accident due to devotion to *Trinath Thakur*, which happened for a social cause.

A farmer named Sadanada did not have a child. For that reason one day he became very sad and attempted suicide. At this time *Trinâth Thâkur* appeared before him in the guise of an old man and gave three leaves for his wife to eat for getting a child. Thus his wife became pregnant and gave birth to a male child. Then gradually his child grew up. His son married and had children. But the man forgot almost everything about the kindness of the old man. One day all the members of the family suddenly stopped talking to each other. This made Sadananda very sad. The house parrot told the man's daughter-in-law that if she did not address her in-laws properly then nobody would love her well. Hearing this question repeatedly, the daughter-in-law became angry and opened the window of the parrot's cage and the bird flew away. The milk cow of the family was also lost at about the same time. After these mishaps, the man sadly walked to the cow market to search for his cow. In the middle of the road, *Trinâth Thâkur* from the top of a banyan tree asked the man where he was going and requested him to bring three things of three paise i.e. betel-nut, betel-leaf, Ganja and oil of one paisa. Thakur requested the man to take *paisa* from the bottom of the bunch of long grass (*bena*) nearby. The man took it but asked where the pot for oil was. Thâkur asked him to use a corner of his towel to take it.

Failing to find his cow in the market, he bought the three things but the grocer cleverly gave him the oil of half *chhatâk* instead of one *chhatâk*. The oil pot of the grocer became empty for his cheating. The clever grocer realized his foolishness and called back Sadananda and requested to pour the same oil in his clay pot. After doing this, the pot became full as before and then he rightly gave one *chhatâk* of oil. The man was amazed to see it. He was amazed at how it would be possible to keep oil in the towel. So he asked the banyan tree, what was the purpose of those three things of three coins (paise)? Thâkur told him to stay there at night if he desired to see the fair of *Trinâth Thâkur* which would be held there with those things. The man accordingly waited there and realized that if anybody had a devotion to Trimath Thâkur and worshipped him, all problems would have vanished. So returning home he arranged to observe it and was rescued from whatever wrong happened in his family.

When Sadananda was busy worshipping, his Brahmin guru ordered one of the disciples to call Sadananda and meet him at the village beside his house. But Sadananda could not meet his guru at that moment and promised to meet after the completion of worshipping. But in the meantime his Guru, becoming angry, went to Sadananda's house and scattered all arrangements of worship with his legs. Consequently, the guru's two sons became senseless by a sudden attack of a disease. After returning home Guru saw the pathetic scene of his family crying.

Trinâth Thâkur himself then reached him in the form of an old man and suggested him to worship *Trinâth Thâkur* for curing the children after begging apology to his disciple Sadananda for his misdeeds. He also suggested taking advice from his disciple for worshipping *Trinâth Thâkur* for getting rid of trouble. The Guru did everything according to the old man's advice and got out of danger. Thus worshipping *Trinâth Thâkur* was introduced in the Namasudras villages of Bengal.

Harichand Thakur, the founder of Matuaism, initiated a weekly religious assembly / *Harisobha*, for fulfilling both the spiritual and cultural aspiration of the Matua Namasudras. It has been an important spiritual feature/ practice of the Matua Namasudras for continuing their cultural spirit. It is a non-stop weekly ceremony, which rounds one family to another in the Namasudras/ *Matua* concentrated villages over the years. The function starts normally in evening with singing/reciting *Vandana* from *Sri Sri Hari lilamrita*[9]/the holy religious book of the Namasudras and with a welcome spiritual song and end up with a sound musical jingle/*matam* playing big drum/

danka, jhaj, korotal mridanga singa and other musical instruments which are used during singing. They performed many devotional and conventional singing and dancing at this function. Their attention and devotion to god during singing sometimes reach too extreme to tear for fulfilling spiritual aspiration. Most of the songs are related to god/ *hari*/ Harichand. Many books of poetry, biography, hagiography and devotional songs have been written by Namasudras relating to Harichand and socio-spiritual activities of the Namasudras. *Sri Sri Hariliamrita* has been a holy religious book of the Namasudras, which narrated the revolutionary, religious-spiritual activities of Harichand and his followers. It has been a philosophical spiritual guidebook of the Matua Namasudras for observing domestic religion. *Sri Sri Guruchand Charit* [10]has been living documents of the deprived Namasudras. Both the social religious life activities of the deprived Namasudras and their guidelines for movements against social injustices have been analyzed in the book. Some poetry and song books are there with spiritual and devotional thoughts. Some songbooks/*Matua Sangeet* have been written by the folk poets of the Namasudras for their spiritual and cultural purpose. *Sri Sri Mahasankirtan*[11] and *Sri Sri Harisankirtan*[12] are two important books of the songbooks of the Matuas. All the Matua devotees of a village assemble in a house of an invitee and perform devotional songs in fulfilling their spiritual aspiration in the weekly *Harisobha*. The Matua -Namasudras believed Harichand as an incarnation of God; some regard him as a great man/saviour of the helpless, some consider him as a great social reformer. The poor Namasudras mostly believed in the incarnation of God, they have been mostly devotional and followed only the spiritual guidelines of Harichand. Some unconscious Namasudras do not follow the socio-educational thought of Harichand and Guruchand but maintain their spiritual guidance. The educated new generation of the Namasudras realizes the true spirit of

Harichand and they can follow the actual aim and objectives of the Matua movement. They followed both the spiritual and material guidelines of Matuaism. The poor and religious Namasudras sometimes worship the idol of Hari-Guruchand, establishing temples at their home.

III

The Worshipping: Vastu, Manasha, Visvakarma, Durga, Kali, Laksmi, Saraswati

The Namasudras believed in *Vâstu Puja*. They observed it for peaceful and prosperous lives and the welfare of all relating to house and family.[13] They had been worried about various kinds of hazards that happened throughout the year. Their houses were made of bamboo, jute, wood, and straw which were highly inflammable. On the other hand, they had to cook their food with inflammable ingredients and wood in the open kitchen. Even the slightest unconsciousness might set the entire house, even the whole village to fire. So, observing *Vastu Puja* was not only to pray to god for keeping them safe from such kind of danger but also to alert them of the danger.

This ceremony was held in December-January /the second week of *Pous* and *Mâgh* with an arrangement of sweets and rice, motor legume/ kalâi, red flower/*ganda* and other necessities. It was organized in the middle of the courtyard by digging a little pond and temporarily planting a small banana tree beside the pond. A temporary soil oven was made on which sweet rice/ *pâyesh*/ *mistânna* was cooked, mixing milk with rice and sugar. Banana and *âtop châl* were necessary for this worship. It did not require a priest to officiate. James Wise believed that it had been in the social practice from the time immemorial as *Poush 'Sankranti'* when the earth was personified and worshipped without a

Brahmin priest.[14] The family members used to fast for a whole day to serve the purpose of the worship.

The peasant Namasudras believed in Worshiping *Manasha*/goddess of the snake. It might have emerged from the idea of saving their lives from the snake bite. They were concentrated in the marshy land of eastern Bengal which remained underwater for more than six months every year. At this time the snakes of the field gathered at the houses of the peasants as they had to build a platform of soil and the snake often bites the peasants and died with the wrong treatment of superstition. They believed in spiritual treatment and also believed in the kindness of the god of the snake. On the other hand, there was a rare arrangement of scientific treatment in the villages of the peasants. Consequently, worshipping Manasha was the only way to save their lives from the anger of the snake's deity.

Chand Saudagar, the famous merchant in the middle age in Bengal introduced this worshipping. It was most popular among Namasudras of the marshy land of eastern Bengal. The worshipping was held at the end of *Shravan* (mid-August) when the rainy season started or water began to rise. James Wise[15] believed that the goddess of Serpents, Manasha Devi, was worshipped throughout *Shravan* (July-August). The worship was simple; the main ingredient of the worshipping was milk and banana which, according to them, was the favourite food for the snake's deity. It was common to all Namasudra peasants including labourers as it was less costly to pray and to satisfy the deity.

The Namasudras believed in *Visvakarma Puja*, the deity of art and creativity. They did many artistic works like carpentry, sculpture, boat making, and the works of a goldsmith besides their basic work of cultivation. They believed that their artistic activities would be prosperous and positive through their devotion and worship to *Visvakarma*. This worship had been common to all the Namasudras. The purpose of the worship was not only artistic but also holistic development. They believed Visvakarmâ as supreme occupational power and they thought worshipping this power would bring prosperous and peaceful lives as well as a prosperous society. They celebrated *Visvakarma Puja* at a scheduled time before *Durga puja*. The Namasudras were attracted to *Visvakarma Puja* more than that of *Durga Puja* as it was less costly. Being financially poor, they were interested in worship which was less costly but fulfilled their spiritual aspiration. They could worship *Visvakarma* with a small idol and at less cost. During the celebration of the Puja, the Namasudra concentrated land remains submerged underwater. In such a situation they as well as the other communities arranged the immersion ceremony with boat racing. It was a noticeable feature of the Puja when all the villagers went out with their racing boats and idols in the evening for immersion of the Viswakarma idol.

Some rich Namasudras observed *Durga Puja* personally at their own family expense with fanfare and some Namasudra villagers celebrated it altogether, namely *Barowari Puja*. The purpose of this expensive Puja was the welfare of all people. Some Namasudras had improved their financial status by taking advantage of various professions under the support of colonial rule. Most of them remained as cultivators and financially poor. The number of these Pujas has been increasing among the Namasudras for their socio-economic development. Many Namasudras, the followers of the *Matuas*, considered the festival of *Baruni* Mela/fair as a great attraction, which is held once per year at Thakurnagar in West Bengal and Orakandi in East Bengal (Bangladesh).

All the Namasudra villagers jointly observed *Kali*

Puja as a common festival after *Durga Puja*. They celebrated this Puja sometimes personally when they desired to fulfil something through this Puja. They arranged this desired Puja any time in the year but the late night of the new moon. Sometimes they observe this *puja* believing that their hazard or diseases in the family would be relieved by worshipping goddess Kali.

Lakshmi Puja was common to all Hindus including Namasudras. The Namasudras as a peasant community observed this ceremony more attentively as they believed that only Laksmi Thakur as a goddess of wealth could eliminate their economic hardship. This worship was costly to the Brahmins and landlords but the Namasudra peasants arranged it with minimum expenditure. They naturally enjoyed the worship using small statues and minimum arrangement but with faith and devotion.

It was held yearly on the day of the full moon after *Durga Puja*. Every house in the Namasudra village is dressed up with various designed *alpana*. Generally, a small statue of *Lakshmi Thakur* was bought by every single family from potters who bring statues to market/ arang held in some particular open places besides a river. All villagers used to take *nâdu*, and various foods made of milk, *gur*, *chire*, *muri*, etc. the villagers invited each other, visiting the entire villager each other, got blessings from elders and took *nadu*, *khai*, sweet, etc. from all the families in the village. A special and attractive feature is seen when they all get the blessing of elders with *dhân* (raw rice) and *durbâ* (grass) on the head during *namaskar* to elders and take blessings from them from all families in the villages in a single day. It made the entire society of the Namasudras coherent, cooperative, and peaceful. A good relationship was built up through this festival. All the Villagers in this festival reach to like a single-family.

Saraswati Puja/pray to the goddess of learning was

also a common festival among Hindus including Namasudras. All the Namasudras in Bengal worshipped this *Devi* of learning with great fanfare. This worshipping was less expensive compare to Durga Puja. The Namasudras were faithful to this goddess and they believed that the goddess of learning would bring holistic development to their community including education. But formal education among Namasudras started from the beginning of the twentieth century with the help of the missionaries and the support of the colonial rulers. They were inspired by the liberal values of the British and the ideals of their leaders. Their great leader Guruchand's vision was 'whether you take food or not, you have to educate your son and daughter. Consequently, worship of Saraswati might have been popularized among them from the beginning of the twentieth century.

IV

The Vows:
Satya Nârâyan & Lakshmi Nârâyan, Charack, Ekadasi, Achara, Surya, Subha Chuni and Sarbajayâ

Satya Nârâyan Puja and Lakshmi Narayan Brata were scheduled to be celebrated on Saturday and Tuesday in *bhâdra* (mid-august to mid-September) for prosperous, peaceful, and secure and for avoiding any kind of difficulties. Various diseases spread at this time in the marshy land in East Bengal. At the end of the rainy season, water is stored in the low land and ponds, consequently, diseases spread easily. The unconscious people among Namasudras did not know the actual causes of the spread of these diseases. They believed in superstitions and arranged to worship and *bratas* to get rid of the diseases.

Milk, un-boiled rice powder, banana, and wheat powder had to be arranged for celebrating/worshipping

Satya Narayan puja. Brahman priests conducted the worshipping; the family members had to fast the whole day. Villagers were invited to take part in the worship. They worshipped Satya Nârayan Thakur jointly at the same time dressing side by side either by idols or photos of the deities. Two separate offerings had to be arranged for two deities. Every farmer in villages arranged the worship weekly on Tuesdays and Saturdays through the whole month of *Bhâdra*. In the same way, they worshipped Laksmi Narayan Brata for removing their poverty.[16]

Many cultural festivals had been organized by Namashudras throughout the month of Chaitra (March -April). *Charack Pujâ* was one of the attractions of these festivals. This festival/ *Puja*/vow was usually observed in the name of Shiva/ Nile. Various songs/ *Ashtak Pala* were performed moving from house to house in the Namasudra villages. Almost all the Namasudras/ backward Hindus throughout Bengal observe the festival for prosperity and removal of sin (*papa*) in the life of *Sanyasi* (worshiper). It had been exciting and enchanting folk traditional worship. The *sanyasis* believed that their lives would be prosperous and sin-free if they would celebrate *Charack Puja* devotionally following the traditional system. The saints (Sanyasi) who took part in this Puja (brata) were dedicated and prepared to accept heavy punishments in expectation of getting the blessings of Lord Shiva. They observed it in the last two days of Chaitra (mid-April) and it had been concentrated mostly in the district of Khulna, Jessore, Pubna, Nadia, North, and South 24 Parganas and Murshidabad. Some considered *Charack Puja* as a part of the *gajan*. Though both *Gajan* and *Charack* had been related to Lord Shiva, Gâjan had been celebrated for one month but the *Charack* for two days only. It seems that *Gâjan* originated in ancient times probably during the beginning of Buddhism with the characteristic of Tantric meditation and strict penance. Some Namasudras as Satish Chandra Biswas, a folk poet, of Radhanagar village of Nadia district, considered that Charack *puja* originated from the ideology of Buddhism, with the concept of tantric meditation, and dedication of saints, who wished to get relief from all kinds of hazards to get prosperous life in the next birth.

A local king named Ban Raja/Nripamoni, in the Pabna district of present Bangladesh, introduced Charak Puja in medieval times. The *Charack puja* was named after a *Charack* tree of thirty to forty feet long and straight stem of a tree named *Del* which had been selected in introducing the worshipping. This stem had to be standing in the middle of a playground beside the village binding long bamboo on the head of the tree in such a way that the saints could be hanged and moved in a horizontal cycle centring the tree. In the introduction of the celebration, the straight tree had to be worshipped and then erected inside a ditch and was balanced by bamboo. This stem was considered as the *Ardhanariswar* (a composite form of Shiva and Pârbati), symbolizing man and nature (*purus and prakriti*). The saints *(Sanyasi)* dedicated themselves by hanging from the stem, being strung with their skin at back. The saints had to move from village to village singing songs for bringing good hope for the villagers against dangerous diseases, natural hazards, flood, and drought of the month of *Chaitra* which has been the main focus of the worship. The strict penance of the saints had to bear to get rid of sin and make life prosperous.

The saints participated in the worship with strict dedication with piercing sharp hooks at different parts of the body, as at the backside, in the tongue, ear, etc. Those *sanyasis* who pierced sharp hooks at the back flew circularly around the *charack* trees, tying up with ropes with the bamboo on the one side and the hook on the other side. The *sanyasi*, who pierced a sharp hook in a tongue, moved around the *charack* walking / riding on the shoulder of saints. They celebrated the festival reciting many rhymes as followings:

(a)Baan Raajaa nripamani garailen delkhani,

lokjan dekhibaar ailo.

Pujaa habe Madhu maase(chaitra),

Pujibe se proti maase raakhiaa atithi ghare.

Taba gotre sanyaas hoile,

duhkha jantranaa sab taraaibe,

bhakti bhare pujile tare.[17]

It says 'The king Nripamoni made the *del,* a deity, the people came to see it, and worship is scheduled to be held in the month of *Chaitra* accompanied by the relatives in the house. If anybody of your clan becomes a saint with devotion, all pains and misery will be driven out'.

(b) *Bhagirathi Ganga ar kalindir jale,*

Dhakpat(del) o sanyasi suddha korlen bhola maheswar.

Dhupati garilen dwadas panke.

Rode dilen shukhaaiye Brahma dilen puriye,

Dhakpat(del)o sanyaasi suddha korlen bholaa maheswar.[18]

It says 'Lord Shiva (Bholaa Maheswar) purified the Del and *sanyasis* with water of river Bhagirathi Ganga and Kalindi, the potter brothers Bhaanu, Baanu and others take soil and mixing it properly make *dhupati* by a wheel with twelve rounds. The suns dry it, the Brahma burns it, and with the water of Bhagirathi Ganga and Kalindi the Shiva (Bholaa Maheswer) purifies it.

(c) *Ohe eso maataa saraswati kaandhe karo bhar,*
Basite aasan debo mastoker upar.
Aamar aasar chhaadaa jadi anya aasare jao,
Dohaai shib parbatir mahadeber maathaa khao.[19]

It says 'Please come mother Saraswati and cheat on my neck, I will give you a seat on my head. Please do not go anywhere other than my meeting, if you go, you are expected to eat the head of Mahadev'.

(d) *Del duaare bandi, bandi deliswar raajaa,*
Upare bandi basumati niche bandhi prajaa,
Baabaa maaer charan bandi galay pari haar,
Bhikshaa sudha korlen bholaa maheswar.[20]

It says 'Del is confined in front of the gate, Dewleswar is confined, and Basumati is captive over, the People are confined on the earth. Praying feet of parents, wearing the garland on my neck, the lord Bholaa Mahaswar, Purifies the alms'.

(e) *Ek dhup swet dhup sat dhup chur,*
Amar dhuper gandha jaabe baishaal pur.
Amar dhuper gandhe naache aapal gopal,
Amar dhupe naache saat bhaai baishaal.
Amar dhup chhaada anya dhupe jaao,
Dohaai laage shiv durgaa mahaadeber maathaa khaao.[21]

It means 'One by one white resin, seven kinds of resin is made of dust. Perfumes of dust spread toward Baisaalpur, Apaal, Gopaal, and seven brothers of Baisaalpur perform a dance taking this perfume. So please don't go anywhere other than my area, if you go, you are expected to eat the head of Mahadev'.

(f) *kothay aachho kshetrapal?*

Amar sanyaasir kaandhe karo bhar,

Jadi naa karis bhar,

tor make niye karis tui ghar.[22]

It says 'Where is Ksetrapal? Come and take possession on the neck of my saints, please do it, otherwise, make a family with your mother'.

(g) *Uttar theke elo kaali chhitke podaa khaao,*

Chhele pule dekhe kaali chheele khete chao.

Maraa naaro maraa khaao,

maraar pristhe diye paao

Mahaadev dhup naao.[23]

It says 'Kaali, coming from the north, eat burnt, wish to eat burnt, and wish to eat children. After seeing them, and moving with the dead, standing on the dead, Mahadev takes the perfume of resin'. During these Bratas the Namasudras used to fast for purification of their mind and body.

Fasting had been a traditional practice among them during all worshipping/ *Puja and Ekadasi, Brato*. They observed a fast periodically for the whole day expecting the blessing of god and sound health. They believed that fasting brings freshness and purity of mind and body of the worshipper without which the worship would not be satisfactory. This fasting was mostly observed during *Ekadasi,* and it was called *Ekadashi upvas*/fasting. They took fruits in the evening of the day and avoided non-vegetarian food in the days before and after the

Ekadasi. All their women and some spiritual men engaged in the observation of this Ekadasi.

The girls of Namasudras observed *Echarâ Pujâ* to pray to god for a disease-free and peaceful life. Some believed that it would bring them a suitable husband. It was observed in the month of *pous* (mid-December to mid-January). The duration of the ceremony was one month. Various flowers like *lâu, lohâgârâ,* pumpkin, *kalâi, champâ,* etc. with *durbâ* grass, had to be collected for the observation. A small soil platform and a small banana tree had to be arranged at the eastern side of the yard. The girls had to worship daily in the afternoon with an arrangement of all requirements. They sang some songs during prayer. All the flowers and constituents had to be changed daily from old to new in the morning through the whole month. At the end of the month, the banana tree had to be immersed in water and the worshiper had to bathe and prepare for the final day of the worshipping. Cooked sweet cake/ *mistânna* with rice, milk and sugar and other requirements had to be arranged on the last day. The prayer herself arranged everything with her companion with the help of her mother. No priest was needed in this worship. They sing some songs during this praying as below:

(a) *Aasan debo jorây jorây basan jata laage,*
moner mato karbo pujâ jadi abhaav saare,
aatop debo serke serke kalaa jato laage,
kalaa debo fanay fanay chini jata laage,
ful debo daalay daaly dhubbaa jata laage,
dhup debo serke serke khosaa jato laage,
moner mato korbo pujaa jadi abhaav saare.[24]

It says 'We will pray with heart and mind giving a pair of seats, necessary dresses and all other requirements such as bananas, sugar, lots of flowers full of the basket, *durbâ* grass, *dhup* with plenty of coconut *khosâ,* please be kind and remove poverty.

(b) *Echarâ thâkur go pacharâ chul,*

tâhâte sobhâ kare lohâgârâr phul,

pârâ bhore brotirâ joy jopâr pâre,

acharâ thâkur âisâ tâke âsirbâd kore,

broti gharer ekti meye khilkharu tar pay,

acharâ thâkur daikhâ tâke niye jete chây.[25]

This means: '*Echraa Thâkur* was dressed and beautified with unleveled hairs and with various flowers. All the prayers played a kind of sound of tongues/*jopaar,* to pray to the god for blessing them. A girl who was dressed and beautified with *khilkhâru* on her legs would bring the attraction of *Echraa Thâkur*. Thus, the Thakur would be desired to accompany'.

The Namasudra women believed in *Surya Puja Brata*. They observed this Brata for two days during Saraswati *puja* in January. On the first day of the observation, a group of observers/ *Brotis*, on fasting, had to prepare a long soil platform for keeping lamps arranged. On the second day after taking bath in the early morning, they prepared themselves for praying the whole day. Brahmans were invited to officiate the worshipping. It was introduced with lighting lamps in a queue on the soil platform after seeing the sunrise in the morning and continued till the sunset. The *brotis/prayers* during worshipping prayed for the happiness and safety of their husband, children, and other members of the family. They sing the following songs during this *brata*:

(a) *Otho otho surya Thakur jhikimiki diyaa,*

Tomar puja korbo moraa asto sakhi loiyaa.

Asto sakhi laagaay baati ghrita pradeep diyaa

Eke eke jaro hoy bratiraa asia.[26]

It says Wake up, wake up the god sun, we eight *brotis*/prayers will pray to you, we the eight *brotis*, lighting the lamps of *ghrita prodip*, have prepared ourselves and we attend all one by one and gather in the place to worship you.

(b) *Sonar thalay phuler mala saajaaiyaa naao,*

Chikan kaalaa aasibe sabe uludhani daao.

Aami maalaa gethe niye go aasi,

O sakhi kon banete Krishna baajaay baanshi?.[27]

It says 'Arrange the gold-plate well with flowers and play tongue music. I am coming, stringing garland, *sakhi* tell me where is Krishna playing the flute?'

The Namasudra women and girls believed in *Subha Chuni Brata* which was observed in the morning once on any day of the year to relieve unexpected hazards and get a secure life. A legend had been in their collective memory, which they narrate traditionally during this *brata*. The legend was that the innocent boy named Dukhiram, a servant of a king was captivated and punished with a stone for stealing a duck. His mother was crying again and again for the forgiveness of her son, while a deity called *Shubachuni* met with her and suggested worshipping *Shubhachuni* for relieving her son. Accordingly, she worshipped *Shubhachuni* with a minimum arrangement and her son was relieved from punishment.

During her worship, the king's cow and members of the king's family died suddenly. The neighbour thought it was the consequence of the sin of heavy punishment of the innocent boy and they suggested the mournful king arrange worship of Subhochuni as Dukhiram's mother did and apologize to her. The king followed the suggestion and worshipped *Subhochuni* and consequently he was also relieved from sin. Being glad, the king decided to marry her daughter with Dukhiram with satisfaction. Hence, following the king, all the villagers introduced the *Subhochuni* brata. This *brata* required Pan supari, plate, sindur, batasha, rice, tulsi leaves, dhup, durbaa, sugar and sandesh (sweet).

The Namasudra women observed *Sarbajayâ Brata* get a better life in the next birth. Particularly the widows had to follow the strict rules and regulations as well as other Hindu widows. They had to fast, wearing jute dress, taking food without salt, for observing this *Brata*. This *Brata* was very expensive, so rare Namasudra widows could observe this brata, but they believed that it was mandatory to get a better life in the next birth. A gold metal idol of Radha Krishna had to be collected; one hundred one Brahmans had to be invited and donated various objects like plates, bed sheets, dress, and utensils along with all kinds of fruits. Relatives had to be invited to take part in this *Brata* from a person's social circle, from a minimum of three districts. But despite having difficulties the widows among the Namasudras tried their best to observe this *Maha Brata* expecting both respect in society and better life in the future.

The Namasudra widows believed in traditional social laws and rituals. They were advised by their Gurus to follow all traditional social laws to make their life purified. Their Gurus believed that widows were the most polluted and sinful in society but they could be relieved from sin by observing rituals and social customs strictly. Those widows who were not able to observe all ritual and social customs properly had to be excommunicated from normal social life. Sarbajaya brata was one of the important criteria to be relieved from the sinful status of the widows.

V

The Festivals: Namsankritan, Baruni Mela, Folk Poetry/Kobigan, Theatre/Jatra Pala/Drama and Boat Race

The Namasudras had been influenced by Vaishnavism. They avoided many of the features of Vaishnavism including leaving the family for their salvation but they have been continuing the attractive features of non-stop singing/ *Namsankirtan* in the name of Krishna/god. They observe this both personally and collectively once in a year non-stop for twelve hours/*Chatusprohar*/twenty-four hours/*Ashtaprahar,* sometimes more than twenty-four hours depending on the financial capability or decision of the committee who organize it. Many special musical parties are invited from various places to perform non-stop *hare-krishna kirtan* with an exchange of some amount of money. The party demands money according to their musical quality. They perform *kirtan,* most of the time, following Indian melodious classical music. All invited musical parties have to share the time of the non-stop *kirtan* dividing equally. After the completion of the non-stop kirtan/singing, they round the village singing the ending song and arrange a grant meal for the entire villager. Their *kirtan* could attract all the devotees of their village and outside.

The greatest festival of the Matuas is the religious fair/ *Baruni Mela/ Barauni Bath/ / fair* on the occasion of the birthday of Harichand Thakur held in Falgun

(February/March) at the *madhu krishna trayodashi tithi* every year. It was initiated by Guruchand Thakur, son of Harichand Thakur, at the village Orakandi on the eve of the twentieth century. All the Namasudra Matuas and other devotees including Muslims[28] assemble at the fair with their musical instruments including big drums/ *danka, kansor, kortal, singa,* picture of Harichand and red triangle flags performing all with musical dingles like a march to the war field. A special feature of the marching was using the red flag as a sign of revolution against social injustices and the sound of a big drum as a sign of war against the exploiters and dominators. They carry a bunch of paddy as a gift to their god Hari. Generally, the fair lasts for seven days from the birth of Harichand. All the religious parties meet with the representatives of descendants of Harichand to get blessings/ suggestions for both the spiritual and materialistic guidelines. Sometimes the leaders of the religious parties discuss with Harichand's descendants for the holistic development of the deprived castes. Particularly the Namasudras and deprived castes from all the corners of Namasudra concentrated areas visit the fairs marching on a footpath. The fairground turns into a battlefield during the fair. The centre of the fair was Orakandi before the partition. After partition, another centre was organized at Thakurnagar of twenty-four Parganas district by P. R. Thakur, grandson of Guruchand Thakur. This fair/mela has been a reunion field of Namasudras and other devotees of Hari-Guruchand. It fulfilled both the spiritual purpose and the community spirit for collective protest against all the evils. They bathe in the pond/*Kamona Sagar* of the fairground for fulfilling their spiritual aspiration and meet with each other to share their experiences. Thousands and lakhs of devotees enjoy this religious festival with great funfair without any complaints of lack of food or shelter.

Folk poetry song/*Kobigan* has been a very important cultural feature of the Namasudras since time immemorial. They arrange this cultural festival on many occasions including *Namsankritan*, local religious fair, funeral ceremony, and propaganda for *Matua dharma*. The main purpose of this folk music and poetry has been for fulfilling the spiritual and cultural aspirations of the village people. Most of the time, the theme of the poetry has been selected by the poets themselves for spreading liberal thought, ideologies, and activities of the Namasudra social reformers to the backward people. The folk poets sometimes select the theme for making consciousness of the village people and for teaching various socio-spiritual mottos, proverbs, and folk education. Hence, the folk poet plays the role of social reformer through their folk poetry.[29] Generally, two contrary poetry parties compete /refute with each other through argument and counter-argument on a particularly attractive spiritual /social theme. They attract the attention of the audiences with their melody singing and creating instant magic of poetry rhythm. Many Namasudra folk poets played an important role in making awareness of the unconscious Namasudras as well as the backward Hindus and Muslims of Bengal. In the last centuries, Tarak Chandra Sarkar (1845-1914) was one of the first poets, of the Namasudras, who not only initiated a new genre in folk poetry but also guided others to write poetry book writing *Sri Sri Hari Lilamrta* and *Sri Sri Harisangeet*. Many of the Namasudras folk poets including Rajendra Sarkar (1891-1970) of village Bainjhaki of Khulna district, Bijay Sarkar (1902-1985) of village Dumdi of Jessore district (settled in village Keotia in North 24 Parganas after partition), Nishikanta Sarkar of Bhairav Nagar village of Faridpur (settled in Palta in 1950 after partition), Gour Pada Sarkar of village Kanaimari of Khulna (settled in Dandakaranya in 1969), Rasiklal Sarkar of Bagerhat of Khulna district, Anadi

Sarkar of Chunkhola of Khulna district (settled in Banga in 1958 after partition), played important role in creating awareness among the Namasudras and writing many poetry songs. Bijay Sarkar wrote over 2000 songs/ *Bijoy Geeti*. The poets' focus was to enlighten those people who were under the superstitions of child marriage, polygamy, untouchability, the sacrifice of a child, etc. They had been enthusiastic to spread the light of education, renaissance, liberty, a message of Hindu-Muslim unity, and so on.

Theatre/Jatra was one of the most important cultural parts of Bengal. The emergence and spread of playing Jatra are also significant in the cultural awakening and social movement of the Namasudras of Bengal. The Hari Jatras played an important role in entertaining and spreading awareness among Namasudras. The Namasudras performed many religious, social and cultural stories through *Jatra pala*/dramas. Guruchand Thakur encouraged those who were accustomed to writing plays and essays among the Matuas for folk education. He first instructed Ramjivan Bala to compose and perform Hari Jatra.

Many *Jatra palas* /dramas/theatres have been written on the activities of Harichand Thakur. Some important *Jatra palas* on Harichand are Ramjivan Bala's (1888 - 1958), Hari Jatra (1925), Upen Biswas's (1896-1978) Gostha Leela (1936), Jagadish Mahato's Hari Jatra (1943) Dhanpati Pal's (1903-1971) Haripaler Haridarshan (1952), Suryakant Thakur's Harichand Agamni Pala (1377 BS,) Nanigopal Bala's Sri Hari Agamni (1296 BS), Usharani Samajpati's Sri Sri Harichad's Atma Katha (1971), Atul Chandra Roy's Gostha Leela (1398 BS).

Besides these there many *Jatra Palas* have been written on the cultural movement of the Namasudras such as, Kumud Biswas's *kamona sagare putra bisarjan* (1413 BS), Raju Das's *Bijyan o juktibadi* Guruchand Thakur, Ramjivan

Bala's *Hiraman* (1921), *Dasaratha* (1921), *Haripal* (1925), *Tinkarimolla* (1925), Upendranath Biswas's *Ramkand Bairagir Akhyan*, (1935) *Tarak Chand* (1937), *Hira Moner Upakhyan* 1939, Ashwini Gosai's *Anurag* 1940, Vijay Sarkar *Bishwanath's Rebirth* 1980, *Hiraman's Upakhyan* (1975) Rosik Chatterjee's *Hiraman Goswamir Upakala Pala* (133 8 BS), Rasiklal Biswas's *Alakar Punarjeevan* (1378 BS), Khitish Chandra Haldar's *Viswa premik sri sri Gopal Thakur* (1411 BS), and Amal Kumar Mandal's *Sprisya banam Aspriya*.

The boat race was one of the enchanting festivals among Namasudras as they were mostly concentrated in the marshy land of Bengal. They considered it as an auspicious ceremony and it was observed as *'Nao-Ka-Pujah'*.[30] Namasudras were numerous among the participants in this enchanting festival in Bengal. All the Namasudra families used boats and it was their pride to have it for conducting all activities during the rainy season when the land around them became flooded by high tide and heavy rain. Sometime in the rainy season, the flood had drowned their houses when they required a boat to save their lives. They had to live on a boat when the water level rose and immersed their houses. They also used their boat to earn money through fishing, carrying goods, and selling them in markets of various places. The Namasudra carpenters were experts in making a variety of boats with woods collected from the Sundarbans.

They made long-shaped boats, for a race, on which seventy to eighty persons could sit on both sides of the boats for using oars for running the boat. A long wooden plate had to be laid at the middle of the boat for standing and dancing with a spear, buckler and a long knife(ramdâ) peacefully saying some rhymes during the race. But, sometimes, they attacked each other in case of any misunderstanding among the competitors in the race. Thousands of visitors gathered on two sides of rivers in which the race was held to see the race. The race was held on some scheduled dates during the rainy season after Visvakarma Puja, Durga Puja, and Laksmi Puja. It had been an important festival of Bengalis as well as the Namasudras.

During the rainy season, many fairs (*ârang)* were held on particular dates in some places beside rivers. They gathered at the fair by boat through a river or flooded land. They organized a particular fair for *Laksmi Puja*, from where they collected the idol of Laksmi Thakur and its requirements before the day of Laksmi Puja. Some special songs were sung when they reached near their house with an idol of Laksmi Thakur. They used to sing a welcome song before landing down from the boat with the idol of Laksmi Thakur. The welcome song was as the following:

O gopaler mâ tor Gopâl elo ghare
Dhan dubba baran kulâ diye gopal tule nâo kole
Âl swarâ baran kulâ, bakulmâlâ diye
Bhagobti bhakti bhare tare baran kare.[31]

It says 'O mother of Gopal, your Gopal has come home, take your Gopal on your arm with *baran kula* and *dhan dubba*, O Bhagabati take your Gopal on your arm with aalsara, baran kula'.

The Namasudras observed various socio-cultural festivals and rituals over the years. Most of their rituals were supervised by their Brahmin gurus called Varna-Brahman. Their gurus supervised not only rituals and ceremonies but also guided them in all aspects of their lives. They supported traditional laws and orders including superstitions. Accordingly, the Namasudras believed in the traditional caste laws and orders and they did not allow even a European to stand or walk over their cooking place/room, boarding on their boat, and if anyone inadvertently did so, the food which was being prepared, had to be thrown away.[32] Risley wrote 'they had their clothes washed by the washerman and used the services of the barber for work during rituals and other needs'.[33]

VI

The Rituals and Customs: Birth, Annaprâsan, Marriage and Funeral Ceremony

The Namasudras had some common customs relating to birth.[34] During pregnancy, their women had to follow some particular disciplines prescribed by the guardian of the family and their gurus for the sake of life. Women were prescribed to be healthy and fresh in mind during conceiving. The pregnant woman had to be normal in activities avoiding some risky works such as moping on a warm clay oven which might be harmful to the health of the baby due to the high temperature of the oven. She was allowed to mop on a normal clay oven but not sitting the opposite side of the oven which was considered harmful because of the positional effect of the baby in the womb. She had to avoid urinating on ashes as it was considered harmful to the baby's hair, sitting towards the backside in a moving vehicle was also considered harmful. The pregnant woman had to avoid some particular food like the water of green coconut, raw papaya, pineapple, and mrigal fish with reddish eyes. These foods were considered harmful for the normal growth of a baby. They believed that doing normal work with necessary rest was better for would-be mother.

In every village, they had some trained midwife who helped during delivery. Relatives and neighbours, after successful delivery, had to celebrate the birth of the baby with a series of tongue sounds (*jopâr*). They had to separate the tripe (nâdi), cutting with a clean knife made of the outer layer of bamboo, which was considered better than a metal knife or instrument. The newborn baby had to be cleaned with normal water as he or she could adapt to normal weather outside the womb.

The newborn baby and mother, according to the advice of their gurus, had to stay separately in a temporary shelter pitching a tent at the side of their inn. In the winter season, the shelter had to be arranged with some warm-keeping utensils like earthenware (*malshâ)* or a fire hole beside their bed on the ground, for a constant warm-keeping fire with *ghasi/ ghute*. Sometimes, this kind of warm-keeping system was made around the bed to keep them safe from reptiles or insects.

The traditional idea of temporary shelter for mother and baby outside of the room came from the ideas of their Brahman guru who used to visit their house. The guru felt uneasy to visit and stay at his disciple's house during the first six days of a newborn baby due to the bad smell and impurity, so to avoid this kind of uneasiness, the guru cleverly advised them to arrange temporary shelter for the newborn baby and mother as a social custom. But some Namasudras rejected the custom realizing it not suitable for a newborn baby due to lack of protection and disruptions of weather and reptiles. But their gurus advised continuing the custom for a better future of their life and fortune. In villages, the customs remained unchanged among some Namasudras who had been loyal to their gurus as they believed in Gurubad. In the cities and towns, the educated and prosperous Namasudras rarely follow this system.

Mother and child had been considered ceremonially unclean for six days, from the birth of a male child but for a female child, it was seven to nine days.[35]They observed *sasti puja* on the sixth day of birth for a male child and ninth day for a female child, with an arrangement of garland/*mâlâ*, yarn /*tâgâ, kâjol*, iron ring /*bâlâ*, banana leaf for both male and female. Mother and baby had to ceremonially be cleaned to initiate into a normal life, washing all clothing of the family member including baby and mother. On the twenty-first day of birth, another ceremony in the same name had to be observed with the presence of the Brahmin priest.

After the completion of six months of babyhood, *Annaprâsan* / *Annaprâsanvidhi*/ the first rice meal-taking ceremony had to be arranged on a special date selected by their priest. This was the first ceremony to invite relatives and neighbours to celebrate. They wished blessings for the baby and took part in the grand meal arranged by the family. The maternal uncle had to feed the baby by initiating a rice meal. The arrangements had been the same as a marriage ceremony. The baby had to be dressed like a bride or bridegroom and the priest had to preside over the ceremony like marriage custom.

The next important ceremony is marriage. The marriage of Namasudra girls usually had to be arranged before reaching adulthood.[36] They believed that early marriage saved the girls from unexpected socio-physical disputes which may bring unhappiness in conjugal life. But the practice of early marriage began to change in colonial times with the influence of western ideas and values. The liberty, equality, and maturity of a girl got importance for the consideration of fixing up a marriage age. Giving bride-price to the father of the bride was another practice for their marriage. Both families of bride and bride-groom believed that bride price was necessary for good relations between two families, for which they could visit each other, freely. Usually, the bride price was Rs 100 to 150 as much as 250.[37] This practice was changed from bride price to bridegroom price (betting practice) during the first half of the 20th century in the form of dowry which has been considered a curse in modern Indian society.

Marriage had been an auspicious convention in social life. It had been considered as an imperative social custom in ethical aspects of society. The Namasudras considered adultery as illegal and peccadillo for both personal and social life. The village head of the Namasudras had the power to excommunicate a person, from their village societies, who engaged him in adultery activities. The village head had to maintain social laws and orders to promote good relations between husband and wife to keep society pure and prosperous. A member of Namasudra society had to arrange a marriage of a daughter or a son with the consent of village society. There were strict social laws and orders to keep marriage relations peaceful and to avoid illegal relations. Love marriage was not allowed in their villages.

The funeral ceremony / *Shrâddha, Pindadan* was another important social custom among Hindus including Namasudras. A person has to observe it for the spiritual peace of the deceased and for continuing the normal life of his family members. The date of the *Shraddha* was normally on the eleventh day of the expiry of a person.[38] Married daughters observed it on the third day of the demise, namely three nights of Shraddha. The participants in the last journey of the deceased have to be cleaned by shaving the beard and cutting nails on the tenth day of the expiry and they have to make a meal of parched rice /*khai, muri,* yoghurt/*dai,* and sweets. The sons of the deceased had to shave their heads on the tenth day and wore a new dress after dipped bathing in the holy water of a river or pond. It was called *Ghat Shraddha* as it was held beside a pond or river. House *Shrâddha* with another *Shraddha* namely *Choury* had to be observed on the eleventh day of expiry. The family members of the deceased had to donate all requirements including dress, ornament, and cows to their Brahman guru who conducted the *Shraddha* ceremony, and they had to arrange grant meals/*bhoj* for villagers, relatives, and others on the thirteenth day. On the completion of one year after expiry, the successor of the deceased had to offer a *pinda* (rice-meal) in favour of the departed soul at Gayâ to free the soul from all encumbrances and for enjoying eternal peace.

Conclusion

The Namasudras believed in the traditional caste system for which they even did not take the help of the missionaries during the natural disaster for the fear of loss of their social purity in the touch of a foreigner. When a cyclone occurred in 1907 the missionaries attempted to help the Namasudras in the village of Basundia, Egarokhan, Tularampur, Chachanda, Betenga, Bansbhita, and the west part of the Narail District in east Bengal but the villagers refused to take missionary help due to fear of losing caste.[39] Nevertheless, Missionary Dr. C.S. Mead, later, realizing their problems, tried again to help them and succeeded. He also realized that the young generations among Namasudras had an interest in new liberal values and ideas of missionaries, and they could be changed socially by getting missionary support.[40]

His endeavour led them to move against the traditional social beliefs and superstitions. Hence, the missionary could influence the unconscious Namasudras. They remained devoted to rituals and *bratas* but moved against some traditional laws and orders of the Brahman gurus as they were influenced by the liberal values and thoughts of the missionaries. They included the birthday ceremony and Christmas in their social practices. Some Matua Namasudras have been loyal to the ideology of Harichand Thakur who founded Matuism in the middle of the nineteenth century avoiding the Brahmanical tradition. He organized a new sect in Hinduism with his ideology of Matuism. It led the Namasudras to move against the traditional social laws and orders prevailing in the Hindu caste system. In place of Sanskritization, the Namasudras were influenced by western liberal values and the revolutionary thought of Harichand Thakur. With this, a professional and occupational change took place among the Namasudras in colonial times.

They were encouraged by the introduction of the modern educational system, new social values, liberal thoughts, and social equality of the colonial rulers. In the early colonial times, it was confined among the conscious Hindus but soon the backward Hindus began to claim the benefits of education and sharing socio-economic rights. The Namasudras urged mobilization demanding equal social status and prestige. Harichand Thakur was able to introduce a socio-religious movement against Brahmanism and Vaishnavism and initiated a new religious sect in Hinduism. The Namasudras under his leadership organized several movements against the social injustice, inequality, and disparity prevailing in Hindu society, influencing the new liberal thoughts of the colonial rulers and the social reformers. Under these circumstances, they initiated many socio-cultural reforms which were significant for the social upliftment of the Namasudras.

ENDNOTES AND REFERENCES

1. Source: Interview with Bhuvan Sarkar, Farmer, Bahirgachhi, Nadia, on 20/12/2014
2. Source: Interview with Bhuvan Sarkar, Farmer, Bahirgachhi, Nadia, on 20.12.2014, *Manik Thakur, Manik Thakur, Cheet cheet cheet, Dâmda diye bakan diyo, Bachar bachar biyaan diyo.*
3. Sri Charan Das: *Tatma Rasamrita Jnanamanjuri,* (P.M. Bagchi and Co. Private Ltd., Kolkata, 2012), p.83. *Adikshitang*

lokonang annang bistha samang, tasya jalang mutra sama, adikshitaopi morone rourabang narakang brajet.

4. *Ibid.*
5. Source; Interview with Sri Chitta Sikdar, Bagula, Nadia, on 25/12/2014.
6. Interview with Prafulla Mondal, Shanti Nagar, Burdwan on 28/03/2015.
7. *Ibid.*
8. Source: Interview with Sri Ramoni, Sarkar, Badalpur, Dakshin Dinajpur on 25/07/2015.
9. Tarak Chandra Sarkar(1845-1914), published in 1916 from village Orakandi of Faridpur district.
10. Mahananda Halder (1902-1972), of village Betkanta of Khulna district, published this book in 1943 from Bagerhat, Khulna.
11. Tarak Chandra Sarkar, Published for the first time in 1900.
12. Sudhanya Kumar, son of Guruchand Thakur, Published in 1928.
13. Source: Interview with Bhuvan Sarkar, Farmer, Bahirgachhi, Nadia, on 20/12/2014.
14. James Wise: *Notes on the Races, Castes, and Trades of Eastern Bengal,* (London. Publisher not Known, 1883), p. 259.
15. *Ibid.*
16. Thakur Abanindranath: *Banglar Brata,* (Kolkata, Gangchil, 2013): 41.
17. Source: Interview with Sri Satish Biswas, Folk poet, Radhanagar, Nadia, on 15/01/2015.
18. *Ibid.*
19. *Ibid.*
20. *Ibid.*
21. Source: Interview with Sri Anil Sarkar, Farmer, Radhanagar, Nadia, on 16/01/2015.
22. *Ibid.*
23. *Ibid.*
24. Source: an interview with Srimati Mira Haldar, Barochand Ghar, Nadia, on 22/08/2015.

25. *Ibid.*
26. Source: Interview with Srimati Kalitar Bala, Housewife Bastala, Egaro Mile, Malda, 07/05/2015.
27. *Ibid.*
28. Tinkori Molla was one of the famous disciples of Harichand Thakur, he visited Baruni mela/fair with his party every year in his lifetime.
29. Biswas Manosanta: *Banglar Matua Andolan: Samaj Sanskriti Rajniti,* (Kolkata, Setu Prakashani, 2016), p. 212.
30. *Ibid.*
31. Source: An interview with Sri Chitta Sikdar, Teacher Bagula, Nadia on 25/12/2014.
32. Wise James: *Notes on the Races, Castes and Trades of Eastern Bengal,* (London. Publisher not Known, 1883), p. 259.
33. H.H., *Risley: Tribes and Castes of Bengal,* vol. 1, (Kolkata: Firma KLM Private Ltd.,1891), p. 188.
34. Source: Interview with Sri Chitta Sikdar, Bagula, Nadia on 25/12/2014.
35. Wise James, *op. cit.,* p. 259.
36. H.H. Risley: *op. cit.,* p. 186
37. H.H. Risley: *op. cit.,* p. 187.
38. Wise James, op. cit, p. 259.
39. Jatin Bagchi: *Jati Dharma O Samaj Bibartan,* (Kolkata, Sanjib Prakashan, 1990), p.141.
40. *Ibid,* p. 142.

3

Reform Movements and Progress of the Namasudras

The Namasudras have organized several movements for socio-economic and cultural reforms being inspired by the liberal values and ideals of the colonial rulers, missionaries and conscious leaders. In pre-colonial times, they had been under the darkness of superstitions and biased traditional social laws and orders. They followed the guidance of their Brahman gurus who were loyal to the traditional social laws and orders prevailing in the Hindu caste system. The Namasudras deprived of education and sharing of wealth for centuries but nobody supported their movement for upliftment in pre-colonial times. The colonial rulers introduced new socio-economic and educational rules and regulations in administration which led them to move against traditional laws and orders. Though a liberal movement in the socio-religious sphere had been introduced by Sri Chaitanya Mahaprabhu in Bengal in sixteen centuries it suffered a decline after his lifetime.

Sri Chaitanya (1486-1534 CE) initiated his movement with the features of saints/monastic and worshipping Krishna with ecstatic song and dance despite the Brahmanical tradition. The Vaisnavas believe that Sri

Chaitanya is the incarnation of God Krishna, who brings the opportunity for the backward Hindus of Bengal to be free from religious domination and exploitation of the Brahmans. Everybody, irrespective of caste, class and religion could enjoy religious freedom in Vaishnavism founded by Sri Caitanya. But Harichand Thakur (1812-1878 CE) noticed a revival of the Brahmanical domination, exploitation and caste discrimination in Vaisnavism and its consequence among the backward Hindus.[1] He felt the requirement of domestic religion, in place of Vaishnavism, that suits the simple lives and activities of the hard-working deprived people of Bengal.

It was the same time when the deprived Hindus had been influencing by the ideology of Islam and Christianity and there had been a chance of mass conversion because of social domination and exploitation of the Brahmans and Zamindars. Harichand appeared at the right time to inspire the deprived Hindus to avoid conversion into different religions. He took an initiative in finding out an alternative religious platform for the deprived people and founded such a religious ideology that encouraged the depressed people. His thought of reforms was different from the movements of Raja Rammohan Mohan Ray (1772-1833CE), founder of Brahmo Sabha/ a socio-religious reform movement and Ishwar Chandra Vidyasagar/ Bandyopadhyay (1820-1891), a social reformer, educator and modernizer of Bengal. Harichand Thakur was the first leader among backward caste communities to dare for the first time to initiate a new religious reform movement violating the traditional caste laws and orders.

Religious Reform

Harichand Thakur started his journey of social reforms from his childhood when he noticed some misdeeds of the Vaishnava Brahmans who often visited their house.[2]

He felt that the backward Hindus were deprived of rights to religious, social, economic and educational opportunities in the society. He could realize the imperativeness of religious reform for protesting the biased social laws and orders which were the main barriers before the upliftment of the weaker sections of Hindus.

He was born in a Namasudra family of ***Madhu** Krishna Tryodasi Baruni Thithi* (March, 1812/ Falgun, 1218 B.S) at Safaladanga village in Faridpur district in Bengal. His parents Jashabanta Thakur and Annapurna Devi believed in Vaishnavism. Harichand did not follow his parents. He had an interest in the pursuit of the realization of god as he had no faith in the complex religious system of Vaishnavism where he noticed domination of the Brahmans. He had an interest in removing social domination since his childhood and did not believe in a biased socio-religious system. He, at childhood, noticed a bad intention of the Brahman Vaishnavas who often visited their house in the form of a guest. Harichand's father was a simple pious man who devoted to the Vaishnavas Brahman blindly. He was interested in serving the Vaishnavas with his group of people. But Harichand witnessed many misdeeds of Vaishnavas and since then he had questioned the behaviour of Vaishnavas and nurtured it in his mind. Once he searched the cloth bags *(jhola)* of Vaishnavas and found tobacco, hemp and cannabis in it. He could not believe in using a drug by religious men. He scattered all the material of the cloth bags with anger. But it made the Vaishnavas angry and unsatisfied and when his father attempted to punish him, he disclosed the secret habits of the Vaishnavas.

Seeing the unspeakable oppression of the deprived castes and the unjust exploitation of the Brahmins in the mismanagement of the society around him, he was always engrossed in that thought. But his conflict with the Vaisnavas, his attitude in society, his playing with snakes and breeding cows led him to be a courageous man.[3] It was the same time when he had to leave his village Safaladanga with his parents and five brothers due to the unjust tyranny of the Zamindars.

The Zamindar of Suryamoni Majumder, of village Safaladanga, imposing a false charge of not paying rent, occupied all the land and house property of Harichand and his family. Suryamoni borrowed seven hundred rupees from Krishnadas, elder brother of Harichand, but had not paid the money as he promised; Seven months later of borrowing money, Krishnadas rebuked Gomasta for not repaying the borrowing. The Gomasta feeling dishonoured informed it to Zamindar Suryamoni. Suryamoni immediately criticized Gomasta but visited Krishnadas to protest his audacity of insulting Zamindar and Gomastha.

Visiting Thakur's house, Gomastha complained that Krisnadas had not paid rent in that year. But Krishnadas asked him to repay the borrowing of seven hundred rupees first and he would pay the taxes next. Hearing these words the steward janitor ordered the pedestrian to arrest all the members of Harichand's family and carry them by boat for punishment. Consequently, a sudden fight took place between them. Zamindar immediately stopped the fight but after returning home he arranged a meeting with another big Zamindar Suryanarayan who suggested the punishment of Krishnadas and his family by making a false charge of not paying rent. Accordingly, a complaint was launched against Krishnadas at the local court. Krishnadas das had not given the scope of the answer of the complaint and the court declared a judgment that Krishnadas was found guilty and for which he was fined thirteen thousand rupees by the court. By this order, the Zamindar himself, with the help of the court clerk, bought the land and property cheaply without any justification.

Thakur family was compelled to leave the house and temporarily got shelter in the house of Sen in Ramdia village. They were respectable to the Sen Family, so they were sheltered. But soon the Zamindar realized his fault when within seven days the property which was shifted to his house fired and lost everything. He came to Krishnadas again to return all the land and property but Harichand and his family refused to return, even though they requested the Zamindar that they already promised to live under another Zamindar and they had no anger to him. The Zamindar was disappointed and returned in vain. They were living temporarily in the house of Sen in Ramdia village for Bhadra to Pous (Bengali). Hence, they settled at Orakandi at the house of Bhajaram Choudhry who was a maternal brother of Harichand. He was a farmer and a renowned person among Vaishnavas, both the family were faithful in the same religion and culture so they began to live there together peacefully.

Meanwhile, Harichand married and began to develop a philosophical thought that began to develop in him at Orakandi. He left the company of his friend and relatives and engaged him in deep spiritual thinking. He used to sit in a secluded place for hours, deep in thought. Once, in the middle of his way to Jaynagar village, while crossing a vast field, sat under a Bakul tree and engaged in deep thought and meditation. In such a meditative state, in the middle of the night, he attains self-realization and self-knowledge, when he initiates a new religion, the Matua Dharma.

He drew the attention of the deprived villagers and made a platform against Zamindars and Brahmins who exploited and dominated the deprived castes and forced the common people to be victimized in different ways.

The Brahman gurus compelled the deprived castes to be their disciples using spiritual threats of sin. But Harichand encouraged the depressed people by uttering his sublime voice 'if a pious person of good character is devoted to Hari, he will no longer need to recite mantras of Brahmin guru'. He inspired the helpless who suffered from diseases and financial crisis due to the exploitation of the Brahmans. Using his healing power and consolation words even he cured the incurable diseases in a moment. Consequently, the helpless people become intoxicated by his spiritual power.

Hence, leaving the work of agriculture he began to wander around the house of helpless people. Many helpless people became his fans all over Bengal. They all came like waves and took shelters at the feet of Harichand. Consequently, he came to be regarded as an epoch maker of the common people. He encouraged the backward Hindus to refrain from conversion to other religions to remain loyal to the good principles of Hinduism. His effort led the deprived castes to be confident and to be loyal to the good principles and ideology of Hinduism avoiding biased laws and orders. He attracted the deprived castes to the modern thought of liberalism founding a new religious idea, Matuaism[4].

He emphasized the idea of *Grihastha dharma*[5] to attain religious aims and aspirations which suited the depressed castes. The Vaishnava principle of leaving the family for getting their salvation seemed to him unnecessary for the laborious communities. He believed that every religious aspiration might be fulfilled within family life. He suggested the deprived castes follow some simplistic paths of honesty and faith to god Hari for fulfilling religious aspiration remaining loyal to domestic religion (grihastha dharma) with spouses considering women other than wife as mother, and to be sympathetic to the misery of others.[6]

He encouraged the deprived castes to be united under his new religious thought, Matuaism, a liberal ideology, considering all good humans equal, paying respect to parents, loving all in the world, having respect to other religions, controlling six instincts and dedicating himself to god Hari. He did not consider paying respect to their Brahman gurus in fulfilling religious aspiration. A noticeable feature in his religious activities was marching with red flags and drums to congregate in a selected place or house, every year in a time of religious fair and every week in a religious ceremony in their villages. They used the red flag as a symbol of revolution during marching and the drums as a warning of the impending fight against the barriers in their religious journey.

His *Matuaism* criticized gender discrimination. It considers women as inspiration, power giver and maker of good hope for society. It advised Matuas[7] consider women, other than wife, as a mother, to be well behaved to other's spouse, to get the blessings of God Hari.[8] Everybody could be free from evil, having peace in the family, behaving well towards women, paying respect to the law and orders and remaining honest with faith in God.[9] The Matuas were encouraged by this ideology and made a good reciprocal relation and bonhomie among men and women. The men among the Namasudras had been considered as most responsible for building a peaceful society. The men could not dominate their counterpart with ideas of patriarchy. The Matua philosophy encouraged them in cooperating women, considering their wives as real-life partners, and lifetime friends. They were encouraged in building an admirable family with a good reciprocal relationship between men and women and to be supportive of each other. Harichand suggested his followers consider men and women equal, sharing of food, dress shelter etc equally. Both the boys and girls required equal social, physical, mental and spiritual atmosphere to develop equally in life. For mental devolvement, the girls and women required friends, peaceful shelter, a comfortable atmosphere etc with their counterpart and all these necessities might be fulfilled through peaceful family life.

With these features, Matuaism took special attention to domestic religion (*Grihasthashram*). The focus was to work hand in hand with spiritual thinking in mind; 'hate cam mukhe nam' avoiding uncontrolled sexual enjoyment. Limiting sexual enjoyment to a certain periodical time had been considered as celibacy (*Brahmacharya*) and living in this manner in the family had been considered as *Brahmachayaasram* in *Matuaism*. The Matuas were suggested to follow *Brahmacharya* and maintain a peaceful family to get holy children for the continuation of prosperous civilization. Both men and women were allowed to enjoy religious and cultural festivals with devotion to god altogether. Their women were allowed to participate in all socio-economic, cultural, educational and political activities. Getting freedom in all activities their girls and women could improve physically, mentally and spiritually as well as the holistic development of their community.

Idolatry was not important in Matuaism. Some Matuas regarded idolatry as instruments of Brahman's domination[10]. Matuas were forbidden to worship many goddesses but to pray to Hari only. They sometimes worship the idolatry of Harichand, imagining as god Hari. They were suggested to organize kirtan (Nonstop singing) with devotional songs and uttering the name of Hari for fulfilling the purpose of their spiritual aspiration. It led them to get a source of inspiration, collective strength, social unity and collective power to protest against social injustice. Harichand had forbidden his followers to take initiation[11] from any human guru for spiritual purpose but to be devoted to god Hari to achieve the spiritual goal. With these reforms, Harichand led his followers to be refraining from conversion to Islam and Christianity but to be loyal to the liberal values and ideas of Matuaism.

Anti-Caste Movement

Their struggle for social justice emerged from the process of formal nomenclature during the census of 1872 when the census authority had depicted 'Chandal' in place of 'Namasudra' in the census report as the collective name of the Namasudras. The conscious leaders among Namasudras had treated the Chandal identification as a social humiliation to them. They did not consider Chandal as their community name but as an objurgation term that was used by the privileged caste due to their jealousy of the Namasudras. The Muslims also used this term following the privileged Hindu castes. Unfortunately, the privileged educated Hindu castes encouraged the census authority and H.H Risley to write down the term Chandal against the Namasudras in the census report and the book 'Tribes and Castes of Bengal'.

The Namasudras regarded it as an act of social degradation and denigration. Therefore, an initiative was taken by them under the leadership of Guruchand Thakur for rectification of this report during the census of 1901 and 1911. The Namasudra leaders of Dacca, Faridpur, Bakarganj, Mymensingh, Jessore and Pabna appealed to The Lieutenant Governor of Bengal for rectification of their community's name through the petition below.[12]

To His Honour
The Lieutenant Governor of Bengal
May it please your honour

The humble memorial of the Nama-Sudras of the district of Dacca, Faridpur, Bakarganj, Mymensingh, Jessore and Pabna in Bengal

Most respectfully Sheweth

I. That the humble memorialists belong to the caste of Nama- Sudras in Bengal.

II. That the Namasudras follow the tenants of Hindu religion and perform marriage Sradha and other ceremonies according to Hindu Sastras and they have no connexion in the origin of occupation with the Chandal who are at present known as Jallad.

III. That the Namasudras are chiefly agriculturist although many of them are Zamindar Talukdar Traders Merchants, Clerks, Smith, Contactors, Carpenters, Teachers, Physician, Postmasters and Muktears like other high castes Hindus of Bengal, and the latter behave with them like the Sahas, Suvarna-Banik and Kaibartts.

IV. That the Hindu Shastra lay down:-

(a) the Chandal and Swaapacha shall beyond the outskirts of villages;

(b) that they shall wear the remains of the dead and iron ornaments.

(c) that dog and ass shall be their chief wealth.

(d) that they shall carry on the transaction with caste man only;

(e) the day shall enter into villagers being market by the king, during the day;

(f) that they shall drug bodies of the dead who had no kinsman;

(g) that they shall execute guilty men sentenced to death by the kind and take their clothing and ornaments;

(h) That good man will not see that in ceremonies; (i) that they shall eat the flesh of dogs;

Most of these occupations are still to be found among the Jallads but none among the Namasudras.

V. That the humble memorialists answer the puranic caste Khuddar and have been certified by many distinguished Brahman Pandits of Bengal to be identified with that caste; press copies of Vyabasthas given and signed by them are annexed herewith your Honour's perusal.

VI. That the Hon'ble Mr H. H. Risley. C.I.E. in his 'Tribes and Castes of Bengal' designates the Nama-Sudras as Chandal without any sufficient Ground, although he admits that no Nama-Sudra acknowledges the term Chandal as his caste designation; and the humble memorialists by reading the census procedure code of 1900 have learned that the Nama are the same as Chandal and their occupation is the same as that of the Chandal, a great mistake which will make them degraded in the eye of the society and which as a statement made by a government will cause damage to their caste and religion.

VII. that it would not be in the humble view of the memorialists, out of place to mention that the memorialists had submitted a petition to the Honorable Mr Risley in February last, representing the above-mentioned facts, with a prayer for correction of the mistake crept as stated above in the said code and the Hon'ble census Commissioner in reply gave the memorialists to understand that communication on the subject had been made with the superintendent of census operation of Bengal. But up until this time the memorialist has not been able to know the result of the said communication.

VIII. That the humble memorialist for the above reasons pray that you honour will kindly pass orders for correcting the statements of the code and Hon'ble Mr Risley's book to draw a clear line of separation between Namasudras and Chandals and that their caste may in future be designated as Nam-Sudras or Kudar but not as Chandal. And the humble memorialists as on duty bound shall ever pray.

ORAKANDI, FARIDPUR.

April 1901.

Eventually, it was rectified in the census of 1911. The caste consciousness and social movement emerged from this event among the Namasudras. It opened the door for movements of the Namasudras against social injustice and inequalities and they became very significant in the determination of social status and caste identity in the first half of the twentieth century. It also unlocked the door of education for them as well as for the backwards. Their anti-caste movement was initiated after the first census of 1872 but it could not solve the caste problems so this movement has been continuing to date. They made several movements against caste discrimination and exploitation during the nationalist movements but without expected result.

Educational Right, School

Namasudras had been deprived of education for centuries due to caste restrictions. They were treated as untouchable by Brahman pundits and privileged castes. According to Hindu social laws and orders education was reserved for Braman, Vaidya and Kayastha in Bengal. The Shudras had to be punished heavily if they would study and utter any hymns violating social laws. The

Namasudras had been guided by their religious gurus following social laws and orders prevailing in old religious texts. It seems that the stigma of untouchability was attached to them in medieval times and since that time they had been confined to manual works only. They had been deprived of education and sharing of resources marginalizing them for centuries in the Hindu society. Naresh Chandra Das believed that they were compelled to be backward due to exploitation and domination of the powerful Zamindars and Brahman since the reign of pro-Brahmin king Ballal Sen, while a social conflict took place and from that time they had been branded as untouchable and deprived of education.[13]

Though they were not allowed in the tole education of Brahmans, the Muslims rulers did not forbid them to enter Madrasha. Some Namasudras violating the Hindu social laws took education from Madrasha in the Mughal era. The colonial rulers introduced English education among the deprived castes in Bengal. The Christen missionaries were interested in spreading education among the deprived castes under colonial rule. This missionary education paved the way for the Namasudras to be conscious of the deprivation of education and exploitation. Dr C. S. Mead came to Orakandi and promised every help to the Namasudras in exchange for conversion to Christianity.[14] But they under the leadership of Guruchand, son of Harichand, refused the proposal of Dr Mead explaining that his people were in the darkness of illiteracy and superstitions, and conversion without education would be in vain; rather he should first arrange their education. Dr Mead helped them without conversion.

Guruchand Thakur (1846-1937), initiated the educational reform movement for the upliftment of the backward and deprived castes. He organized the deprived castes, for the first time, for mass education and government jobs.[15] The first revolt, demanding mass education and government jobs, was held in 1872 under the leadership of Guruchand. Guruchand invited all the backwards in Bengal to join in his movement for spreading the light of education among the deprived people. His first and foremost slogans towards the deprived people was 'no misery either take food or not, but education is must for your children'/*Khao ba na khao tate duksha nai, chhelepule shiksha dao ei ami chai*.[16] Hence, they arranged several meetings in many villages of their community, to discuss their problems and the way out. The first big meeting, under his leadership, was held in 1881 in the village of Dattadanga in the Mollarhat police station of Khulna district.[17] They made a plan for the future movement of the community and sent a deputation to the Lieutenant Governor of Bengal Sir Lancelot Hare demanding educational rights and government jobs, in 1906. Mr Hare later made a report and submitted it to the Governor-General of India.

Consequently, a declaration was made in the Morley-Minto Reform Act in 1909 for education and government jobs for Namasudras as well as the backward castes in Bengal. The colonial government realized the requirement of reservation for education and government jobs for the backward castes of India in response to the movement of Namasudras. Ultimately it was passed in the Montagu Chelmsford Reform Act of 1919. Consequently, they got the opportunity for taking education in government schools and the right to government jobs.

Though the colonial rulers offered an opportunity for taking education and government jobs for them, yet the conservative Hindus sustained the traditional social restrictions despite the endeavour of the colonial rulers. They tried to prevent the movement of the depressed people and when the Namasudras tried to establish schools by their effort with the support of the colonial rulers the Brahmans and Zamindars continued their non-cooperation by all means.

The Namasudras had no educated persons to teach their students. The only way was to hire teachers from upper castes who did not want to help the Namasudras. In primary education, they faced fewer problems than higher education in the first decade of the twentieth century. For the first time a Kayastha educated teacher, Girish Basu at Fukra village near Orakandi took the initiative to help the Namasudras in teaching and establishing a secondary English school at Orakandi. But his attempt did not succeed due to the opposition of the Brahmans. The Brahmans boldly opposed his attempt and arranged to punish him for the help to the Namasudras. The upper castes arranged a meeting in the village Fukra for refraining Girish Basu from any help to the Namasudras, while he was advised that 'the Namasudras are peasant caste by birth, who should not be encouraged in education, and it was not possible to educate them, they suit only for manual and agricultural work, and if they are given the scope of education, there would be a crisis in manual and agricultural work, and consequently, they might face difficulties in future.[18] Girish Basu was suggested to help the Namasudras by establishing a hospital in place of school at Orakandi, which would be suitable for them as they suffered from many diseases due to manual work and unconsciousness about health and hygiene. All the Brahmins including Bhattacharya family members of the Fukra village assured Girish Basu that 'if the Namasudras were given the scope of education they would be out of control and this might destroy the traditional social system'.[19] Hence, Girish Basu became frustrated and decided to refrain from helping the Namasudras and went to Calcutta.

But Guruchand encouraged the Namasudras to continue their movement with self-help and missionary support. He thought that the Namasudras should not be frustrated by the non-cooperation of privileged castes who always opposed their developmental activities and movements. He inspired the villagers to arrange several meetings regularly, to achieve success, to make self - respect, self-confidence to unite and go ahead without the help of privileged castes. He organized a mass movement with his fellowmen for establishing a school in every village of the deprived castes with the help of missionaries.[20] He organized the Bengal Namasudra conference in Khulna town in 1923 to establish a school in every village of deprived castes including Namasudras. The discussion in this conference led to the formation of the 'The Bengal Depressed Class Association' (BDCA) in 1926. Hence, they established many schools in the villages all over Bengal in the first half of the twentieth century with the support of the missionaries and colonial rulers.

The missionaries demonstrated democratic ideas in promoting English education and social services. They tried to implement their aims and objectives by spreading their culture and religion through the medium of English education and social service under the aegis of colonial rule. They drew the attention of the backwards promoting democratic attitude in their social activities irrespective of castes, class and gender. The Namasudras among the backwards were mostly attracted to the socio-educational activities of the missionaries and got their support in the struggle for education for both girls and boys.

Guruchand, for the first time, established a primary school at Orakandi in 1880.[21] He established an English school in the same village under the supervision of the Australian Baptist missionary Dr C. S Mead and Miss Tuck in 1906. A higher English school was established in 1908 and teachers were appointed with the help of missionaries.[22] They established a day school and a Sunday school for girls with the help of Miss Tuck.[23] The missionary education played an important role to ignite the movement against social injustice and inequality. The difficulties of the Namasudras in promoting education had been swept aside with the effort of reformers and the support of colonial rulers. The missionaries influenced the backwards with the liberal social ideas and values. They got the liberal values and democratic concepts from the missionaries and became courageous to move upward despite traditional social laws and orders.

The missionaries converted primarily some Namasudras to Christianity. But the Namasudra leaders were loyal to the good principles of Matuaism and Hinduism. In this context, Sasibhusan, son of Guruchand, worried about the disgrace of conversion of the depressed Hindus to Christianity and he conveyed his worry to his father. On the other hand, Dr C. S. Mead promised Guruchand to help them in all means in exchange for the conversion of their people to Christianity[24]. But Guruchand convinced Dr Mead explaining that his people were in the darkness of illiteracy and superstitions while conversicn into Christianity without education would be in vain; rather he should at first arrange their education before conversion. Guruchand also told Dr Mead that if his people would get a chance of education, they themselves would be grateful to him.[25] Dr Mead was convinced and arranged for their education and helped to establish several primary and secondary schools for them.

Thus, the door of education, the backbone of all strength, opened for the Namasudras in the last decade of the nineteenth century. Keshablal Sarkar, of Pabna District, graduated for the first time among Namasudras in 1902.[26] The second graduate was Sidheswar Halder of Kotalipara, the third graduate and first Deputy Magistrate were Kumud Bihari Mallick. The first three doctors among them in government service were Dr Dinabandhu Mondal, Dr Kalicharan Mondal and Dr Tarini Charan Bala of Gopalganj district.[27] Since the first decade of the twentieth century, their progress has been initiated. Jogendranath Mandal, P R Thakur and many reformers among the Namasudras contributed to the development of the backwards in Bengal. Gopal Sadhu was one of the Namasudra reformers who established an ashram cum educational institution in 1932 in the Khulna district, on a plot of hundred *bighas* of land for the students of Namasudras backward castes.

Gender Disparity Reform

The Namasudra leaders were enthusiastic about removing gender disparity and empowering their women during colonial times. In pre-colonial times they believed in patriarchy according to the guidance of their Brahman gurus. It was difficult to change the rules and regulations regarding women without changing the guru system which had been continuing for centuries. Their gurus supported the 'sati' system, the restrictions for widows in taking food and participating in social activities, the system of child sacrifice in the water of Ganges, the '*antarjali jatra*'/ last journey in the water of Gangues, the system of '*Jogini*', *devadasi*/ service of pretty girls to religious gurus in the name of god. All these inhuman practices on girls and women were familiar in Bengal as well as in India. The colonial rulers, for the first time, recognized these social practices as most inhuman and uncivilized. But they had very little interest in abolishing these inhuman social practices.

Nevertheless, the missionaries' social liberal values and ideas, and the spread of English education influenced the inhuman practices of Hindu society. Many Indian reformers were influenced by the revolutionary thoughts of Europeans and took an initiative to abolish the inhuman practices. They were influenced by the Christan missionaries who provided the ideas of gender equality and the utility of women empowerment. They showed the path for establishing a school for girls, for the first time, in India in Madras in 1715. In Bengal, Raja Rammohan Ray introduced a movement against the inhuman practices of women with the help of missionaries. He initiated the movement by preaching on the support of girls and women in two newspapers *'The Friend of India'* (presently *'The Statesman'*) and *'Samachar Darpan'*. His writings against the most sorrowful sati system influenced many conservative Hindus in Bengal. His spirit of social reform ultimately passed the law for the abolition of Sati in 1829, and Vidyasagar passed the widow marriage act in 1856 with the help of the colonial rulers.

The Namasudras were influenced by the revolutionary activities of Rammohan and Vidyasagar. They moved for equal rights and freedom of girls and women in all activities. They were able to establish girls' schools and gymnasium for girls alongside the boys' schools.[28] They became liberal towards female education.[29] But many leaders among Namasudras allowed their girls to take education and were free in every social activity up to matriculation. They thought that higher education might change the mindset of the girls, which could divert them to be arrogant against the social reputation of their parents in the villages.

The rate of female education at a higher level among the Namasudras had been low in the last century. The rate of female education at the matriculation level had been comparatively better than higher education. The effort of social reformers and the missionaries encouraged female education among the Namasudras but their people could not free themselves from the mindset of patriarchy. Even in the twenty-first century, they hesitate to allow their girls in higher education. But they consider some girls to take higher education if they score excellent results in the examination of matriculation.

They allowed their girls to participate in all social activities and cultural programmes including singing, dancing and playing with their counterparts up to a certain age. They even allowed their girls to take part in physical exercise and gymnastics. Guruchand encouraged his followers in establishing gymnasiums and training schools for women. The first women training school was set up at Orakandi with the help of the missionary lady Miss Tuck in the first decade of the twentieth century.[30] Guruchand thought that the advancement and prosperity of a nation would not be possible if women are deprived of the right to education. He considered, about one century ago, that 'mother is the first teacher of every child, so a child's mother has to be educated properly for the development of their child's life, the children would be misguided and spoil the next generations if their mothers are not educated properly. Many leaders among Namasudras supported Guruchand and engaged in the movement for women empowerment in Bengal. Jogendra Nath Mandal, P. R Thakur, Rasiklal Biswas, Mukunda Behari Mallick et.al were enthusiast in the reform movement for uplifting the women's social status in their community as well as for the backwards, establishing schools for both boys and girls since the midst of the twentieth century. They abolished many inhuman practices prevailing in the society, including child marriage, widowhood, sati system and polygamy.

Child Marriage Reform

The Namasudras believed in child marriage in pre-colonial times while their gurus encouraged them in continuing it. Harichand introduced, for the first time, the ideas of gender equality among the Namasudras in the middle of the 19th century. He, for the first time among Namasudras, thought for the empowerment and liberty of women. He opposed the patriarchal system and biased orthodox laws and orders which considered women as men's consumption and machine of production.

The traditional social laws and orders prescribed five to six years as the average age of a girl's marriage in pre-colonial times. In 1891, the colonial ruler opposed it and passed a bill against child marriage and the first decision was taken that the age of a girl should be 10 years, later it was changed from 10 years to 12 years. An act was again passed by Lord Lansdowne against child marriage.[31] The Namasudra leaders agreed with this act and encouraged their people to preach that the marriage of girls under a mature age was harmful to a girl's life and society.[32]

Guruchand campaigned against child marriage and opposed the old traditional marriage laws. He preached that child marriage had very negative effects on society. Most of the girls who married at an early age lost their husband at a young age, which led them to face many difficulties in widow life. Remarriage of the widow girls was not allowed in that society. Therefore, a child widow had to bear misery for her whole life due to strict social laws and orders. Guruchand argued against the traditional social laws and tried to create a public opinion against them on the eve of the twentieth century. He suggested the end of child marriage and polygamy for saving women from the misery of widowhood.[33]

The girls lived at the house of their parents until they attained puberty and some lived at their in law's house after marriage. Their guardians had to negotiate in this regard. This system had been in practice among Namasudras as well as the other Hindus in Bengal. Even in present times, some villagers among the Namasudras married their daughters before reaching the age of eighteen years. One of the reasons was their fear of losing a good reputation in the village society as it never allowed girls in love marriage or marriage according to the choice of their girls. Sometimes they married their girls forcefully at an early age due to their unconsciousness. They could not realize the consequence of an immature girl's marriage. This has been taking place because of their poor financial condition and their traditional beliefs.

Dowry practise was not rigid among Namasudras in pre-colonial and colonial times. The gift of rupees had to be given to the family of the bride; the family of the bridegroom could not take any gift in the form of dowry as the modern marriage system. The family status had been more important than dowry for making a better marriage. The elder members in a family considered the social position and status of the family to determine the marriage. The economic status of the family was less important than social status. The gift which was given to the bride's family was just for a socially introduced marriage relation, and it was not so rigid and complex. The Namasudras generally considered a minimum amount of rupees or gift to pay to the family of the bride to make a good relationship between the two families. The members of both families could visit each other after introducing the minimum payment of the gift or rupees. It had been a social law that without payment of a minimum amount of rupees to the family of the bride, they could not visit each other before the birth of a child of the married couple. It seems that the number of males was more than females at that time due to the effect of child marriage and polygamy.

Child marriage led to the continuation of the misery of widowhood in Hindu society. The widows had to follow some strict social rules and regulations. The remarriage of a widow even at the time of childhood was considered as one of the most illicit acts in Hindu society. Vidyasagar, for the first time in Bengal, attempted to abolish this cruel system. But the conservative Hindus attempted to dampen down his effort and made sufficient campaign movements against this reform movement. Nevertheless, they could not stop these revolutionary activities of Vidyasagar who passed the widow marriage act in 1856 with the help of colonial rulers.

Widow Remarriage

It was about the same time when Harichand among the Namasudras encouraged his people to promote widow marriage and to allow the widows in all social activities. He invited all the widows to his religious and cultural ceremonies. His son, Guruchand, organized several campaigning programmes in support of widow marriage in the last decade of the nineteenth century. During his time many widow marriages took place among the Namasudras in Bengal. However, the Brahman gurus criticized them for this reform as they considered widow marriage illegal.[34] But the Nmasudras continued their campaign in support of their reforms and effort. Their social reformers Rasiklal Biswas, Manmohan Das et.al organized several campaigning movements for spreading widow marriage among the Namasudras in the first half of the 20th century. Consequently, it became in vogue among the lower castes of Bengal in colonial times.[35] Dhananjoy Biswas of Maldanga village was the first man among Namasudras, who married a widow. Guruchand arranged the marriage of his widowed sister with Srinath. Rashiklal Biswas (MLA), Muktar Roy, Manmohan Das (MLA) and many among them married widows. Debichand arranged thirty-four widow marriages in a single day.[36] Guruchand praised him for this attempt and suggested undertaking this social work as a greater spirit for social upliftment.

Guruchand supported the widow marriage act of Vidyasagar as legal and encouraged their men to marry widows.[37] He got the support and help of the missionaries in promoting widow marriage among them. Dr C.S. Mead had been supportive in the activities of Guruchand who was the most enthusiastic about promoting widow marriage. Guruchand invited Dr C. S. Mead to encourage widow marriage and other reforms as legal social activities. He had been present before many widow marriages for encouraging the courageous persons who did not hesitate to marry widows.[38]

He considered that the lives of widows were miserable, aimless, and hopeless because of all-time negative criticism towards them. The widows had to be victimized by the malpractice of the antisocial people. He felt the requirement of proper social campaigning and arrangement for alerting their people against the cruel social laws and orders for widows. He established an ashram for sheltering the helpless widows at his village Orakandi. He was also an enthusiast in abolishing immature girl marriage and in introducing freedom for the widow in all social activities including physical exercise. He established schools and training centres for empowering their girls and women.

Many leaders beside Guruchand had been an enthusiast for women empowerment among Namasudras. Pagal Chand (1854-1956) played an important role in creating consciousness among the Namasudras regarding gender discrimination in his areas of Khejurtala in the

Barishal district. He was one of the prominent social reformers and philanthropic men among Namasudras. He preached the ideology of gender equality and fraternity considering that men and women are equal in every right and opportunity in society. If a woman pays respect to her husband and is worshipped as Narayana, a man should equally pay respect to his wife. There should not be a disparity in respect and responsibility between men and women. He argued that if a wife of a man is called *ardhangini* (half-female body), in society, then why would a husband not be called *ardhango* (half-male body)? They both might enjoy spiritual, physical and mental pleasantness in the family considering equal social rights and responsibility.[39] Sons and daughters should respect and pray to their parents in place of praying to god or deity as parents are their real creators for fulfilling spiritual aspiration. Everybody should find their creator in real parents before the imagination of spiritual parents. If they pray to spiritual gurus avoiding the real creator, confusion and conflict would appear in human society. Pagalchand suggested respecting parents at first then pray their spiritual gurus, the deity, to reach their spiritual goal.[40] He attacked the traditional system of patriarchy and guru system where the only male got importance and the female got ignorance.[41]

He was a great supporter of widow marriage. His simple argument for support of widow marriage was that 'if a man can marry after the death of his wife, a woman also can marry after the death of her husband'.[42] The gender disparity in remarrying led to disharmony and conflict which promoted illegal activities in society. So he encouraged his people in abolishing gender disparity and promoting women empowerment in building a prosperous society. He married a widow to encourage widow marriage and made many campaigns through the entire Bengal by arranging meetings and ceremonies by using a boat namely *pansy*. He delivered several lectures in front of gatherings in many places all over Bengal. His followers continued his social movement organizing weekly and yearly socio-cultural programmes at his village of Khejurtala of Barishal district.[43].

With the effort of these social reformers, the missionaries tried to influence the women among the backward castes to their liberal social values. Many girls and women got light of education with the effort of the missionaries. They were encouraged to be financially self-dependent earning money through handicrafts and to enjoy their life with satisfaction studying at school and taking training from the training centres established with the help of missionaries in the Namasudra concentration areas in Bengal. Miss Tuck and Miss Thomson helped them in multi-dimensional activities for women's socio-economic empowerment. Guruchand established a*n ashram* for widows for their accommodation and education at Orakandi. The helpless women also sheltered there with the widows and got the support of Guruchand and missionaries.[44]

Abolition of Sati

The Namasudras did not believe in the Sati *pratha*/ self-immolation system, the worst superstition prevailing in Hindu society. It was banned in 1829 for the effort of Rammohan Roy. According to Mahabharata, it had originated from the wife of Daksha, named Sati, who regained the life of her husband by immolating herself on the funeral pyre of her husband following her desire. Since then the Sati system / the self-immolation of widows among Hindus came to be familiar in Indian society after her name Sati.

This practice had been there among the Namasudras until the rise of Buddhism in Bengal. They were influenced by Buddhism which discouraged them from following sati pratha and gender disparity. They all did not believe in conversion to Buddhism but accepted the new liberal values and ideas of Buddhism rejecting the conservative laws and values of Hinduism in the middle age. During colonial times, they again were influenced by liberal social thought and rejected the sati pratha. They followed Matuaism which did not support the cursed customs of sati, child marriage, and dowry. For the rejection of this traditional custom of Hinduism they were criticized by their Brahman gurus, but their social leaders did not hesitate to abolish the sati.

Though the goddesses Lakshmi, Saraswati and Pârbati have been given priority in worshipping than gods Brahma, Vishnu, and Maheshwar, yet women had been treated as inferior among mankind. Women had not been given liberty even to select their bridegroom in pre-colonial times. The emergence of liberal values and laws of the colonial rulers changed this social system gender disparity in India. There was not a single record of violence against the patriarchal social laws among the women in pre-colonial times. It was because of their ignorance, theological beliefs and faith. Many Namasudras accepted the values that women are the most valuable part of human beings and men could not reach any goal without cooperation with their counterpart, the holy women. A household would be valueless without holy women. The goddess of wealth would be compelled to present at home with the presence of holy women in the family. Divine sage would present in that home where holy women are respected. But the holy women would be present in that house where gender discrimination did not exist.

Conclusion

The influence of liberal values on society and belief in revolutionary activities led the Namasudras to many reforms in the late nineteenth century and the first half of the twentieth century. The reform movements changed the socio-economic, cultural and religious attitude of the Namasudras as well as the other deprived castes. But they could not be united as required for gaining the political power for holistic development and upliftment of the community. Their great leader Guruchand Thakur, realizing the weakness of the Namasudras had advised them to take part in political activities for their upliftment.

Many changes in socio-economic, political and professional aspects took place in this period. The Namasudras became more coherent and organized and ran through rapid changes getting the ideas of new liberal values of the British. Violating the biased traditional rules and regulations, they organized several movements against the domination and exploitation of Varna Hindus; they attempted to shape a new identity for their community. They initiated a struggle to make a separate socio-religious self-image. Their socio-economic and political activities, anti-caste movement and attitude during this time were significant in the history of Bengal as they were a numerous, prominent and influential peasant community. Playing a multidimensional role in agricultural production, boat making, furniture-making, and cultural activities they enhanced the holistic development of Bengal.

ENDNOTES AND REFERENCES

1. Pramatha Ranjan Thakur: *Atmacharitra ba Purbasmriti*, (Thakurnagar: Binapani Press, 1995), p. 101.
2. *Ibid.*, p. 99.

3. Tarak Chandra Sarkar: *Sri Sri Hari Lilamrta*, (Thakurnagar, Modern Press, BS 1347), p. 47.
4. A new religious sect in Hinduism.
5. Religion within the household.
6. Tarak Chandra Sarkar: *op.cit.*, p. xxiii, *'Karibe grihastha dharma loye nijo naaari, Grihe theke nyasi vanaprastha brahmachari, Paranaari maatribat mithyaa naahi kabe, Para dhukshe dukshi sadaa satcharitra rabe'*.
7. The followers of Matuaism.
8. Harpada Biswas: *Prochar Noy Satya*, in Santosh Kumer Barui (ed.) *Matua Darpan*, (Aanath, Durgapur 2008) pp. 17-19.
9. Harpada Biswas, *op.cit.*, p. 18.
10. S. Bandyopadhyay: *Caste, Protest and Identity in Colonial India; The Namasudras of Bengal, 1872-1947*, (New Delhi: Oxford University Press, 2011), p. 39.
11. *Diksha* had been as the initiation of the spiritual guidance of Brahmin guru.
12. Sarat Chandra Biswas: *Namasudra Samprodayer Atmakatha*, (Srimali Computers Kolkata 2005), p. 247.
13. Naresh Chandra Das: *Namasudra Samproday o Bangladesh* (Kolkata, Dipali Book House, 1997), p. 125.
14. Acharya Mahananda Haldar: *Sri Sri Guruchand Charit*. (Thakurnagar: Resolution, 2009), p. 160.
15. *Ibid.*, p. vi.
16. Acharya Mahananda Haldar, *op.cit.*, p. 161.
17. S. Bandyopadhyay: *op.cit.*, p. 51
18. Acharya Mahananda Haldar: *op.cit.*, p. 141.
19. *Ibid.*, p. 139.
20. Jatin Bagchi: *Jati Dharma O Samaj Bibartan*, (Kolkata, Sanjib Prakashan, 1990), p. 143.
21. Haldar Acharya Mahananda: *op.cit.*, p. vii.
22. Promothranjan Thakur: *Atmacharit ba Purbasmriti*, (Thakurnagar: Binapani Press, 1995), p. 57.
23. S. Bandyopadhyay: *op. cit.*, p. 56.
24. Haldar Acharya Mahananda: *op.cit.*, p. 160.

25. *Ibid.*, p. 161.
26. Naresh Chandra Das: *Namasudra Samproday o Bangladesh* (Kolkata, Dipali Book House, 1997): p. 125.
27. *Ibid.*
28. Acharya Mahananda Haldar, *op.cit.*, p. 171.
29. *Ibid.*
30. Acharya Mahananda Haldar: op.cit., p. 371.
31. Jatin Bagchi: *Jati Dharma O Samaj Bibartan*, (Kolkata, Sanjib Prakashan, 1990), p. 12.
32. Acharya Mahananda Haldar: *op.cit.*, p. 253.
33. *Ibid.*, p. 253.
34. *Ibid.*, p. 254.
35. Rakhi Mandal: *Matua Biswase Narir Abasthan*, in Kapil Krishna Biwas (ed), *Sri Harichand Thakur Matua Dharma Andalan* (Kolkata, Nikhil Bhara Prakashani, 2012), pp. 139-148.
36. *Ibid.*
37. Acharya Mahananda Haldar, *op.cit.*, p. 245.
38. Acharya Mahananda Haldar, *op.cit.*, p. 277.
39. Naresh Chandra Das, *op. cit.*, p. 47.
40. *Ibid.*
41. *Ibid.*
42. Naresh Chandra Das: *op.cit.*, p. 125.
43. Jatin Bagchi: *op.cit.*, p. 161.
44. Haldar Acharya Mahananda: *op.cit.*, p. 371.

4

The Namasudras in Bengal Politics, 1901-1947

Introduction

The political awareness of the Namasudras had emerged from the social protest movement that took place after the first census of Bengal (1872). Guruchand Thakur, for the first time among the Namasudras, felt that they need participation in politics for their upliftment. He encouraged his people with the words 'the king is the source of all power and a religious community can be lively having king power' (*Sakal saktir utsay rajsakti…Je dharma rara achhe se dharma taja*).[1] He arranged a conference at village Dattadanga in Mollarhat police station in Khulna district for the political unity of the Namasudras. More than five thousand Namasudras from Faridpur, Barishal, Jessore, Khulna Dacca and Mymensingh districts attended this conference (1881). Guruchand encouraged them in strengthening their organizations at this conference against social injustice. He emphasized the education of their children for the holistic development of the community. A memorandum had been made at this conference for rectification of their nomenclature sending a deputation to the census authority.

The Namasudra representatives from Bakarganj, Faridpur, Jessore, Dacca and Pabna jointly appealed to the Government of Bengal for changing their community's name from 'Chandal' to 'Namasudra' in 1901. Many members of the Namasudra Associations jointly led the movement and supported the affirmation of their claim. Some British officials including the Magistrate of Faridpur and Collector of Dacca had supported them and considered their demand as rational. They agreed with the Namasudras in this regard and promised to implement their demand. Hence, a deputation of the Namasudras had submitted a memorandum to the Lieutenant Governor of Bengal Sir Lancelot Hare for rectification of their community's name and ensuring equal rights in socio-political activities and government jobs (1906). Mr. Hare later submitted a report of the memorandum to the Governor-General of India and a declaration had been made in the Morley Minto Reform Act in 1909 for extending permission to have the education and government jobs for the backward castes of Bengal. Consequently, the colonial rulers had changed their community's name from 'Chandal' to 'Namasudra' in the census record and agreed to open government jobs for them as well as the other deprived castes. The Namasudras were encouraged by this support of the colonial rulers and they initiated political activities.

The upper castes political leaders had no interest in incorporating the deprived caste leaders with the nationalist politics as the primary target of the deprived castes was to reform the traditional social laws and order which was not liked by the nationalist leaders. The upper caste leaders had an interest in continuing the traditional laws and orders for sustaining their privileges. They had also an interest in securing their rent collection from the Namasudras peasants under their domain of landlords and social institutions. Consequently, the

Congress leaders did not support the social reform movements and political participation of the Namasudras.

The Demand during Anti-Partition Movement

But the Congress leaders required the participation of all the native people in the anti-partition movement against the British. They called all the castes communities including Namasudras and Muslims for boycotting British goods for success in the *Swadeshi* movement.[2] But the Namasudras and Muslims had been non-cooperative with the Congress leaders because of their financial crisis and dominative attitude of the nationalist leaders. They both shared a similar standpoint of avoiding the Swadeshi movement and supported the colonial ruler as they got support from the British. They were the peasant communities and subjected to the same socio-economic constraints due to the domination of the high caste Hindus. From 1905, they became united against Congress leaders and politicians in the context of the anti-partition movement.

Ambika Charan Majumdar, a Congress leader had made an effort to rally with the Namasudras for the anti-partition movement, but very few of the Namasudras participated in his rally. He lived in a village (Ghritakandi) beside Orakandi in the Faridpur district. He tried to motivate the Namasudras for supporting the *swadeshi* movement by organizing several meetings in the southern part of the Faridpur district. But Guruchand Thakur of village Orakandi was a very influential leader of Namasudras in that area. He discouraged the Namasudras from participating in the anti-participation movement. Mr Majumder requested the Namasudras to convince Guruchand and his son Sasibhusan for participating in the movement but failed. Guruchand and his son campaigned that the Congress leaders had ignored the upliftment movement of the deprived castes.[3] They analyzed that the congress leaders never tried to reach out to them till they faced trouble in the movement against the British. The Congress leaders had suddenly developed a great interest in the backward castes since they required their support.

The Namasudras already had the support of the colonial rulers and moved close to the British. They appraised their socio-economic deprivation to the British officials and bestowed their support against the upper caste Hindus in the context of the anti-partition movement. The Namasudra leaders felt that the Congress leaders were enthusiastic to move against the British for their self-interest. Before the beginning of the anti-partition movement, they never thought on behalf of the Namasudras' development. They did not utter a single word against the exploitation of the landlords and Zamindars. But the British rulers appeared to be more impartial to them. The colonial rulers never went against the interest of the backward castes as they upheld a view of social equality. So the Namasudras were interested in being loyal to the British rather than to the upper caste Hindu politicians who were trying to oppose the British during the *Swadeshi* Movement. Besides this, the poor peasants needed to buy cheap British goods. The poor Namasudras had no financial capacity to participate in the anti-partition movement.

The Namasudras came close to the British since the Governor of Bengal passed a resolution in 1907 to distribute the government jobs in proportion to all castes and communities, including the peasants. They got important jobs in the post of the sub-registrar, government doctor and deputy magistrate which encouraged them further to promote the upliftment of their community. Their educational upliftment was promoted by giving government grants to establish and run their schools well. So they decided not to take part in the anti-British movement.

But they were numerous among the deprived castes of Bengal. Without their cooperation, it was difficult to succeed in the *swadeshi* movement. *Swadeshi* leaders had been to secure the support of the Namasudras but they could not convince the Namasudras who had grievances against those leaders who had ignored their social upliftment. They did not even allow the Namasudras to take their seat beside an upper caste person. Several meetings were held in Namasudra concentrated areas since 1908 for social justice but failed due to non-co-operation of the Congress leaders.

Under this circumstance, the leaders like G.G. Pattandar and Ambika Majumdar promised to arrange for raising the social status of the Namasudras if they would cooperate with the *swadeshi* leaders. Sricharan Sen, a *swadeshi* leader of the Barisal district, acknowledged that the Namasudras were the only fighting community among the Hindus in Bengal and without the cooperation of the Namasudras the movement would not be successful, in the conference held on 17-19 August in 1908. He further argued that if their people could demand rights to freedom against British domination, then why should the Namasudras not assert rights to freedom against the domination of the upper castes? He tried to encourage the Namasudras to adopt a resolution for their upliftment where he included that the washermen *(dhobi)* and barbers *(napit)* should serve the Namasudras as they were also Hindus. Surendranath Sen added that the caste system should be abolished for promoting equal social rights. But all these lectures were only empty promises and not a single step had been taken by them to translate their promises into action. They continued the practices of social restrictions, commensality and separations with the Namasudras. The Namasudras realized that the promises made by the *swadeshi* leaders were only to get support and success of the *Swadeshi* movement.

Some of the Namasudras supported the nationalist leaders. Kesab Chandra Das, a leader of the Bengal Namasudra association, for example, worked for the *Swadeshi* leaders. His centre of activities was Calcutta. His brother Mohini Mohan Das was also sympathetic to the nationalist leaders. Mukunda Behari Mallik associated with them and tried to get the support of his people for nationalist movements. In association with the nationalist leaders, these leaders organized several meetings and conferences for getting the mass support of the Namasudras in the context of the *Swadeshi* movement but they did not succeed because they could not influence the mass of the Namasudras with welfare and developmental activities like the colonial rulers and their missionaries.

The nationalist leaders had been always indifferent in the question of caste discrimination. Sometimes they showed interest in solving the caste conflict and in the improvement of the socio-educational status of the Namasudras but all these were without effect. On the other hand despite the caste restrictions, the colonial rulers put into effect many plans and prospects of the Namasudras. They opened the door of education for the first time for the depressed castes in the late nineteenth century. The nationalist leaders, however, continued to subscribe to prejudice even during the days of the *Swadeshi* movement. They promised to uplift the caste status of the Namasudras only to get support in the Swadeshi movement. They never allowed the Namasudras to be socially equal with them. Even the then Vice-Chancellor of Calcutta University, Debaprasad Sarbadhikari, was unable to arrange for the Namasudra students in accommodating them in the same hostel with the students of the upper caste due to caste prejudice. Nor could he build a separate hostel for the Namasudra students for the objection of the upper caste Congress leaders (1916).[4]

Under this circumstance, the Namasudras could not overcome the doubt regarding the discriminatory attitude of the Congress leaders. Consequently, the Namasudra leaders continued their non-cooperation with the Congress leaders.

Formation of Association

They formed some associations for their unification and growing consciousness, both socially and politically for their upliftment. The *'Namasudra Hitaishini Samiti'* (NHS) was formed in 1902 in Dacca for political consciousness and for challenging the Congress leaders. The 'Bengal Namasudra Association' (BNA) was founded as a political organization for the Namasudras of all the districts of Bengal in 1912. It led to communication with all the Namasudra leaders of Bengal for their socio-religious and political aspirations. It was the same time when a greater section of the community was organized under the platform of Matuaism. The popular Namasudra leader Guruchand Thakur founded the *'Matua Mahasangha'* (MM) for the unification of the Matuas. He led the Matuas to be united, organizing religious programmes under the platform of Matua Dharma. Guruchand and his son Sasibhusan encouraged the Matuas to be loyal to the colonial rulers as the British had supported the upliftment of the deprived castes. Promoth Ranjan Thakur son of Sasibhusan Thakur supported the Congress leaders and carried out his political activities under the aegis of the Congress party but he had been an enthusiast to the progress deprived castes including Namasudras. He joined the political activities in Bengal in 1929, organizing 'All Bengal Depressed Castes Association' (ABDCA), he protested against the allocation of only ten reserved seats for the backward castes of Bengal, by Ramsay Macdonald, the Prime Minister of England, in 1932.

Demand during the Home Rule and Non-Cooperation Movement

The nationalist leaders continued seeking the support of the Namasudras and invited them to participate in home rule movements. They showed more eagerness to improve the socio-educational status of the Namasudras for strengthening Hindu unity. The Home Rule League was organized by Annie Besant and B. G. Tilak for the demand of self-Government in 1917. The league's leaders urged Namasudras' participation in the league but the Namasudras, as well as the Muslims, had a similar stand as it was during the *Swadeshi* movement. The Muslims doubted that the Home Rule would be nothing for them but Hindu domination in India. The Namasudras in a similar way considered self-government as an instrument of upper caste Hindus' domination to the deprived castes in place of liberal rule of the British. Hence, 'Home Rule' for them would be deprivation and exploitation of dominant Hindus, which might lead the British to discontinue the support to the Namasudras if they support the Home rule. Therefore, they opposed the Home Rule movement and preferred to rely on the British.

Rather they organized several campaigning programmes against the Home Rule movement through their organizations. Several articles had been written in their journals '*Pataka*' and '*Namasudra Hitaishini*' on the support of colonial rule. In Calcutta, Mukunda Behari Mallick, the editor of *Pataka*, was one of the prominent leaders of the Bengal Namasudra Association. He expressed his faith in colonial rule through his writings in 'Pataka' published in Calcutta. Many of the Namasudra leaders supported colonial rule through writings and campaigning. They had discussed their desires and aspirations directly with the then Governor of Bengal, Lord Ronald shay and apprised him of their support to the backward castes. The Governor on his part assured them of an equal opportunity for their community based on capability under the British administrative support in the context of their impending political conflict with the upper castes.

This assurance encouraged the Namasudra leaders to make their community stronger and politically organized for future scopes in Bengal politics. They arranged a meeting under the leadership of Purna Chandra Mallick in Calcutta (3rd November 1917). More than thirty leaders from different parts of Bengal attended the meeting. They unanimously passed sixteen resolutions for future aims and objectives. They decided mainly to be loyal to the British Government through these resolutions, to make a powerful protest against social injustices, exploitation, and inequalities, to make arrangements for the upliftment of the community and to form a committee to communicate with the government for appraising the Governor of their grievances. Next year they arranged a big conference for a similar purpose on the same date and place, under 'The Bengal Namasudra Association'. All the famous Namasudra leaders from all regions of Bengal province, including Rasiklal Biswas, Mukunda Behari Mallick, Prasanta Kumar Das, Birat Chandra Mandal and Chaitanya Krishna Mandal attended the conference. Chaitanya Krishna Mandal presided over the conference. Different associations and committees including two constitutional enquiry committees for transferred subjects and franchise were formed at this conference. Thus, the Namasudras organized themselves against the leaders of the 'Home Rule' movement.

The nationalist leaders, on the other hand, tried to make the Namasudras understand that the 'Home Rule' would not be against their interests. They promised to uplift the socio-political status of the Namasudras and tried to convince the Namasudras, organizing several meetings, that the upper caste Hindus would not be based on the caste question. One of the prominent leaders among the upper-caste Hindus, Manoranjan Guhathakurata, explained that 'the Home Rule would not be Brahmanic oligarchy and that democratic system would be most beneficial to the lower caste masses'.[5] Srinath Dutta, a nationalist leader had made an effort to make them understand through writing in '*Nabyabharat*'. He argued that Congress was not a political institution of Brahmanical domination. It was a platform where there would be representatives from all the sections of the people including all deprived castes like the Bagdi and Keora who would have equal rights in the political sphere. In the same way, many famous intellectuals including the scientist Meghnad Saha tried to make a compromise between the Congress leaders and the deprived castes in the context of the Home Rule movement. But they could hardly change the antagonistic situation involved in the caste question.

The Namasudras did not believe in lectures of the upper castes but the implementation of the promises. They thought that they should not participate in either the 'Home Rule' movement or the 'Non-cooperation' movement as their people were poor and depressed and were unable to understand the politics and movement for independence without securing their freedom from caste restrictions and without getting an education. Unless they could eliminate caste discrimination their participation in the political movement would be useless.

On the other hand, Congress leaders like Bipin Chandra Pal thought that they should first attain freedom then they could think of social reform for the deprived castes.[6] M.K. Gandhi, who had given the call for the 'Non-cooperation' movement wanted to upgrade the status of untouchables, changing their name from untouchables to Harijan. He suggested his fellowmen treat the Harijan not as untouchable but as the men of god. Thus he wanted to get the support of the deprived castes but he never thought of abolishing the discriminatory laws and social inequalities prevailing in the Hindu society.

The standpoint of the depressed castes and the nationalist leaders remained the same as before during the 'Non-cooperation movement. The deprived castes had been less interested in this movement all over the country. Firstly, they had no clear conception regarding the significance of their participation in the movement. Secondly, they were detached from education for centuries and were unconscious of their role in the movement. The conscious deprived caste leaders had no interest to move against the British as they could not see any opportunity from this movement because they were always deprived of the fruits of political activities.

The leaders of the deprived caste demanded firstly to remove the social convolution then think about the participation in the non-cooperation movement. Guruchand Thakur argued that the deprived caste people had to engage in their work of earning their bread daily as they had no other options to maintain their family. Consequently, they had no scope to participate in the movement. On the other hand, they had no future in supporting the nationalist leaders because the fruit of the movement would be appropriated by the upper caste dominant Hindus only. Besides this, the upper castes had enough time for organizing movements as they had either service or sufficient wealth. They could invest their time for their interest in acquiring political and social power after the victory in the movement. All the opportunities would go to the upper castes after getting freedom if the present social system would not change.

So without social change, the freedom would be valueless to the underprivileged castes. When the British would give freedom without changing the traditional discriminatory system then the upper caste would occupy all the administrative posts including local boards, central boards and any other platforms of the society.

Therefore, the conscious leaders among the Namasudras, organizing several conferences and local meetings, tried to unite the depressed castes against the nationalist movement and analyzed the reasons why they did not need to participate in the non-cooperation movement. They could join the movement against the British only after asserting equality in society. Eventually, Guruchand, keeping the Namasudras alienated from the non-cooperation movement, drew the attention of the nationalist leaders for organizing the national movement with the holistic development of the nation. He was not against the nationalist movement but he tried to protest against the confusion prevailing in the mind of the conservative leaders. He repeatedly drew the attention of the upper caste Hindu leaders for social reform and upliftment of the Namasudras but failed.

The reason for his failure was not only the disinterest of the upper caste leaders but also the disunity of the Namasudras themselves. The lack of consciousness and want of education had been responsible for their disunity. The poor peasants among the Namasudras had no idea of their scope and opportunities during the time of movements. They, therefore most of the time, were motivated by clever nationalist leaders rather than their conscious leaders. Besides this fact, some of the Namasudra leaders were interested in getting personal profits by supporting the nationalist leaders. The Nationalist leaders showed interest in eradicating the problems of the deprived castes during the need for mass participation in the non-cooperation movement but they developed cold feet when it was the time to take action to their interest. This was understood only by a few of the Namasudras. This trend of manipulating the politics and policies of the leaders made the Namasudras confused and complex.

The Election of 1923

The Namasudras could not be united and confused about their role to play in Bengal politics and anti-British movements. The average Namasudras could not understand the significance of casting votes in the election of 1923. Their average casting of votes was very low in almost all the constituencies of Bengal. It was only 33.95 per cent in north Bakarganj, 46.91 per cent in south Bakarganj, 46.09 per cent in North Faridpur, 36.85 per cent in south Faridpur and 45.47 per cent in Khulna in the election of 1923. As a result, all the Namasudra candidates were defeated by the opponent candidates. Mukunda Behari Mallick got 22.08 per cent from Khulna; he was defeated by Sailaja Nath Ray Choudhury. Nirod Behari Mallick got 41.84 per cent of votes from south Bakarganj and was defeated by Satyendra Nath Ray. Kesab Chandra Das got 15.90 per cent of votes from North Bakarganj and was defeated by Nisit Chandra Sen. Braja Mohan Mandal got 24.23 per cent of votes cast from North Faridpur and was defeated by Kumud Sankar Roy Choudhury. The Namasudra candidates from Dacca and Jessore were also defeated in the election of 1923. The main cause of these defeats was their economic backwardness and lack of education.

The result of the election led the Namasudras leaders to be worried about the unconsciousness of their people. Consequently, they associated with the colonial rulers more actively in respect of social reform for creating awareness of the Namasudras. The Namasudras sent a deputation to the colonial government for supporting the British (1928). They highlighted their socio-economic hopelessness, educational crisis and need for consciousness to the rulers. On the other hand, the colonial rulers had sympathy for Namasudras and they had a disinterest in the discriminatory approach of the upper caste Hindu leaders. The Namasudras, therefore, decided not to be led by upper-caste leaders in the future but by the colonial rulers.

Non-Cooperation with the Civil Disobedience Movement

M.K. Gandhi tried to unify all the caste communities for the success of the civil disobedience movement (12th March 1930). He visited Bengal and urged the Congress leaders to cooperate with all the castes communities of Bengal. But almost all the leaders of the deprived castes including Namasudras decided to oppose the Congress leaders. They could not find rationality in joining the movement. They rather organized a campaigning programme to motivate the peasants against the anti-British movement. The Muslims supported the Namasudras. They jointly kept themselves alienated from the civil disobedience movement in the Namasudra concentration areas of Khulna, Jessore, Bakarganj and Pirojpur. The Congress leaders had to face strong confrontation in these areas in the weekly *hats*. Birat Chandra Mandal, one of the Namasudra leaders, attending a meeting of All India Depressed Classes Association' (AIDCA), at Simla (30th June 1930), asserted that the Namasudras of Bengal would be antagonistic to the civil disobedience movement as the dominion status should not be granted in such a situation where there was no social equality. He called for the implementation of the system of the separate electorate to provide a safeguard for the depressed classes. The other Namasudra leaders including Rasiklal Biswas supported him.

The Separate Electorate, Reservation in Education and Government Job

The Congress leaders worried about the demand for a separate electorate of the Namasudras and deprived castes. The Namasudras demanded it for socio-economic and educational development. It had emerged from the Morley-Minton reforms of 1909 when the demand for a separate electorate of the Muslims had been granted by the British administrators. The tension of the Congress leaders increased when the Census Commissioner E.A. Gait promised the deprived castes to enumerate their separate identity in all kinds of activities including politics in the census of 1911. It made the Congress leaders apprehensive of the intentions of the British rulers. They sensed a hint of separation of the Hindus to weaken their strength by giving a separate electorate to the Namasudras and other depressed Hindus by the British rulers.

Under this circumstance, the nationalist leaders established the 'All India Hindu League' for the unity of the Hindus for serving their political purpose. They took an initiative to protest the intentions of the divide and rule policy of the British. The Namsudras were numerous among the Hindu communities who could contest with the Muslims of eastern Bengal but if they would be motivated to move against the Hindu gentries then it would be harmful to the political interests of the Congress. Consequently, the Namasudras became indispensable in the nationalist political sphere since the 1910s. On the other hand, the Namasudras realized that it was the right time for the deprived castes to demolish entire social barriers and to move against all social injustices through this changing wave in Bengal politics.

Some Namasudra leaders supported the demand for a joint electorate with reserved seats. The Bengal

Namasudra Franchise Bar and the Namasudra Association of Jessore district supported the Joint electorate with reserved seats. The Bengal Namasudra Association supported a separate electorate, which was demanded by Dr B. R Ambedkar. It was about the same time when the 'Communal Award' was declared by the British government. The Namasudras of Bengal were granted ten seats for the special electorate in this award. But only ten reserved seats were not logical according to the population ratio in Bengal. So the Namasudra leaders were not satisfied with this award.

It was about the same time, when Promoth Ranjan Thakur, grandson of Guruchand Thakur, returned from England after the completion of his study. He joined Bengal politics in 1929. Organizing 'All Bengal Depressed Castes Association' (ABDCA), he protested against the allocation of only ten reserved seats for the backward castes of Bengal, by Ramsay Macdonald, the Prime Minister of England, in 1932. Consequently, the reserved seats were increased from ten to thirty in the same year[7]. He tried to organize the Namasudras to support the demand for a separate electorate. He arranged a meeting two days after the commencement of Gandhi's fast unto death against a separate electorate. He discussed with other Namasudra leaders and decided to protest against Gandhi's ideas of a joint electorate. They did not care for the threat to Gandhi's life. P. R Thakur considered that the interest of the depressed caste, as well as the Namasudras of Bengal, was much more important than the life of Gandhi who did nothing for the welfare of the deprived castes. Thakur argued that Gandhi had no right to deprive the Shudras by impeding the separate electorate which would ensure the share of political power to the deprived castes.

In this circumstance, all the backward castes including Chamar, Kapali, Malo and Kaibarta were supporting a separate electorate. All the leaders of backward castes attended the meeting organized by P. R Thakur and decided to demand a separate electorate. They jointly appealed to the Government of Bengal to increase the number of reserved seats or to arrange a separate electorate. They demanded increasing the reserved seat minimum up to fifty in the legislative assembly of Bengal and ensuring a minimum of two ministers in Bengal. They decided to disobey the resolution of the provincial Hindu Mahasabha (HM) and the direction of the Congress leaders on the question of sharing political power.

But the event turned in favour of a joint electorate when Gandhi opposed the issue of a separate electorate. He had a doubt that the Hindus would be disintegrated and weakened if a separate electorate was granted. He had an interest in the unification of all the Hindu castes for ensuring the strength of the national movement for freedom but he did not consider the interest of deprived castes. He was determined to ensure the joint electorate by any means and pledged his life for this crucial issue. Therefore, ultimately Ambedkar and other leaders including Rasiklal Biswas of Namasudra were compelled to sign the Poona Pact (1932) on behalf of Gandhi with the allocation of thirty reserved seats instead of ten for the Bengal Legislative Assembly.

All the deprived castes including Namasudras were displeased by the Poona Pact. The allocated reserved seats were also inadequate considering the proportion of the deprived castes' population. Most of the Namasudra leaders of the 'Depressed Castes Association' (DCA) of Bengal believed that the joint electorate enactment was detrimental to the interests of the Namasudras as well as the backward castes. And there was also a chance of its being abused due to the discriminatory attitude of the caste Hindus. It would not be able to ensure the reservation policy in the

Legislative Assembly. But they were compelled to accept it with the thirty reserved seats of the joint electorate.

The Namasudras and other deprived castes leaders demanded one-third reservation in the educational institutions and government jobs. Already the government had enacted the provision of one-third reservation in education and employment for the Muslims of Bengal (1930). The Namasudra leader Mukunda Behari Mallick explained that they ought to have such reservation because the dominant upper-caste Hindu employers always remained biased in education and employment in Bengal. They would also influence the recruiting authorities in the recruitment of government jobs. They also would influence the activities in the educational institutions. The display of sympathy by the high caste Hindus during the mass movement against the British had impressed the backward people but they had done nothing to keep their promise for the benefit of the depressed castes of Bengal.

P.R. Thakur had a similar standpoint, so he supported the demands of the depressed castes. He added that at least one judicial post should be reserved for the Namasudras in Bengal. He argued that the Namasudras had the requisite qualification to hold such a post but due to the discriminatory attitude of the upper caste they had been deprived. On the other hand, most of the depressed caste candidates were not conscious regarding the recruitment process and even the requirement for governmental jobs. Most of the time, they could not appear before the recruiting authority due to their lack of consciousness. In addition to this the conscious upper caste leaders and officials most of the time influenced the recruiting authority due to the fulfilment of their self-interest. They never allowed the depressed caste candidates to get recruited to the important posts. Therefore the percentage of recruitment of the depressed castes was not satisfactory up till 1935.

Under these circumstances, the deprived caste leader P.R, Thakur and Mukunda Behari Mallick drew the attention of the recruiting authorities to enquire about the fact and to make proper arrangement for the recruitment of the depressed caste candidates including Namasudras according to their rights. They discussed the matters of organizing a conference at Orakandi in April 1935 and ascribed all the problems including their deprivation of recruitments to the government of Bengal for ensuring their rights. Consequently, the government arranged to ensure their recruitment as per communal ratio in various posts according to their rights in all the districts of Bengal. The authorities extended the recruitments for the depressed castes up to fifteen per cent of the total vacancies in Bakarganj, Khulna, Twenty four Parganas, Burdwan, Birbhum, Murshidabad, Dacca, Faridpur and Jessore.

The Namasudras were comparatively progressive among the depressed castes of Bengal in the political context and employment. The opportunity of reservation led them to be prosperous in education and politics in Bengal. The progress led the upper castes to be jealous of the Namasudras and began to campaign before the Government against the reservation of Namasudras in education, employment and politics. P.R Thakur requested the government to avoid such kind of intention to keep them aside from the influence of the upper castes leaders. On the other hand, he tried to unify the Namasudra leaders to win the election of 1937 but failed. The leaders of the community could not be united for the first general election of 1937 (declared on 6th February 1935).

The Election of 1937 and Jogendra Nath Mandal

Some of the Namasudra leaders including Rasiklal

Biswas and Mukunda Behari Mallick joined with the Congress before this declaration. They accepted the Congress ticket to compete in the election and drew the attention of Muslim voters to win the election. They won the election in reserved seats only, with eleven other Namasudra candidates. Pulin Behari Mallick won against the Congress candidate from Howrah. Dhananjoy Roy won against Mohini Mohan Das from Dacca. Madhusudan Sarkar, Amritalal Mandal and Manmohan Das won from Bogra-Pabna, Mymensingh and Tripura respectively. Some of the well known Namasudra candidates including P.R. Thakur, Birat Chandra Mandal and Lalit Chandra Ball were defeated. On the other hand, J.N. Mandal defeated a popular Congress leader Saral Kumar Dutt, nephew of Aswini Kumar Dutt, from Bakarganj North. It was an exceptional victory of a Namasudra leader, which indicated the growth of political consciousness among the poor Namasudra peasants of Bakarganj.

J.N. Mandal as a lawyer had an influential role in the political activities of Bakarganj. He became familiar with Bakarganj through his welfare activities for the deprived castes. He started it after joining as a lawyer (25th July 1936) in the district court of Barisal. The deprived castes suffered from the victimization of false charges due to their educational and financial weakness and lack of lawyer in their communities. Under these circumstances, he stands for the support of poor victims and serves without fees. He won several cases on behalf of deprived castes including Namasudras and became popular among the people of Bakarganj as a successful lawyer. These developments prepared him as a political leader in Bengal.

There was no reserved seat in north Bakarganj where he was familiar. Besides this, it was almost impossible for him to fight an election without experience and financial support. But some lawyers, service holders and friends stood for him and forced him to contest. They collected money (about Rs. 250) for campaigning and submitting the nomination paper. Further J.N. Mandal had to fight against a popular Congress candidate. It was almost impossible to win the seat against a popular leader. But Namasudras and others including Kaibarta, Jalia Kaibarta, Jhalo, Dhoba Patni, Muchi voluntarily engaged in campaigning for him. Through their support, he won the election (6th February 1937). His strong opponent Saral Kumar Dutta secured 10653 votes while Mr. Mandal got 12069 votes.[8]

It was a great opportunity for him to be a member of the Legislative Assembly (MLA) for the upliftment of the deprived castes. In the first year as MLA, he developed the Madhyamik English educational institution, 'Agailjhara Bheegi Halder Public Academy' (ABHPA) to be a higher English educational institution for the students of backward castes. He encouraged the Namasudra students who could not attend this school due to the financial crisis. This institution had various difficulties including the financial crisis and land property.

Mr. Mandal called a guardian meeting to resolve the problems. In the meeting, he impressed them with a very influential lecture. He appealed to them to send their children to school, assuring the solution to their financial problems. Consequently, the Namasudra student's strength increased from ninety-three to three hundred in a year. The land of the school was under the lease of the district board of Barisal. The board refused to renew the lease as it expired earlier. Jogendranath, as a member of the district Board, requested the secretary of the board to include the issue as an agenda of discussion in the next meeting but the secretary did not do it. Mr Mandal informed the matter to the president of the school committee and district magistrate Mr John

Lister Leulin and ultimately it was included in the agendas of discussion and solved the problem. It was possible due to the financial support from the government through membership as an MLA and support of the then education Minister of Bengal Abul Kasem Fajlul Huq, financial Minister Nalini Ranjan Sarkar and the educationist Dr Syamaprasad Mukherjee.

Inspired by his welfare activities, a police constable from the Namasudra community appealed to Mr. Mandal for a remedy of discriminatory residential arrangement in governmental police quarters. The police of backward castes could not live in the governmental quarters with the upper castes as they were treated as untouchables. Mr. Mandal regretted the problem during the budget discussion in 1938 and appealed to the higher authority to solve it. The then home minister Khwaja Nazimuddin promised to do it. He formed an enquiry committee and sent this committee to Dr S.N Dasgupta, the principal of Kolkata Sanskrit College, to know whether the caste Hindu police constables would have any chance to be contaminated if they live in a separate room with the untouchables in the same building. The Principal suggested arranging a separate room without a roof for residing the untouchables alongside the upper caste's room to avoid contamination.

It was the same time when an appeal was sent to Mr. Mandal to arrange for the construction of an embankment at the north side of the Harter bill (a water body) in the Ujirpur police station in Bakarganj. The poor peasants of the north side of the *bil* area had to lose their crops due to the flood caused by the river water flowing from the south side, so they appealed to him for a remedy. Mr. Mandal drew the attention of Minister Sris Chandra Nandi, district magistrate and the district Board of Bakarganj in a meeting held on 6th March 1939, describing the unknown miseries caused by the damage of crops due to lack of embankment there. In response to this, the honourable Minister replied that 'I may state here for the information of the honourable members that the Government is aware of the drainage difficulties of the area and we are certainly trying our best to find out its remedy.[9]

Another similar problem was there in Baghar of Barisal where 360 Namasudra families were socio-economic and educationally very poor and suffered from the damage of crops for storing water in the bil area at the NorthWest side of the village. There was no arrangement for the drainage of stored water during heavy rain. If an arrangement was made for the drainage by digging a canal from the bil to the big canal of Mahilada situated at a distance of one mile to the east, then hundreds of acres of lands would be suitable for cultivation. They tried earlier at their best but no arrangement had been made. The peasants appealed to Mr Mandal for digging the canal. Mr. Mandal visited the place and promised to do his best. He further promised them to improve their economic and educational condition. Arranging a meeting with peasants he declared that if the government would not take any step to do it then all peasants should refuse to give tax to the government. Ultimately the administrator of the Mahakuma visited the place with Mr. Mandal, and realizing the urgent need for the canal, solved the problem. This success encouraged the Namasudra peasants. After this event, Durga Mohan Sen, the editor of the 'Barishal Hitaishi', a very influential critic of the backwards, praised Mr. Mandal calling him 'Megasthenes of Bengal', in his article published in the journal. This publication created a good image of Mr. Mandal in Bengal politics.

It was at the same time when the students of depressed castes drew the attention of the higher authority of the colleges and universities in Bengal for their separate hostels. Mr. Mandal requested finance

Minister Nalini Ranjan Sarkar for the fulfilment of this demand. Mr Sarkar commented that it was an age of interaction with each other and the proper time for scheduled caste students to reside with the upper caste students. He arranged for a hostel free of charge and for giving them monthly fifteen rupees with a stipend for their study.

Mr. Mandal realized the necessity of reservation in governmental service for backward castes. He raised the issue before the scheduled caste MLAs and decided to appeal to the Governor of Bengal for taking action. The upper castes MLAs were against this reservation and they tried to postpone the issue. But Mr. Mandal immediately applied to be the governor and chief minister of Bengal. Eventually, the authority made an arrangement for reservation in government services both for Muslims and scheduled castes. Fifteen percent of seats were reserved for the scheduled castes in Bengal (1938).

It was the same time when Mr. Mandal came to the close to Sarat Chandra Bose who introduced him with Subhas Chandra Bose. Subhas Chandra appreciated and inspired him by providing moral support for the welfare activities of the backwards. Mr. Mandal wanted to cooperate with Subhas Chandra when he, after establishing 'Forward Block' went to visit Barisal for organizing his party. During the rally in the road of Barishal Subhas Chandra accompanied Mr. Mandal standing side by side in a car. A big conference was arranged for a lecture of Subhas Chandra at the Banipith School campus in Barishal. Mr. Mandal had to preside over the meeting according to the wish of Subhas Chandra while Mr. Mandal was quite young among the present respectable persons. The huge gathering of people was out of control during the lecture of Subhas Chandra due to the lack of a loudspeaker. But Mr. Mandal managed the crowd with his loud voice and speaking capacity. Hence, the attachment with the great leader Subhas Chandra and his leadership skill made Mr. Mandal famous among the deprived castes of Bengal.

He had been working in the co-operation of Congress leaders during the year 1939 and 1940. But the ex-communication of Subhas Chandra Bose from the party meeting at Wardha displeased him. Despite having been elected as president, Subhas Chandra's resignation from theAll India Congress Committee (AICC) led Mr. Mandal to be doubtful of the existence of healthy norms of democracy in the Congress. He could see that Subhas Chandra Bose was compelled to form a separate party due to the meanness of some conservative Congress leaders. From the time onwards, Mr. Mandal decided to avoid proximity with Congress leaders. With the resignation of Mr Bose, Congress held no appeal for him anymore.

He could not accept the ideology of M.K. Gandhi who instructed his party members to improve the financial condition of the Harijans by arranging small industries, charkha and collecting subscriptions from village to village and opening the doors of temples for untouchables. It was not enough to remove the untouchability and sustainable development of the depressed castes. The actual development for the untouchables was possible by allowing them in education, employment and health service. But the Congress leaders including Gandhiji avoided the sustainable development of the deprived castes. Henceforward, he cut off all relations with the Congress realizing the disinterest of the Congress leaders in welfare activities for the deprived castes.

But Congress was the strongest party in India. It was difficult to bypass the Congress party for overcoming the problems of the deprived castes. So he realized the need for a strong organization for scheduled castes to remove their problems. It was necessary to have representatives of SCs in the administration to overcome their problems. So he attempted to organize a 'Scheduled Castes Federation' more strongly to share political power.

Scheduled Caste Federation

The scheduled castes were about seventy-five per cent among the Hindus in undivided Bengal. Most of them were poor peasants who had to pay taxes according to the demand of the upper caste Hindu landlords who deprived the peasants in many ways. The peasants made a lot of contribution to the state but they had no representative in the administration and politics. There was no scheduled caste representative in any of the local board, police station, district board, district school board, union board and Municipality.

Under these circumstances, the Namasudra leaders initiated a separate federation in Bengal. Mr. Mandal had already prepared for forming the federation through his 'Independent Scheduled Caste Party'. He initiated it by selecting Hemchandra Naskar as the founding member of the party and himself as the secretary (1938). S.C. Bose, during the construction of 'Forward Bloc' after the ex-communication from Congress, suggested Mr. Mandal organize a 'Scheduled Castes Federation of Bengal' as an integral part of the 'All India Scheduled Caste Federation. Now, Mr. Mandal took more responsibility for the unification of the deprived castes by forming the Federation for all the districts of Bengal.

According to the resolution and guidelines of the third conference of 'All India Backward Classes Association' (July 18-19, 1942, Nagpur), N. Shibraj and Dr B. R Ambedkar initiated a central political organization 'All India Scheduled Castes Federation (AISCF) for the scheduled castes. It was also instructed in that conference to set up a local political organization of the scheduled castes to merge into the central organization and to work together. Hence, Mr. Mandal formed the 'Bengal Provincial Scheduled Caste Federation' (May 1943). He took up the post of President and MLA Manmohan Das of Mymensingh and MLA Shyamaprasad Barman of Dinajpur jointly took the post of secretary.

The centre of the activities of the 'Bengal Scheduled Caste Federation' was a rented house at 1/2 Sitaram Ghosh Street in Calcutta. Mr. Mandal bears all the expenses for this federation till the partition of India. After partition, it was shifted to Patuatuli in Dacca. 'The objective of the 'All India Scheduled Caste Federation' was to attain, a distinct status by the scheduled castes, and to form a separate constituent body in the national sphere and to obtain political, economic and social rights to find a new path for national progress[10].

The Namasudra leaders, considering Dr Ambedkar as the supreme leader of the Federation, worked with full encouragement. Mr. Mandal met with Dr Ambedkar first time in October 1943 in Bombay during the all India conference of ministers of cooperative societies. He attended the meeting, as the representative of the ministers from Bengal. Dr Ambedkar was then the Labour Minister in the central Government. Here, Dr Ambedkar inspired Mr. Mandal by giving some valuable suggestions for constructive activities for the backward castes of Bengal.

It was the same time when the people of backward castes in Bengal suffered from a food crisis caused by the scorched earth Policy (*Poda Mati neeti*) of the British for fear of Japanese attack in India. The British rulers kept the stored foods and crops of Bengal aside in some unknown place for preventing the Japanese attack. It was a self-deprivation and man-made crisis which affected mostly the backward and poor peasants of Bengal. The deprived castes reached a miserable condition due to a lack of food. During the Assembly meeting of the Ministers (10th March 1943) Mr. Mandal drew the attention of the ministers about the crisis and the victimization of the SC. Most of the SCs were landless peasants who lost all the means of survival. They even did not have the means to buy the minimum dress to cover their bodies. He appealed to the honourable speaker for making an arrangement for their minimum requirements for survival irrespective of caste and colours[11].

This year Mr. Mandal published the aims and objectives of the SCs of Bengal through the Journal 'Jagran'. The objectives were (i) to get separate political right for SCs, (ii) to arrange reservation in the central law council following the ratio of caste population and reserve services in different sector of the state and central government, (iii) to establish a separate university, separate educational institutions, with separate necessary grant and finance and arrangement for elder's education (iv) separate leather workshop, a separate institution for cloth workshop, separate metal workshop, a separate institution for the science research centre, and separate institution for engineering, (v) to arrange their self-administration, (vi) to make arrangement for separate business, (vii) to make freedom for agriculture, and (viii) to annihilate untouchability.

He, as leader of the Federation, appealed to the honourable speaker during the Shyama-Huq Ministry in the Assembly House Calcutta to fulfill their demand according to right (24th March 1943). He said 'Sir I move this motion to raise a discussion on the policy of Government in ignoring the legitimate right and claims of the scheduled castes in the matter of their representation on local bodies such as District Boards, Municipalities, District School Boards, local Boards etc.'[12].

It was at the same time when the 'Shyama-Huq Ministry' broke down after the resignation of Huq (28th March 1943). MLA Khwaja Nazimuddin (Muslim League) began to collect support from others to be the leader of the opposition of Mr Huq. Mr. Mandal, at this time, arrived at Savoy Hotel of Calcutta with his SC MLAs. He decided at first to support Nazimuddin as he promised to fulfil their demands.[13] On the other hand, the representatives of Mr Huq and Dr S.P. Mukherjee (HM) approached Mr. Mandal for his support but he refused as they did not agree upon the demands. Nazimuddin and his companions promised to fulfil their demands in exchange for the support of twenty SC MLAs. Mr. Mandal and his MLAs accepted the condition and selected Nazimuddin as the leader of the MLAs. Eventually, the new Ministry was formed and Nazimuddin was selected as the Premier (April 1943). According to the previous condition, three SC MLAs were included in the ministry. Mr. Mandal and Mukunda Behari Mallick, with 13 ministers, were included with the new post of parliamentary secretary in this ministry.[14] Mr. Mandal was appointed as the Minister of cooperative societies and loan, Prem Hari Barman was appointed as the Minister of forest and excise department and Pulin Bihari Mallick as the Minister of campaigning department[15].

This ministry fulfilled all the demands of the depressed castes according to their promise. Barrister Suresh Chandra Biswas was appointed as the Judge of Calcutta High Court (small), Barrister B.M. Mandal was appointed as 'General Deputy Administrator', Sukumar Mallick and Subodh Mallick were selected as ICS. Thus, many leaders from deprived castes were appointed in various departments of services including Inspectors, Auditors, development Officers and clerks of the governmental services in the ministry of Najimuddin

(April 1943-March 1945). Many cooperative inspectors and sub-registrars were promoted to the post of Deputy Magistrate for the effort of Mr Mandal.

But some conservative ministers appointed food and rationing departments without following the communal ratio (1943). Mr. Mandal complained to Prime Minister Nazimuddin and supply Minister Mr Suhrawardy about the irrational appointment. In response to this complaint, Nazimuddin made a proper arrangement, enquiring the facts, and the SC candidates were appointed rationally. Another complaint was the appointment of a general candidate on a reserved seat as per the advertisement of Calcutta Gazette (July 1, 1943) and (November 23, 1943). Mr. Mandal wrote to Secretary P.B. Rudra Rai Bahadur, Bengal Public Service Commission, requesting the formation of an enquiry committee for that recruitment. It was found that a general candidate was appointed in a reserved post of commercial tax officer showing the reason that there was no qualified candidate among the scheduled castes. Mr. Mandal in his letter informed the commissioner that there were available qualified B.Com and M.Com candidates among scheduled castes for the post.[16].

Mr. Mandal took an initiative to arrange to solve the problems of deprivation from the right to education for the SC students forming an advisory committee. He ensured the reserve seats for SC students in Calcutta Medical College and Campbell Medical School. The committee was formed for selecting eligible SC students for admission to these colleges. Mr. Mandal had doubts about the fair selection in the process of admission in these important institutions. He included SC members in the selection committees. During the admission to Campbell Medical School, Sashibhushan Halder, one of the members, found that the SC student's seats were not filled up according to the ratio. He drew the attention of Minister Khan Bahadur Maulavi Jalaluddin Ahmed and increased the number of reserve seats. Jamini Mohan Biswas, a Lawyer and Sashibhusan Halder accompanied them in protesting the anti-SC activities in the educational institutions.

Jamini Mohan Biswas organized a big conference at his village in Faridpur for discussions of the problems of Namasudras as well as other backward castes (January 1944). Mr. Mandal presided over the meeting and he encouraged thousands of deprived students delivering his lecture on the development of the backwards. He criticized the prescriptions of 'Manusmriti' mentioning its negative impact on society in a meeting at Batajor village of north Bakarganj. In response to this critique, the privileged castes accused him as anti-Hindu and campaigned against him calling him an iconoclast of modern times (*kalir kala pahad*).[17]

One of the female leaders among Namasudras, Santoshkumari Talukdar, arranged a big conference in Bakarganj (1944). She described the importance of women in society. She encouraged all the SC women to be united for fighting against social injustice and removing their barriers. She demanded the right to education for SC women, organizing a campaigning programme for their need of education in the society for looking after children properly and making their society strong. Mr. Mandal had been encouraged by her spirit of thoughts and became more enthusiastic about the upliftment of women and established many girls' schools in the Namasudra concentrated areas.

The SCs of Bakarganj and Gopalganj were interested in the activities of Dr B.R. Ambedkar. The SCs of Gopalganj invited Dr Ambedkar, to attend a meeting of the 'Bengal Provincial SCs Federation' (24th & 25th April 1945) in the town of Gopalganj. Thousands of deprived caste people attended the conference. But for an unavoidable reason, Dr. Ambedkar could not attend the meeting. Though Mr. Mandal felt sorry for this absence, he managed the meeting properly, as the president of the meeting, delivering an encouraging lecture on their aims and activities. Dr Ambedkar sent a letter (23rd April 1945) to Mr. Mandal informing the cause of his absence and promising every endeavour to attend the next conference of the SCs of Bengal late that year.[18]

They decided (i) to make an arrangement of a new colony for the landless scheduled caste peasants based on distributing land (Khasmahal) under government, (ii) to eradicate the jurisdiction system of the landlord and middle man and to make an arrangement for direct tax collection on a legal basis, (iii) to ascertain the justifiable and minimum price for crops and to establish a market on a cooperative basis, (iv) to allow fishermen to catch fish directly from marshy land, (v) to introduce need base minimum salary for the labour in the municipality and other industry, (vi) to grant insurance for unemployed, old man, old women, ill, and to grant pregnancy allowance for would-be mothers among labours.

In the same year, a conference of AISCF was held at Urdupark in Delhi. Mr. Mandal as a representative of Namasudras delivered a lecture criticizing Gandhi's disinterest in removing untouchability and barriers of the deprived castes. He expressed his realization that Gandhi would be pleased if the deprived castes stayed with the stigma of Harijan in place of untouchable and the status of helpless. He lamented that the Congress leaders including Gandhi should be cooperative with the deprived castes, tribes and Muslims conceding their demands. He appealed to them to be united for a prosperous and liberal India, considering the demands of the deprived castes and understanding their agony of deprivation and social injustices. His view was that if all the depressed castes, tribes and Muslims, whose interest was almost the same, would protest jointly then the dominant privileged castes would not be able to exploit them.[19]

The General Election of 1946

Under these circumstances, the general election was held (1946). All the leaders of the Congress, the Muslim League and the SC Federation became enthusiastic to ensure their proportionate power in the election for the formation of the interim government. Their political strength would depend on the number of winning seats. The leaders, therefore, prepared and campaigned well to win the election. But the AISCF was only three years old; further, the financial condition of the federation was poor. So, it was difficult for the leaders of the federation to fight in the election. But their future and fortune would depend on it. Members of the Federation in Bengal discussed the fact and predicted that after the completion of the election Lord Wavell would arrange a meeting where certainly the members from the winning party would be invited for forming the 'Constitutional Assembly' of India. According to the previous reservation rule, three members out of thirty winning members from BSCF would be selected for this council. If they could not participate in the constituent Assembly' with their full strength, the congress members would be active against the interest of scheduled castes.

However, the AISCF competed in some of the seats of some of the states where a total of 151 seats were reserved for SCs, STs. The candidates nominated from these castes and tribes were against three seats from Punjab, three seats from Bombay, four seats from MP, ten seats from Madras, two seats from the United States and six seats from Bengal. It was not possible to contest all the reserved seats due to the financial crisis and lack of consciousness of the backward castes.

Apart from the financial crisis and lack of consciousness, the manipulation of opponents was crucial for the election. The supporters of SC candidates, in this election, had to suffer a lot due to manipulation. Many of the Congress supporters assaulted SC candidates and SC supporters. In the general seat of the centre of north Bakerganj, supporters of J.N. Mandal had to suffer more due to the arrogant activities of their opponents due to an incident at the Kirtipasha polling station. Some of the upper caste women cast their vote several times changing their dresses. The Namasudra supporters complained about this illegal casting and a dispute appeared there. The goons of the Congress candidates assaulted the people of Namasudra villages Batajor, Horror, Deopada, Bachhar, Bankura, west Chandrahar, south Chandrahar Singa etc. (15 Feb 1946) anticipating the defeat of their candidate Manoranjan Gupta against Mr. Mandal. Many Namasudras were injured including some Namasudra women. Further, the powerful Congress leaders complained to the police against Namasudras, and the police tortured and arrested the Namasudras. The police, bribed by Congress leaders, filed a false case of murdering and looting against them and sent them to Barishal Police Station for punishment.

The SC leaders were helpless. They only tried to protest and help the sufferers by giving emotional and financial support. Mr. Mandal informed the then governor of Bengal and sent a telegram describing how the 'Congressmen prevented SC voters from casting their votes and attending many polling stations by force and intimidation. The upper caste Zamindar Talukdars, Mahajans and school teachers threatened and stopped SC voters from casting their vote. Polling stations were selected intentionally in the upper caste concentrated areas, caused inconvenience to SC voters and gave undue privilege to Congressmen. Promulgation of section 144 was utilized by educated and clever Congressmen to threaten illiterate SC voters with fear of imprisonment for attending polling stations. Upper castes presiding and polling officers hobnobbed with caste Congressmen at all centres and encouraged proxy and false personating by turning a deaf ear to and disregarding objections raised by many polling agents at many polling stations. More than 50% of the upper caste poll of the congress candidate were proxy votes. Upper caste polling officers snatched ballot papers at many polling centres from SC male and female voters and put them in the Congress candidates' box despite protest. They instructed and persuaded many voters to vote for the Congress candidate. Elections were stopped before due time for which many voters could not cast their votes. At some polling stations in the areas of majority SC voters, the upper caste presiding officers opened the polling booths much later than the due time and harassed scheduled caste voters by making undue delay in issuing ballot papers for which these voters had to wait till late at night and many of them could not cast their votes. Many SC voters were refused to issue ballot papers on frivolous grounds. The Congressmen delivered lectures showing a picture in which they depicted the candidate as a man of very immoral character and narrated many false stories to prove him to be a man of vicious character which adversely prejudiced his voters and materially affected the election. All these facts affected the whole election so much that led to an appeal for kind orders for re-election.[20]

However, only one Namasudra candidate won from the Federation's nomination out of the thirty reserved seats in undivided Bengal in this election. Three neutral candidates won from scheduled castes.[21] The remaining twenty-six out of thirty reserved seats were occupied by Congress's nominated candidates. Mr Majumder and Mr Dhali from SCs were defeated by very marginal votes. Mr. Mandal won two seats with huge support. In Pirojpur he got 28560 votes against Upendranath Edgar who got 15445 votes.[22] Muslim league won most of their selected seats. So the League formed the ministry of Bengal (24th April 1946). Mr. Hussain Sahid Suhrawardy was selected as Bengal's premier who formed his ministry with eight ministers among whom Mr. Mandal, from scheduled castes, was selected as minister of justice, public works, and house building department.

Dr. Ambedkar, after the election, delivered a long lecture before the scheduled castes, in a meeting (30th June) at Indian Association Hall in Calcutta, describing the actual situation of the eight crores deprived castes in the country and appealed to them to act collectively targeting their rights and demands. Mr. Mandal as the president of the meeting also appealed to them to act for their future generation as they can live without discrimination and exploitation of the privileged castes.

After this meeting, Jogendraath organized 'Satyagraha Movements' for creating awareness among the SCs throughout Bengal to protest against the arrest and imprisonment of about two hundred SCs Satyagrahi in Poona. On 8th August, he organized a big procession in Calcutta after long deliberation in the meeting at the office of the 'Jagaran' and made a declaration. Several processions and meetings were organized on 15th August as a day of protest' and 'Nikhil Bharat Poona Satyagraha Dibas' throughout Bengal. It was organized at the Ochterlony Monument in Calcutta under the leadership of Mr. Mandal, at Khulna in the Gandhi Park under Ramdayal Das, at the Kalibari in the Gopalganj district under Satish Chandra Biswas, at Pirojpur in Barishal under Kiron Chandra Roy.

The Constituent Assembly

In this circumstance, Mr. Mandal decided to be a member of the Constituent Assembly' from Bengal and he desired that Dr. Ambedkar would also be a member of the Constituent Assembly. But Dr. Ambedkar himself was defeated in this election, so it was almost impossible to elect Dr. Ambedkar as a member of the Constituent Assembly without the support of Bengal. He needed five votes. Ultimately six Namasudra members including Mr. Mandal voted for Dr. Ambedkar. MLA Nagendra Narayan Roy, Rajbanshi, was elected from Rangpur and voted for Dr. Ambedkar. Mukunda Behari Mallick, Congress MLA of Khulna, decided to support Dr. Ambedkar because he doubted Gayanath Biswas and Dwarakanath Biswas about their support to Dr. Ambedkar. Dwarakanath Biswas, Congress MLA of Faridpur and Gayanath Biswas MLA of Tangible were threatened by the high command Congress leaders for not supporting Dr. Ambedkar. Kshetramohan Singh, a Rajbanshi Congress MLA from Rajshahi, also voted for Dr. Ambedkar. The election was completed on 18 July and the result was published on 19 July. Dr. Ambedkar won and became a member of the Constituent Assembly.

It was significant for the future and fortune of the deprived castes of India. If it had not happened, the depressed castes of India would have been deprived of many opportunities. If Dr. Ambedkar did not get the opportunity to frame the Indian Constitution the rights and opportunities of the SCs might take a different turn. Many of the members of the Constitutional assembly hesitated to co-operate with Dr. Ambedkar, not for his quality and efficiency but his birth as a lower caste. Nevertheless, Ambedkar did not leave his duty for non-cooperation but did his best for drafting the Constitution.

The Muslim League

Muhammad Ali Jinnah prepared a list of members for sending to Lord Wavell for forming interim-Government. He included Mr. Mandal in the list of the Muslim League.[23] He chose him from SC even avoiding some famous leaders of the League. Experienced leaders like Khaja Nazimuddin, Nawab Ismail Khan were excluded from the list. The inclusion of J.N. Mandal was unexpected to other Indian leaders and Lord Wavell. In the Congress list, there were Hindus, Muslims, Sikhs, Parsi, Christians and SCs. The League's members wanted to include more members from SC for their idea that the interests of both the Muslims and SCs were the same. The League's members tried to prove that they were closer to the SCs than the Congress. When Suhrawardy founded the Muslim League in Bengal, Mr. Mandal was enlisted as a single non-Muslim Minister in his ministry; he was almost unknown to the high command at that time. Mr. Mandal was appointed as a Law Member in the ministry of Lord Wavell.

The interim Government was formed (2nd September 1946), under the leadership of the Congress president Pandit Jawaharlal Nehru. The Muslim League did not join this Government. Two seats were vacant which were kept for Muslims. Those who joined from the minority community were Congress nominated. So, the Congress MLAs from SC were not satisfied with the formation of this government. Only one minister Jagjivan Ram from SCs was included in this Government, but he was under the control of the Congress high command.

Some of the SC MLAs in this time left the Congress and joined the Federation to protest against this deprivation. Joining with Federation, the SC MLAs including Dwarakanath Baruri, Bholanath Biswas, Haran Chandra Barman and Gayanath Biswas argued that the

Congress high command leaders had no concern for the depressed castes. They blamed Congress for their effort to deprive the SC MLAs. They got only one seat in place of three seats as per the communal ratio. Despite being the best leader of about eight crores of minority people, Dr Ambedkar did not get a seat in the interim government.

On the other hand, the chief of the League in Bengal, Mr Suhrawardy, requested Mr Mandal to join the central ministry with the League. But Mr Mandal refused it because he knew the League attempted to join in the ministry only to compete politically and they would return from it within a short period after quarrelling with the Congress leaders while he would be helpless. Further, it would require resigning from the ministry of Bengal and membership of the law council but it would not be permitted by the members of the Federation. Suhrawardy told him to join the centre ministry for the moment and return from the central ministry again and join in the local ministry.

Ultimately, Mr. Mandal agreed to join the central ministry but after taking the consent from Dr Ambedkar and the leaders of the Federation Mr Suhrawardy, could not spare much time for it. Then Mr Mandal agreed with a condition that he should be allowed to resign his post whenever his leader Dr Ambedkar would ask him. Mr Suhrawardy agreed. Hence, five ministers from Bengal were included in the interim government. Mr Mandal was appointed as the law minister on 15th October 1946. Dr Ambedkar from London sent a telegram to Jogendranath with the word "You have my Blessings". Some members of the Federation and the secretary of 'Jagaran' were pleased and congratulated him. The members of the Federation met Md. Jinnah at Delhi on 16th October and thanked him for the inclusion of Mr. Mandal as a Minister.

Md. Jinnah promised that he would do his best for the welfare of SCs with the cooperation of the League. The Congress leaders including M.K. Gandhi were not pleased by this inclusion. Gandhi commented 'it will be deceiving myself if I tell that I am happy that a person from SCs is appointed by Muslim League in the Administrative Council of the Governor-General (18th October 1946)'[24]. According to the population ratio, the SCs should get three seats and the League should get five seats. Congress allowed only one seat to SCs but as Congress candidate not as SC candidate. The Congress leaders had no interest in providing any seat to SC M L As. But the League nominated one seat from SCs within their five seats the Congress became displeased.

Under this circumstance, Mr. Mandal felt a common cause with the Muslim League's demand for a separate domain. He argued that the economic and educational interests of Muslims and SCs were the same, so the SCs would have a chance to get equal opportunities in Pakistan, which would be uncertain in the Congress dominated state where no rights had been given to the SCs. On the other hand, Md. Jinnah, the chief leader of the League, had the interest to include a united Bengal and Punjab with a separate Pakistan State. For this, he required the support of the 'Scheduled Caste Federation' of Bengal. Similarly, most of the Bengal Federation's leaders desired either united India or united Bengal. The demand for united Bengal was supported by most of the leaders of the S.C Federation.[25] Eventually, after partition, Mandal was selected as chairman of Pakistan's Constituent Assembly. He agreed to serve as the Minister of Law and Labour. Thus, he fell into the trap of the Muslim leader and allowed the Namasudra movement to die out.[26]

The Muslim League leaders neither fulfilled the demand of the minority people of East Pakistan nor saved their life from communal violence. Hence, the

Namasudras including the other backward Hindus of the eastern part of the divided Bengal became helpless and had to undergo unimaginable sufferings due to communal clashes and conflicts. Mr. Mandal could not comprehend the actual motive of the Islamic leaders. Joining Namasudras with the pro-farmer Fazlul Huq Ministry (1937-41) and Shyama-Huq Ministry (1941-43) was not detrimental because Fazlul Huq was interested in the people of Bengal. He was also sympathetic to the depressed castes including Namasudras.

Mr. Mandal could not realize the intention of the pro- British ministry (1943-46) Nazimuddin who tried to sideline the pro-farmer Mr Huq and desired to control the League under the Islamic ideology. This pro-British Jinnah centric Ministry had a desire to make a separate Muslim state but also promised to look after the interests of the Namasudras as well as the Hindu minority of Bengal. Md. Jinnah made an effort to fulfil his interest in forming a separate Muslim state with the support of the SC leaders. So he offered the post of temporary chairman of the Pakistan Constituent Assembly to Mr. Mandal.[27]

But after becoming Law Minister in the Md. Jinnah led ministry Mr. Mandal could do nothing for the Namasudras. A decision was taken, in the meeting between the League and a part of the Namasudra leaders, that if the Namasudra leaders would support the League then they had not to leave their homeland and their demand would be fulfilled, their lives, wealth and land would be saved. Most of the Namasudra leaders considered that Mr. Mandal would be able to secure the interests of the Namasudras. Therefore immediately after the partition, they did not leave East Bengal.

But it did not happen as they expected. Mr. Mandal could not manage the problem which appeared after partition. The riots of Kolkata in 1946 were stopped.

But the communal clash, looting of land and wealth of the minority and inhuman and brutal activities of the Islamic goons in East Bengal continued for years after years. When Mr. Mandal understood that he would not be able to protect the minority despite being a Minister, he decided to resign (October 1950) from the ministry and came back to West Bengal in utter frustration and disillusionment. The brutal activities and looting increased so highly after 1950 that the Hindus could hardly save their life and wealth. Thousands of them were able to hide themselves scattering to various unknown places of Indian provinces.

ENDNOTES AND REFERENCES

1. Acharya Mahananda Haldar: *Sri Sri Guruchand Charit*, (Thakurnagar: Resolution, 2009), p. 148.
2. It was the first pre-Gandhian successful anti-colonial movement organized under the leadership of Aurobindo Ghosh, Bipin Chandra Pal, Balgangadhar Tilak and Lalarajpat Rai, during 1905 to 1911, against Bengal partition-policy of Lord Curzon.
3. Acharya Mahananda Haldar: *op.cit.*, p. 169.
4. S, Bandyopadhyay: *Caste, Protest and Identity in Colonial India: The Namasudras of Bengal, 1872-1947*, (New Delhi: Oxford University Press, 2011), p. 102.
5. S. Bandyopadhyay: *op.cit.*, p. 112.
6. *Ibid.*, p. 116.
7. Naresh Chandra Das: *Namasudra Samproday o Bangladesh* (Kolkata, Dipali Book House, 1997), p. 194.
8. Jagadish Chandra Mandal: *Mahapran Mr. Mandal*, Vol. I, (Chaturtha Dunia, Calcutta, 1382 BS), p. 33.
9. *Assembly Proceedings*, Bengal, Vol. LIV, No. 2, p. 136.
10. Jagadish Chandra Mandal: *op.cit.*, p. 98.
11. *Assembly Proceedings*, Bengal, Vol. LXIV, No. 3, p. 36.
12. Jagadish Chandra Mandal: *op.cit.*, p. 68.

13. The demands were: i) to appoint three Ministers and three Parliamentary Secretaries from Scheduled Castes, ii) to grant Rupees five lakh as a recurring grant for the educational purpose of the Scheduled Castes, iii) to appointed the scheduled caste candidates in the governmental services according to the communal ratio.
14. Amalesh Tripathy: Indian National Congress and The Struggle for Freedom,1885-1947, translated by Amitav Tripathy, (New Delhi, Oxford University Press, 2014), p. 334.
15. Mandal Jagadish Chandra: *Mahapran Mr. Mandal,* Vol. I, (Calcutta: Chaturtha Dunia, 1382 BS), p. 83.
16. *Ibid.*
17. *Ibid.,* p. 103.
18. *Ibid.,* p. 113.
19. *Ibid.,* p. 94.
20. *Ibid.,* p. 151.
21. Mukunda Bihari Mallick from Khulna, Pramothranjan Thakur from Faridpur and Nagendra Narayan Roy from Rangpur.
22. *Ibid., op.cit.,* p. 146.
23. M.A.K. Ajad: *India Wins Freedom,* (New Delhi, Orient Longman, 1978), p. 161.
24. Mandal Jagadish Chandra: *Mahapran Mr. Mandal,* Vol. I, (Calcutta: Chaturtha Dunia, 1382 BS), p. 197.
25. Amalesh Tripathy: *Indian National Congress and The Struggle for Freedom, 1885-1947,* translated from Bengali by Amitav Tripathy, (New Delhi, Oxford University Press, 2014), p. 488.
26. Babul Kumer Pal: *Barishal Theke Dandyakaranya* (Kolkata, Mitram, 2010), p. 58.
27. Madhav Godbole: *The Holocaust of Indian Partition: An Inquest,* (New Delhi, Rupa Publications India Pvt. Ltd., 2011), p. 130.

5

Partition and Struggle for Survival, 1947-1971

Introduction

Among the minorities in East Bengal, the Namasudras suffered most from the Indian partition. They were dispersed and divided geographically, politically and culturally due to the communal violence during and after the partition. The radical posture of the Muslims compelled the Namasudras to leave their homeland and scatter throughout the Indian provinces. The goons of Muslims forced millions of minorities to evacuate the Hindu villages of eastern Bengal. The hooligans among Muslims initiated genocide for the minorities by setting fire to their villages and raped their girls and women. Thousands of Hindus were killed and millions were displaced. The Islamic fundamentalists wanted to convert East Bengal to an Islamic state. They, therefore, attempted either to convert all the Hindus to Islam or to drive them all out from their state occupying the land, wealth and resources of the Hindus. The Muslim friends of the Namasudras turned into enemies and played an active role in driving them out from Bengal.

On the other hand, the backward Hindus, mostly Namasudras, who could migrate to India, suffered from a lack of shelters. The Congress leaders, after getting the administrative power, dishonoured their promises made during the partition regarding the rights and security of the minorities. They could not protect the minorities of East Pakistan from the tyranny of Muslims hooligans but took steps to create a secular image. The Congress high command did not care for the socio-economic, religious and political interest of the backward Hindus. Eventually, those backward Hindus who were compelled to migrate to new India had to struggle a lot for survival. They had to protest against the anti rehabilitation policy of the Hindu high command who took the administrative posts in independent India.

The partition of Bengal did not generate any acute difficulty for the upper caste Hindus of Bengal. Their number was very few in the marshy land of eastern Bengal. They were mostly concentrated in western Bengal which was included in new India. On the other hand, being highly educated, politically conscious and having employment opportunities in advanced professions, the upper caste Hindus of eastern Bengal could easily migrate to new India. Most of the Hindus, near about five million, who were inhabitants of Khulna Jessore, Barisal, Dacca, Faridpur, Rajshahi and Pabna in eastern Bengal, belonged to lower castes[1] and they were uneducated and unconscious regarding their political future. The highly educated Hindu castes being politically conscious migrated to new India before the partition but the lower castes, the uneducated and politically unconscious Hindus most of whom were Namasudras did not think of migrating to new India, due to their financial crisis and lack of opportunities, before the beginning of riots, killings, rape, threats and plunder organised under the process of Islamization.

The Pakistan government and Muslim high command did not take any action against the hooliganism of ruffian Muslims due to their interest in creating an Islamic state. On the other hand, the Muslims in West Bengal were secured by Jawaharlal Nehru's attempt of making India secular. The Nehru government allowed an exchange of population in Punjab but it was discouraged and prohibited for the Hindus of Bengal.[2] Consequently, the Namasudras, among the Hindus of Bengal, suffered from the partition most. They were numerous among the backward Hindu communities in East Pakistan. Their incomprehension of political matters made them unable to predict the impact of the partition and its reaction among the Muslims. The conscious Namasudras began to migrate after the great killings of Noakhali. But most of them who were politically unaware and financially poor were not able to migrate immediately after this riot.

But the Muslims took an initiative to drive them out forcefully from East Pakistan. Consequently, millions of poor and unconscious Namasudras were compelled to migrate to new India and gathered in West Bengal where there was no sufficient place for rehabilitation. Therefore, they were dispersed in various places out of Bengal which were not familiar to them. They had to stay in camps in West Bengal and outside year after year while they had to suffer a lot due to the lack of food, a crisis of shelter, unhealthy living and so on. Thousands of them had to die suffering from various kinds of diseases and lack of food. Hence, they became aimless and segregated. Their movements for political upliftment, social injustice, socio-economic and cultural development faded away. The partition marked a major shift in their movement. It led them to struggle for the survival of their lives in place of the movement against social injustice.

Divide and Rule Policy

The British encouraged the Muslim leaders in a separate electorate, even in creating a separate state for securing their self-interest in India. They had an interest in dividing the Indian continent for weakening the united strength of the freedom fight to sustain their rule. On the other hand, the Congress High Command had an interest in dominating the Muslims and the backward Hindus which led the Muslims and Shudras to be interested in securing their political rights. This conflict encouraged the British rulers in applying the divide and rule policy in India. It led to the weakening of the Indian nation breaking their unity. The Hindus and the Muslims were disintegrated and the Hindus themselves also were segregated. The people of the Indian sub-continent had been split into three main groups - (i) the high caste Hindus, (ii) the backward Hindus and the (iii) Muslims, which led to many difficulties among the Indians.

The British masters applied the 'divide and rule' policy on Bengal for the first time to dismember the Bengalis by partitioning it in 1905. Thereafter, they applied the policy in promoting separate seat arrangement for the Muslims in the Legislative Assembly of Bengal passing the Indian Act in 1908. Hence, the disintegration and conflict began between the Hindus and the Muslims under the scheme. On the other hand, the Congress High Command endeavoured to bring the Indian dominion under the supremacy of the high caste Hindu gentry. Before Md. Jinnah declared the two-nation theory, Hindu Mahasabha leader V.D. Savarkar, in 1925, declared that the Hindus were the only nationalists of India. [3]

During the transfer of power, many of the renowned Muslim leaders including Khan Abdur Gaffar Khan and Maulana Abul Kalam Azad tried to bring back the

Hindu–Muslim unity but failed. Rather the idea of a separate nation of Md. Jinnah was more attractive to the Muslims.[4] The Namasudras as well as the SC Hindus were attracted more to the liberal policies and principles of the British and to the call of SC leaders than the call of conservative Hindu nationalist leaders who tried to unite the Hindus against the British and the Muslims. Most of the Namasudras could not be faithful to the hegemony of the privileged caste Hindus.

During the transfer of power, the leaders of the Scheduled Caste Federation (SCF) of Bengal became divided into two. Some under the leadership of Mr. Mandal joined with the League receiving the invitation of Md. Jinnah who nominated Mr. Mandal as a member of the League and as the only representative of the SCF. Some joined with the Hindu Mahasabha and the Congress. When according to the plan of Lord Mountbatten, votes were being collected on behalf of partition and against the partition, a part of the Namasudras as the representative of the SCF, under the leadership of Mr. Mandal, cast their votes on behalf of partition demanding united Bengal and United Punjab with Pakistan.[5] Nevertheless, their votes could not influence the decision of the High Command of Congress and the League.

Md. Jinnah, the sole spokesman of the League, committed to making a separate state for Muslims. He needed the support of the SCF of Bengal for the formation of the Interim Government. So, he invited Mr. Mandal to support him and promised to fulfil the demands of the SC Hindus and to look after their interest expecting undivided Bengal in the impending dilemmas of Hindu-Muslims conflicts. Considering these promises Mr. Mandal joined the League. But Md. Jinnah's focus was on the interest of the Muslims only.

The Calcutta Killings, Partition and Creation of Islamic State

The League refused not only to join with the Central Council (16 August 1945) of the United Front for independent India but led to riots in Calcutta.[6] Md. Jinnah's effort to see the interests of the Muslims and to make a separate Muslim state made the situation critical in the Hindu-Muslim conflict. The conflicts reached their highest point after his declaration of the 'Direct Action Day' to achieve a separate Muslim state (July 1946). He announced before the press conference in his residence in Bombay that 16 August would be the 'Direct Action Day' for achieving his target.

Hence, the then Chief Minister of Bengal Mr. Huseyn Shaheed Suhrawardy asked the Governor of Bengal, Sir Frederick Burrows, to announce a holiday and strike on the declared 'Direct Action Day'. He agreed to do so. But the Congress leader Prafulla Chandra Ghosh urged the Hindus in Calcutta to run normal activities disregarding the holiday and strike. The members of the League in Calcutta began to rally according to their prior plan on the declared day at 7 a.m. They began to gather at Harrison Road in Calcutta by Lorries armed with big sticks, bottles, brickbats and other weapons.

Thus, violence took place and more than four thousand people were killed and over fifteen thousand were injured. The Hindus were killed and injured more than the Muslims. The Muslim rioters made preparations for the hooliganism, and they were criticised as more responsible for the great Calcutta Killings.[7] Thus, a horrible situation appeared which changed the course of history in India. The violence continued for more than a week. The Viceroy, on 21 August, asked the administrative responsibility of dismissing the Government of the Muslim League to manage the bloody rioting and clash, and it was stopped in Calcutta.

But the Calcutta Killings led to several riots in Bengal and Tripura in October-November in the same year. The Muslim's hooligans, from the first week of October 1946, began to be organised for forcing the Hindus to convert to Islam and to marry their beautiful girls with Muslims of many areas in Noakhali and Tripura. Those Hindus who rebelled against these actions were killed and their land and wealth were occupied. Thus, a horrible panic situation appeared throughout Bengal.

The massacre of Noakhali left more than five thousand dead and fifteen thousand injured and it led to huge destruction of the wealth of Hindus. About two million Hindus migrated to West Bengal after the Noakhali and Tippera riots in 1946 and after the Khulna riots in 1950.[8] The Hindus left their villages and scattered to different places to hide them for saving lives. More than fifty thousand Hindus, most of whom were Namasudras took shelter in the relief camps under the British and thousands of them scattered in different places of Hindu concentration areas in Assam and Western Bengal.[9] This communal violence led to a large-scale migration from eastern Bengal to West Bengal and Assam.

Mr. Mandal, as a minority leader and as a supporter of the League, tried to save the minority Hindus but failed. The reasons behind this failure were the uncontrollable situation that appeared for the indifference of the Muslim political leaders. Those Namasudra leaders who joined with Congress and Hindu Mahasabha condemned Mr. Mandal for his joining with the League.

Though all the Namasudra leaders shared the same standpoint of national unity many of them had decided to join the League. They opposed partition and wanted a United Bengal.[10] Some of the Namasudra leaders participated in the pro-partition campaign organised by Hindu Mahasabha and Congress demanding a Hindu homeland. Radhanath Das, the chief leader of the

'Depressed Classes League', became close to the Congress leaders. He drew the attention of the depressed classes to join the Congress. Birat Chandra Mandal, the foremost leader of the 'Depressed Classes Association' was interested in acting as a part of the Hindu Mahasabha. But all the leaders among the Namasudras wanted at least United Bengal if India would be divided.

Ultimately India was divided into three parts after a lot of inexplicable debate, intense discussion and unforeseen violence. The Partition Plan of the British was agreed upon by the Congress, the Hindu Mahasabha, and the Muslim league. The Muslim League leader Md. Jinnah began public campaigning in favour of a separate Muslim state, while Jawaharlal Nehru of the Indian National Congress (INC) tried to keep India united. As independence approached the country began to descend towards a virtual civil war. Ultimately the Islamic Republic of Pakistan was founded on august 14, 1947. The Republic of India was established on the following day.

The Partition could not solve the communal problems. Many massacres took place; and thousands of Hindus, Muslims and Sikhs were murdered and displaced after Partition. On January 30, 1948, M.K. Gandhi was assassinated for his support of a multi-religious state by young Hindu radicals. Since August of 1947, India and Pakistan have fought three major wars and one minor war over territorial disputes and many problems since then are continuing including the displacement of the minority Hindus until the present times.

Bengal was divided in such a way that the Namasudra concentrated districts like Rajshahi, Pabna, Jessore, Faridpur, Khulna, and Barisal were included in East Pakistan. The Namasudras could not play any role in decision making on Partition. Their effort on keeping Bengal undivided could not influence the decision-makers.

Even the demand of HM members was ignored by the Congress High Command. Bengal, as well as Punjab, was divided according to the plan and decision of the British masters, the Congress and the League.[11] The Boundary Commission considered the opinions of Congress and the League. The minority Hindus of divided Bengal and Punjab could not play any role in decision making for a boundary but to migrate to new India.

The minorities of West Pakistan were able to migrate to India and the Congress leaders arranged their rehabilitation. Though the process was difficult it was done with the effort of the Congress leaders. Particularly Jawaharlal Nehru was very much enthusiastic to do his best to solve the problem of West Pakistan to create his secular image. He had made proper arrangements for their rehabilitation in proper places.

But this scenario was different for the minority of East Pakistan. Here the minorities were not able to migrate like the Hindus of West Pakistan due to different socio-economic and political situations. The foremost leader of the minority Hindus in eastern Bengal, Mr. Mandal fell into the trap of Md. Jinnah, and on the other hand, the Congress High Command had no interest in the SC Hindus of Bengal. These backward Hindus were almost ignored by the Congress High Command. This ignorance had originated from a caste conflict. It began with the caste reform movement organised by the Namasudras of Bengal during colonial times. The Namasudras were uncompromising in caste reform and share of political power. Hence, most of the Congress leaders were not interested in the fate of the minority Hindus of Bengal, most of whom were Namasudras.

On the other hand, the upper caste Hindus consciously supported the partition of Bengal. Because they doubted that the united Bengal would be included with Pakistan and if it was divided then West Bengal along with Calcutta would remain with India, where the upper caste Hindus of Bengal were concentrated. Thus, in the divided Bengal, the Congress leaders were almost indifferent regarding the problem of the Namasudras, the majority SC Hindus, who were almost unable to migrate to India. Eventually, the fate of the Namasudras in East Pakistan sank in deep dilemmas and dreadful miseries.

From the moment of the partition, the Islamic leaders began to play the role of fundamentalists preaching the Islamic ideas and values throughout West and East Pakistan. They organised several meetings and conferences to campaign for Islamic laws and orders based on the Koran. One of the fundamentalist Maulana Abdur Raf, declared, in the meeting held in September 1947, that there would be no laws and orders beyond the Islamic laws in Pakistan. The members in the meeting demanded the Urdu language as the state language and demanded Pakistan as an Islamic state. Hence, they attempted to remove Hindus and non-Muslims from Pakistan either by evicting or by killing them and destroying their wealth.[12] One of the victims, Bibhuti Bhusan Das reported "We all embraced with Islam within ten nights, all villages of locality (Chatkhil, Rampur, Dasgharia, etc.) accepted Islam, a huge mob came and gave us an ultimatum to either embrace with Islam or to be ready for burnt in a fire, their High Command/directive was to complete the conversion of Hindus in the Noakhali district within a week".[13] The situation became out of control of the then government. J.N. Mandal as minister of the Pakistan government tried to solve the problem but failed due to the communal interest of Muslim High Commands.

The communal interest of some Islamic leaders became so intense that the Hindu-Muslim conflicts assumed a horrible mood after partition. Mr. Mandal had to resign from the ministry for the sake of his life and came to

India. But the SC Hindus, who had faith in him as their efficient leader, had to remain in the darkness and debacle. They were compelled to remain in East Pakistan giving up all their hopes, their land and wealth. Their land and wealth were occupied by the Islamic fundamentalists. The Hindus who remained there after the partition had not thought of their future. They did not know how they could escape from the tyranny of the Muslims. They knew their motherland as the only place to live or to die. So they did not try to leave their home. There were only two options: either to surrender to the Muslims or to die fighting with them. Those Hindus, who crossed the Indian border, for saving their lives from the brutalities of the Muslims, had faced the problems of rehabilitation and the blame of being intruders. The Congress High Command did not care about the rehabilitation and security of the minorities which were declared during the Partition.[14]

A panic appeared in the lives of the minority Hindus of East Pakistan. A large number of Hindus, about one million had been killed there, about 75000 girls and women had been sexually harassed and raped, and nobody knew how many of them were missing due to the holocaust of Partition. The SC Hindus who are sheltered in West Bengal had to receive lots of ignominy and negligence from the central government. They had to stay on platforms, at the roadside under a tent, in a warehouse of jute and take such types of food which were unworthy of human consumption. Thousands of children, men and women died in front of their survivors and hundreds of young women and girls had to be prostituted.[15]

The Noakhali Riots, Migration, Postpone of Exchange and Relief Camp in West Bengal

Their pathetic history instigated by the effect of the

Noakhali riots which took place before the Partition. They were confused about their duties and destination during the hooliganism. They were not able to migrate easily due to their lack of knowledge and fiscal crisis. On the other hand, they were advised by the Congress leaders to remain in their homeland and keep the peace. Gandhiji visited the place after the Noakhali riot but he suggested remaining in their homes despite receiving threats from the Islamic hooligans.

But the torture and brutality in some places were too much for remaining there. The rise of Islamic fundamentalism made the situation worse. But the Congress leaders continued to advise them to remain there. Jawaharlal Nehru repeatedly suggested, through the Chief Minister of West Bengal, Dr Bidhan Chandra Roy, to remain in East Pakistan. He advised the C.M. to arrange temporary shelter for the refugees who had already migrated to West Bengal, instead of rehabilitation. Nehru hoped that after the end of the violence the refugees would return to their birthplace. Under these circumstances, most of the Namasudras and other minorities tried to remain in their home despite receiving inhuman torture.

But they could guess that their lives were going to be endangered and it would be impossible to save women and girls from the brutality of the Muslims. In the places where the Muslims could not drive out the Hindus, they applied their different policy to harass and drive out the Hindus. The Hindu women during bathing were surrounded by Muslims to harass them commenting *'Pak Pak Pakistan'* from one side of the bathing pond, and *'Hndur Bhartar Musalman'* from the other side.[16] Not only harassment but also the persecutors molested the women and girls when the victim became senseless. In a hostel, the Hindu students were forced and compelled to eat beef.[17] In villages, the Hindus were compelled to buy goods from the shops of Muslims. The Muslims immediately after the Partition set up shops beside every Hindu shop and threatened the Hindu shopkeepers to stop their business. They forcefully harvested the ripened crops of the Hindu farmers and looted the fishes from the fishermen. The teachers were harassed by the Muslim students; the Hindu patients were compelled to go to the Muslim doctors, clients were compelled to go to the Muslim lawyers. Thus, various types of means were taken by the Muslims to drive out the Hindus from East Pakistan. The Pakistan Government had been indifferent to these inhuman tortures.

Under these circumstances, the minorities, in some places, realized that the time had come for them to leave their home to save their lives, their women, girls and their self-respect. Hence, mass migration from East Pakistan started after the Noakhali killings in October-November 1946 and the great Calcutta Killings. During this riot five thousand Hindus were killed, thousands of Namasudras were converted to Islam; many villages were plundered and destroyed by the Muslims to occupy the land and wealth of the Hindus. It was done in the Namasudra concentrated areas of Sandwip, Chhagalnaiya, Lakshmipur Raipur, Begamganj, and Ramganj of Noakhali, many villages in Gopalganj and Chittagong. It affected the areas Hajiganj, Faridganj, Chandanpur, Chauddagram and Laksham police station of Tripura. It also affected many areas of Bihar and Punjab. Holocaust was started on 10 October on the day of Lakshmi Puja and continued up to 18 October in 1946 in Noakhali. The Namasudras, in most of the villages in the affected areas, were surrounded by the Muslims who directed the Hindus to obey their command and to convert to Islam. They were forced to contribute a huge amount of subscription to the Muslim League according to their demand and were given the warning not to violate their orders to keep the peace. The Government arranged a temporary relief camp in Comilla, Chandpur, and Agartala for the survivors of the riot. In Tripura more than 350 villages were affected, over 2053 Hindu shops and houses were destroyed. More than 35000 Hindus took temporary shelter in the relief camps set up by the Government.

The successful police action (August 1948) against the effort of Nizam, of Hyderabad, who wanted to make a separate independent Muslim state, influenced the Muslims of Pakistan.[18] The Muslims in East Pakistan again attacked Hindus to protest the police action which led to another mass migration. The Hindus who were displaced from Barisal, Khulna, Jessore, Faridpur, Pabna and Rajshahi migrated to West Bengal, their nearest places in India.

West Bengal was a part of Bengal and almost similar to their language, culture, weather, so most of them decided to come and settle here. Primarily Calcutta was their destination for getting shelter. They reached at first to Sialdaha station with all their family members expecting suitable places to be rehabilitated under the support of the Indian Government. Most of these evacuees, who took shelter at this station, were poor and unable to be self-dependent as they came without any resources. Some of the families had no adult men to look after them. So they began to wait in the station for the help of the Government.

But they had to stay there for a long time without the bare necessities of living. About 1000 to 3000 refugees gathered daily at the station. But there were no necessary arrangements to send them to camps or to rehabilitate them in barren lands. Only two toilets for women, twelve for the men and three taps for water, had been arranged at the station for their use. The government arranged some minimum dry foods and dole (two rupees) per family for their survival.

They had to use open places for a toilet and wear the same dress day after day without cleaning like beggars. This situation continued year after year which led to pollution, diseases and several deaths. Various kinds of diseases including indigestion, dysentery, cholera, influenza and diarrhoea appeared. Many of them were attacked by diseases and died. Besides these harrowing problems, they had to face another kind of dilemma that was the manipulation of some hypocritic men who kidnapped their women and girls for prostitution enticing them with promises of a job and good shelter.

The West Bengal Government arranged to dispatch them by a van from the station to relief camps set up in barren lands in some places of West Bengal for their shelter. Some temporary shelters were made to control the situation. Nearly 300 evacuees were dispatched daily. The vacuum was filled up by a new group of fresh evacuees. This was continued up till June 1949, when Hiranmoy Bandyopadhyay had been appointed as the Rehabilitation Commissioner under Chief Minister Dr Bidhan Chandra Roy who was anxious to solve the problem of refugee gatherings at the station.

More than 70,000 evacuees in this time required to be rehabilitated. It was difficult to arrange a settlement for all of them. But Dr Roy and Hiranmoy Bandyopadhyay tried their best to manage the situation. They arranged for rehabilitation in some suitable places in West Bengal. Most of the evacuees near about 62500 (12,500 families) out of 70000 were energetic enough to earn their living by own-effort without government help. This group of evacuees tried to rehabilitate themselves seeking vacant land and houses in various places of West Bengal.[19] They were ready to build houses on the given land with their effort. The evacuees, among this group, with small business and shop, desired to be settled near Calcutta, as they alone were able to earn their living. These evacuees were, according to their necessity, sheltered at different places like Habra, Bygachhi and Gayespur, making necessary arrangements for living. They became self-sufficient. Some of them settled in barren lands chosen by themselves.

But about 7500 refugees in this phase were unable to be rehabilitated by their effort. They could not earn their living and look after their children due to the absence of adult men in their families. Dr B.C. Roy and Mr. Bandyopadhyay were very much anxious to rehabilitate them properly when the influx of the refugees slowed down at the end of the year 1949. At this time Dr Roy decided to rehabilitate all the evacuees to vacate the relief camps. They selected barren lands to arrange temporary rehabilitation.

Those families who had no adult or efficient men to look after their families were rehabilitated at Habra, Bygachhi, and Gayespur in the vacant Military camps which were set up during the Second World War. It was made for the temporary living of foreign troops. In these places, the flat rooms and dormitories were selected as suitable for the rehabilitation of a weaker section of the evacuees who could not build their houses and earn their living due to the absence of able men in their families. Self-sufficient evacuees, who were able to settle themselves making their houses, were allowed to rehabilitate in other types of barren lands which were not ready for rehabilitation. Such places were Hamidpur and Khosbas Mohalla near Chakdaha situated beside the railway, and Habra near Calcutta. About 300 small houses, with two small rooms for each, were made at Habra for evacuees. It became a small township that was named Ashok Nagar by the evacuees. A similar colony was set up in the vacant land at the north side of Habra which was named Kalyangarh. In this colony, each family of refugees was given 10 Katha of land to be rehabilitated. They were suggested to build their houses and to cultivate vegetables and plant trees beside houses.

Some evacuees were agriculturists. They were given some minimum land in some places of Burdwan. A political leader of Burdwan, Sri Basanta Kumar Bandyopadhyay was anxious to make rehabilitation arrangements for the evacuees. There were some uncultivated vacant lands on the western side of the Bhagirathi River, under Kalna and Katwa subdivision in Burdwan. The evacuees who were interested to settle here were given a loan to buy land for their cultivation and for making houses. Many of the evacuees successfully settled here and improved their financial condition within a short time through hard labour and cultivating skill and became self-sufficient.

They began to cultivate jute which was a very profitable crop. The jute industrial units of West Bengal, situated beside the Hooghly River were lacking the raw material which was coming from the eastern part of Bengal but after partition, the flow of raw material from East Bengal was almost stopped. Under these circumstances, the efficient farmers, mostly Namasudras, initiated the jute cultivation in West Bengal and revived the dying Jute Industry. [20]

The Namasudras among these evacuees who were weavers needed such places to rehabilitate from where they could sell their product without difficulties. They desired to settle near Calcutta which was suitable for their occupation. Such a place was there at the south of Garia near Rajpur which was preferable for them. So they were rehabilitated there. Some of the evacuees were fishermen who needed a different kind of living place from where they could earn their living by catching and selling fish. Most of the refugees of fishermen were given shelter at Gayeshpur relief camp on the west side of Kanchrapara. This group of refugees wanted to be rehabilitated near the Bhagirathi River. So a vacant land was selected for them near Majherchar which was situated beside Bhagirathi on the westside of Kachrapara. It was also situated beside Kalyani, the planned township of Dr Bidhan Chandra Roy. So these groups of people were very much satisfied finding such places for rehabilitation. They were given some materials for building a house. Thus all the relief camps were made vacant within January 1950.

But it was at the same time when the Hindus were attacked again in East Pakistan. It was started by Bagerhat. The Hindus of this place migrated to West Bengal due to fear of killing. The Hindus in West Bengal hearing the news became excited and began to attack the Muslim houses at some places in West Bengal. Dr Bidhan Chandra Roy worried about further migration but he was ready to control the situation. The news of the riot of West Bengal spread to Pakistan and consequently, the intensity of attack on Hindus increased there. In these circumstances, the government of West Bengal had to be prepared to receive another phase of the refugee influx. It was difficult to rehabilitate more refugees in West Bengal. But Dr Roy was trying to manage it.

The displaced Hindus, mostly Namasudras who migrated after 1950, due to the horrible activities of Muslims, were also poor cultivators. They were also unable to be rehabilitated by themselves as they came with a bare hand. So, Dr Roy had again arranged some temporary relief camps for the predicted influx of refugees. According to his decision, a border slip was issued against each of the refugee families who crossed the West Bengal border and sheltered them at Banga and Darsana. Hence, the refugees had to be rehabilitated necessarily in barren lands or to promote an exchange of population with Muslims of West Bengal, who desired to do it.

But, at this time, J. Nehru decided to stop the exchange of population thinking of secular India. He declared it improper and inhuman for the nation. But in Bengal, it was necessary due to the insufficiency of barren land to rehabilitate the refugees. In response to this declaration, S.P. Mukherjee replied that 'our prime minister says that exchange of population goes against his faith; he had kept his faith in cold storage when he had himself organized population exchange in Punjab.... here also at another time, he could put his faith in cold storage for Bengal'.[21]

In the meeting held on second March 1950 at Writers Building, the then central rehabilitation minister Mr. Saxena declared that the central government would be responsible for temporary shelter of the evacuees, and not to rehabilitate them permanently in India.[22] He argued that the refugees would return to their home after the riots subsided so the Indian Government would not arrange their settlement in India. Dr Meghnad Saha was present at the meeting. He strongly protested the declaration of Mr. Saxena telling that it would be illegal action of the Indian Government if rehabilitation for the new refugees was not made. He argued that the Indian leaders had promised during the partition to rehabilitate the minority Hindus, so it would be ignominy of their promise if they refused to rehabilitate them. This decision of the Nehru Government was intriguing where the rehabilitation arrangement was made for the minority coming from West Punjab but not for the minority coming from East Bengal.

India was divided following the religious conflict and decision of Congress, League and British. They had accepted the responsibility of the minorities who would be victimized by communal violence. Therefore, if the minorities in Pakistan were tortured and uprooted then it was the duty of the government to protect and rehabilitate them. So, the decision of the Nehru government to delay the rehabilitation of the uprooted Hindus of East Pakistan was wrong and inhuman.

J. Nehru had an interest in creating a secular image in the context of the Kashmir war which was anonymously started by Pakistan to capture Kashmir where the Muslims were a majority. The Hindu Maharaja of Kashmir becoming afraid of the tyranny of Pakistan joined India and included Kashmir with it. In this context, J. Nehru took a policy to make a secular India for dissolving the Kashmir Problem. He changed the previous standpoint of population exchange which was applied immediately after Partition.

With the new policy, J. Nehru sent Mr. Saxena to West Bengal to convey the plan to Dr. B.C. Roy, Chief Minister of West Bengal. He suggested making temporary arrangements for the refugees expecting the refugees would return to their home after the situation became normal. He predicted that a minimum of two lakhs of the upcoming refugees would be unable to rehabilitate them. But it would not be possible to accommodate so many refugees only in West Bengal due to the insufficiency of barren land in the state. So he suggested allocating the responsibility of 25000 evacuees to the government of Orissa, 50000 to the Government of Bihar, 25000 to the Government of Tripura and the rest to West Bengal.

According to this suggestion, temporary relief camps were set up at Chandipur near Basirhat, Bagda and Tangra villages in Banga Mahakuma, Rupasripally near Bagerhat, and Dhubulia near Krishnanagar in West Bengal. Most of the refugees had entered through the Banga and Banpur border. The arrangement was made for giving them a border slip as an entering document.

With this slip, they reached Sialdaha station and then they were dispatched to relief camps and outside. The influx of evacuees increased from February 1950. The number of new evacuees was only 1002 in February, but it became 75000 in March and 27000 in May.

All the evacuees coming from East Pakistan desired to settle in West Bengal due to the geographical, meteorological and cultural similarity with their homeland. They did not want to go outside of West Bengal. But the density of population in West Bengal was too much[23] to settle here. In this context, there was a chance of conflict between the evacuees and the residents of West Bengal. Nevertheless, a huge number of Namasudra evacuees went to Tripura and Assam due to its nearest position in the eastern and northern parts of East Pakistan. If they could reach West Bengal they would arrive shortly and it would be difficult to receive them.

Nevertheless, the rehabilitation of the minority Hindus would not be difficult in West Bengal if an exchange of population was permitted. But it was prohibited. Even the interested Muslims of West Bengal have stopped the exchange of population. For this prohibition, the problem of rehabilitation in West Bengal remained unsolved. A conflict between the evacuees and the residents of West Bengal began to grow due to the crisis of barren land.[24]

The Hindus of East Pakistan were driven out by the tyranny of the Muslim but the Muslims in West Bengal were secured by Nehru's declaration of secular India. Even Nehru - Liaqat Pact (February 1950) was signed for encouraging the refugees to return to their homeland. After this pact, some Namasudras returned to their homeland but had to face a horrible situation. On the other hand, the remaining refugees had to be confined in unhealthy conditions in the relief camp for a long time due to the push back policy of the Congress government. The refugees in camps were helpless and aimless. They could not protest the domination of the officials of the camps.[25] But the refugees outside camps began to unite to protest against the anti-refugee, anti-rehabilitation and push back policy of the central government.

Refugee Movement in West Bengal

The refugees, mostly Namasudras, organized several movements protesting against the government's policy of keeping them in relief camps for a long time and against the conspiracy of dispersing outside of West Bengal. They drew the attention of the government demanding proper arrangement for rehabilitation. They felt the necessity to be organized politically to move against the Government's anti-rehabilitation policy. Most of them were antagonistic to the Congress before Partition, only a section of them were supporters of the Congress.[26]

But after Partition, as refugees and friendless in exiled places they all became Congress supporters. In other words, the Congress was in power in West Bengal and the backward Hindus of East Bengal were refugees in the state. So these displaced Hindus had to change their previous antagonistic stand. Now they needed to co-operate and to support the Congress to get rehabilitation in West Bengal. On the other hand, they reminded the Congress leaders' promise of rehabilitation and security of the minority Hindus during partition. Dr Bidhan Chandra Roy, the then Chief Minister of West Bengal (1948-1962), was sympathetic to them in this regard. He was anxious to cooperate with them to get their rehabilitation right in West Bengal with the support of the Nehru government.

Nevertheless, PM Nehru had no interest in rehabilitating the SC refugees in West Bengal. The refugee leaders appealed to the central government for rehabilitation in West Bengal. But the government did not respond to the refugees' appeal; even the distribution of dole/ the minimum foods had been discontinued. They had to face a lack of minimum food in relief camps, further; they were not permitted to work outside for collecting food. So anger grew among them and they organized protest movements strongly against the central government.

The first attempt was taken by the refugees in September 1948 organizing 'Nikhil Banga Bastuhara Karmi Parishad' (NVBKP). The effective leaders in this attempt were Bijay Majumder, Binay Ray, Nagen Das, and Mahadev Bhattacharya. They organized several movements demanding rehabilitation in West Bengal. Besides this movement, the leaders encouraged the refugees to occupy barren lands in West Bengal forcefully for their settlement. It was started in 1949. Bijay Majumdar encouraged the refugees to occupy barren lands for rehabilitation.[27] Being an active leader of the CPI (M), he desired to engage the party to make an absolute movement for the rehabilitation of the refugees. But the other leaders of the Party did not agree with him. Consequently, a separate Refugee Council was required to be set up. A big meeting was held at the commercial Museum hall in Calcutta inviting leaders of all the organizations of the refugees on 4 June 1950. About 200 members of forty-three organizations attended the meeting and formed the big organization namely United Central Refugee Council (UCRC).[28] At the same time, the influx of refugees increased for the effect of the introduction of passports in Pakistan in June- July 1952.

It was the same year for the general election in India. The SC Hindus who came to West Bengal became influential in West Bengal politics. On the other hand, the UCRC was set up to secure the interest of the refugees. Now the political parties in West Bengal became careful to influence the vote bank of the refugees. So they drew the attention of the refugees to the question of their rehabilitation. Congress could not win all the reserved seats in the West Bengal Assembly election of 1952. Three out of thirty-nine reserved seats were won by CPI (M), two seats won by forward Bloc, two seats by Krishak Mazdoor Party (KMP) and one seat by Janasangha.[29] This result showed the beginning of an anti-Congress trend among the refugees due to the anti-refugee rehabilitation policy of the central government.

It was the same time when the members of UCRC encouraged the refugees to draw the attention of the central government through various ways including rail occlusion. A noticeable rail-occlusion took place in the Kurmitola near Lalbagh in Murshidabad. The refugees of the camp attempted to stop the running train near the camp on 25 August 1955, on the issue of lack of dole for week after week. But the train did not stop and left many refugees dead and injured.[30] This incident led the refugees of other camps to move against the anti-refugee policy of the central government.

Consequently, the central government took the initiative to arrange rehabilitation. With this action, the Dandakaranya and Andaman Project were taken to solve the refugee problem in West Bengal. J. Nehru, realizing the problem of the Bengali refugees, tried at first to influence the government of Pakistan for the security of minorities but failed. In this context, he decided to change his earlier stand of pushback policy and initiated rehabilitation for the camp refugees. He decided that those evacuees who would desire to settle in India would be rehabilitated and those who would desire to return homeland would be allowed. The government of West Bengal, after this decision, made more arrangements for relief and rehabilitation. Some new camps were set up at Kashipur, Ultadanga near Calcutta, Ghusari beside the West side of Bhagirathi, Nababnagar and Kansha in Burdwan. All the Hindus who immigrated within 30 April 1950 were rehabilitated without any major problem, except at Cooper's Camp which was the biggest of the camps. It was under the direct maintenance of the central Government.

About 85% of the refugees in Cooper's camp were Namasudras who were poor peasants. They had neither the capability to rehabilitate themselves nor were allowed to go outside of the camp. The gatekeepers were directed to confine them in the camp till the decision of the central government to dispatch them to other places. It was under the responsibility of the central government so the state government had nothing to do regarding their rehabilitation or to enquire about the condition of the people in the camp. Year after year they were confined in the camp. The central authority made arrangements only to distribute some dry foods and did not take care of the living condition of the refugees in the camp. There were about 70000 refugees in the camp but with only twenty tubes well for water and eighty temporary toilets for their use. The dole of dry foods, rotten rice, decomposed wheat and milk which were given to them were not sufficient to fill their stomach at least two times a day. Even it was not given regularly according to the need for which they had to fast day after day.[31] They had to wait in the queue hours after hours before the toilets and tube well to get a chance to use it. They often had to quarrel and fight with each other to get a chance. Year after year they had to stay in the unhealthiest condition.

Consequently, various kinds of diseases appeared. Hundreds of children and old people died without treatment. The dead bodies were piled up beside their living rooms at the wall of the camp. They had to stay in the malodor of the rotten dead bodies until removed by the authorities. The authority sent a lorry per week to remove the rotten bodies but within this time the situation became horrible with the unsavoury and unhealthiest condition of the camp. The refugees who were alive in this condition in the camp had given up all hopes to get a normal life. Their lives turned worse than that of a beast.[32] But no one from outside was allowed to know the condition of the camp residents. The authorities did not disclose the horrible situation of the camp to the people from outside.

But some members[33] of the UCRC under the leadership of Anil Singh collected the information cleverly by eye washing of the commandant of the camp. They found that the refugees were spending their times hysterically in malodor in the same room where the rotten dead bodies were piled up. They became nervous to see the horrible situation in the camp and could not imagine such a dreadful situation.

After finding this information, the UCRC became arrogant to protest against the policy of the central government and to encourage the refugees to make colonies by occupying barren lands. They organized them more strongly, collecting information from all the refugee camps showing the present situation to the authority of the central government. Under this pressure, the government took the initiative to form a 'Fact-Finding Committee' with fifteen members for the refugees in West Bengal, on 15 November 1952. A report of the Committee had been received by the Ministry of the central government and it was granted in 1954. But the government did not take any further action to solve the problems of the refugees of West Bengal.

The situation of the refugees in Bettiah camp at Champaran district of Bihar was almost similar to Cooper's camp. It was as big as Cooper's camp. The population of the Camp was about 70,000, which was similar to that of Cooper's camp. The authority of the camp campaigned to the general people of the areas that the refugee problem would make the local people poorer to poorer due to the presence of refugees. Consequently, negligence for the refugees grew among the local people which created the life of refugees bitterly in Bettiah camp.[34] Further, the distribution of a minimum food in the name of dole was irregular. So the refugees decided to leave the camp for West Bengal and joined in the struggle for survival with the refugees of West Bengal. Hence, a mass movement was organized under the leadership of the UCRC throughout West Bengal against the Government's policy.

This mass movement was supported by the leftist leaders of West Bengal. The Namasudra refugees leaned to the political activities of a leftist to mobilize their movement politically. Hence, the Congress leaders felt the need to keep the refugees out of the influence of the communist party due to political interest. They knew that the election result of 1952 where the leftist parties got a noticeable vote in the districts of 24 Parganas, Nadia, Howrah, Hooghly, Burdwan and Darjeeling where the refugees were concentrated.[35] So it was the result of the refugee leaning to the leftist due to their frustration with the congress activities regarding rehabilitation.

On the other hand, the leftist parties were trying to organize a movement for the refugees. They combined the refugee interest with their political agendas. The refugee leaders Bijay Majumdar, Dharani Goswami et.al who worked silently for the Communist party now became active and enthusiastic with the encouragement of the Communist leaders. Consequently, a scope for the leftist was being developed to get the political majority in West Bengal. Thus the percentage of votes for the Communist parties increased noticeably in the general election of 1957 with the support of the refugees. The Left Front got 51 seats and the Congress got 99 seats in this election. Jyoti Basu became the opposition leader from CPI (M).

Most of the Namasudra refugees who arrived in West Bengal in the 1950s became antagonistic to Congress due to the ignorance of the Congress leaders regarding the interest of these refugees. The 'Namasudra refugees did not get a fair deal in West Bengal...like the first wave of the upper caste refugees'[36]. But these refugees made the Congress leaders worried about the increasing power of CPI (M) due to the refugee factor in West Bengal politics.[37] J. Nehru predicted that the refugees' support would bring a political change in the next election if they would not be dispersed from West Bengal before the next election. Hence, J. Nehru became anxious to disperse the refugees out of West Bengal to eliminate the refugee factor from West Bengal politics. He accelerated the Dandakaranya project for the rehabilitation of the refugees.

Forced-Rehabilitation in Dandakaranya and Massacre of Marichjhapi

It was the same time when the refugees' influx increased again due to the incursive policy of the Muslim leaders in East Pakistan. These leaders were required to cooperate with the ministry of liberal-minded Fazlul Haq who had formed the United Front Government in East Pakistan in June 1954. It was dismissed by the Muslim high commands of the League. It affected the minority Hindus in East Pakistan in an adverse manner. They became afraid of the Muslim leaders and began to migrate to West Bengal. More than 15000 refugees, per month, took shelter in the relief camps in West Bengal from the middle of the year 1955.[38] The West Bengal

Government was unable to rehabilitate this vast number of refugees in the state.

Under these circumstances, Shri Ram Murti, the retired minister of the Madras Government, proposed the Dandakaranya project for dispersing the new coming refugees and the camp refugees. The central government was already trying to promote such a project. Though the project was very risky and expensive it was to proceed due to the interest of the central government. The place was not suitable for the rehabilitation of the Bengali refugees. Most of these refugees were Namasudras, the poor peasants who needed at least some agricultural land for cultivation for earning their bread, but it was almost absent there. Besides the crisis of agricultural land, there was also a lack of water, communication and other basic requirements for their living. But honourable Prime Minister J. Nehru became very enthusiastic in dispersing the refugees to these infertile lands.

The Nehru government could not save the minorities from the tyranny of the hooligans during and after the partition. The government had failed to influence the Muslim leaders of Pakistan on the issue of the minorities' security. The Muslim high command was not interested in the security of the minority Hindus. On the other hand, the Muslims of post partitioned India had been assured of security under the secular policy of J. Nehru. The Muslims were given tight security and encouraged to stay here. So without any tension, the Muslims of West Bengal felt secured and did not allow the Hindu refugees to enter their areas. But the Hindus in East Pakistan were targeted and driven out and their land and wealth were occupied by the Muslims. J. Nehru expected, up till 1955 that the refugees of West Bengal would return to their home but that did not happen.[39] So, he decided to take action to rehabilitate the refugees in India but outside of West Bengal due to the refugee's influence on the vote bank of West Bengal.

The Bengali refugees were entirely unfamiliar with the land of Dandakaranya. They heard the story of Dandakaranya in Ramayana that it was a horrible place where even the heroic person Ramchandra had to face a terrible situation due to its horrifying environment. But now the government has committed to rehabilitating the refugees to this dreadful land. A committee was formed on 12 September 1958 for the rehabilitation of the refugees in Dandakaranya. The project covered a vast area of infertile land and unhealthy forest under Bastar district (Parul Khot, Kondogaon) in Madhyapradesh and Koraput (Malkangiri and Umerkote) in Orissa. The government decided to generate about 300 villages in this dreadful area with the effort of digging some big ponds for water, cleaning deep forest for cultivating and arranging some other minimum requirements for the settlement. Some aborigine people were living there but they did not cultivate the land and could not live like general people. They earn their living collecting food from forests and hunting different kinds of animals and birds. The land was full of red soil, kakor and stone which made it impossible to prepare land for cultivation but the government was enthusiastic to rehabilitate the refugees there.[40] The rehabilitating authority campaigned for the success of the project. The political activities and movement of the UCRC for rehabilitation during 1952-54, led the Congress government to rehabilitate the refugees anyhow in Dandakaranya.[41]

The refugees did not want to settle in Dandakaranya, they organized against this project under the leadership of UCRC and SBBKP. Their leaders thought that though barren lands were scarce in West Bengal it was not impossible to rehabilitate them here. Some suitable areas of marshy and barren lands were there in West Bengal for the rehabilitation of the refugees. They thought that if the Congress government would take some positive steps following the need and nature of the Bengali refugees it would be possible to rehabilitate them in West Bengal because there were huge scopes for creating industrial and agricultural projects. The refugees, who were selected for rehabilitation in the Dandakaranya were poor peasants and labourers who had an intense interest to stay in West Bengal. They did not demand sufficient land for rehabilitation but just an opportunity to live and earn their living through hard labour. So, according to their argument, it was not difficult to utilize their labour in the production of West Bengal. The local political leaders of West Bengal had some positive plans and prospects to rehabilitate them in West Bengal but it was discouraged and dismissed by the central government.

Dandakaranya authority decided to stop doles of the refugees and decided to close all the relief camps to force the refugees to leave for Dandakaranya. The central government was aware of the fact that the refugees had organized several movements demanding their rehabilitation in West Bengal and they were not interested in departing for Dandakaranya. They supported the CPI (M) and influenced the vote bank of 1952 against Congress.[42] More than eighty percent of the refugees, at this time, were supporters of the Communist Party of India.[43]

On the other hand, the refugees' leaders could understand the reason behind the effort of the Congress government to rehabilitate the refugees in Dandakaranya. They detected a political conspiracy behind this enthusiasm of the government. They knew that the Nehru government which did not take any action before the election of 1957 to rehabilitate them now became very busy rehabilitating them outside of West Bengal. They suspected that this was nothing but to eliminate the refugee factor from West Bengal politics. They also predicted that the election results of 1952 and 1957 indicated a political turning in West Bengal.

Nevertheless, the refugees neither united against Congress nor could influence the government's policy of rehabilitation. Under these circumstances, the exiled leader of the SC Federation Jogendranath Mandal, who was isolated and out of political activities from 1950 to 1958, entered in Dalit movement in West Bengal. He was unacceptable to the Namasudra refugees in West Bengal due to his failure in East Pakistan.[44] But now 'an isolated Mandal found a new support base among the Namasudra refugees to reinvent his political leadership as they felt also marginalized and torn between identities'.[45] He was invited by the members of Sara Bangla Bastuhara Karmi Parishad (SBBKP)[46] to lead the refugee movement for the demand for rehabilitation in West Bengal. He was welcomed by Hemanta Biswas, the then spokesperson of SBBS, to attend the meeting held at Bagjola in 1958. Mr Mandal became a primary member of SBBS and was promised an opportunity to lead the organization after faithfully working among the refugees. He was warned not to think of the movement on the issue of caste.

Nevertheless, he found a separate Dalit organization namely Purba Bharat Bastuhara Sansad (PBBS) on 9 July 1958 organizing a meeting, at Mahabodhi Society Hall, under the presidency of Hemendranath Dasgupta.[47] Hence, he tried to mobilize the Namasudras on the Dalit issue and the refugees' interest in their rehabilitation in West Bengal. He reactivated the Satyagraha movement which was started earlier after the threat by the Nehru government in 1956 for the stoppage of dole and which was organized under the leadership of communist leaders of the UCRC. The campaigning of the Satyagraha movement of 1958 lasted for about one month (March-April) which was organized under the leadership of Mr. Mandal against the Dandakaranya policy of the Nehru Government. He organized several campaigning meetings in 1958, in 24 Parganas, Howrah, Burdwan, Birbhum and Nadia on behalf of the refugees demanding their rehabilitation in West Bengal.[48]

Thus, he tried to be faithful to the Namasudra refugees for accepting him as an active leader in West Bengal politics. He tried to bring back the previous image of Dalit leadership through the movement against the government policy of rehabilitating the refugees in Dandakaranya. But the leaders of the UCRC were not faithful to him, so they condemned him on the issue of responsibility during Partition. On the other hand, Mr Mandal campaigned against them giving warning to the audience that the leftist leaders of the UCRC had made a false promise for working for the refugees, and they had only tried to embezzle the money which was sanctioned for the refugee. During the conflict, he attempted to prepare against the leftist leaders by setting up another organization namely the East India Refugee Council (EIRC). This conflict between the refugee leaders weakened their movement.

It was at the same time when a conflict appeared between the PBBS and UCRC on the issue of rehabilitation of the refugees who were peasants. The leaders of SBBS were trying to move against the rehabilitation of peasant refugees in Dandakaranya. But the UCRC did not support this movement. The SBBS argued that 70 per cent of the refugees were Namasudra agriculturists who needed agricultural land to earn their living but it was absent in Dandakaranya, so its leaders attempted to protest strongly against the Dandakaranya project. But the leaders of UCRC did not respond to this movement.

The existing inhabitants of West Bengal found the Dandakaranya Project of the Nehru government quite reasonable. They were not interested in rehabilitating the refugees in West Bengal due to the fear of overpopulation. The leftist leaders who supported the movement of UCRC were conscious of the political support of non-refugees. They did not want to lose the average support of voters in an election. Therefore they abandoned the joint movement with the EIRC in the interest of refugees. But the Namasudra refugees under the leadership of Mr Mandal organized several Satyagraha movements and strikes in Calcutta and 24 Parganas demanding their rehabilitation in West Bengal. The protest movement became so massive in Calcutta that Mr Mandal was arrested on 18 January 1960. But after his release, he again mobilized the refugees to move against the Dandakaranya project. He appealed to the government to utilize the sanctioned amount of rupees for rehabilitation plans in West Bengal instead of spending it on the Dandakaranya. The government refused his pleas and proposals. His repeated protest marches with about 3000 camp-refugees in front of the Writers' Building and his appeal to rehabilitate the refugees in West Bengal were ignored and refused by the government.[49] But he continued his struggle for the refugees without success till he passed away in 1968.

It was at the same time when P. R. Thakur, Guruchand's grandson, did not support the refugees' demand for rehabilitation in West Bengal. He was a supporter of Congress during Partition and did not engage himself in the movements of refugees in West Bengal. Though he established a refugee colony in Thakurnagar in North 24 Parganas buying a plot of land and organizing a religious-cultural movement in 1948, he did not discourage the refugees to go outside Bengal. He even suggested that the refugees should settle anywhere in India where they could get land for rehabilitation.[50] He won the election of West Bengal Legislative Assembly with a Congress ticket in 1957 and 1962 from Haringhata SC constituency and Hanskhali SC constituency respectively and became a successful politician in West Bengal under the aegis of Congress. He was conscious about how the communist leaders had attracted a false promise to the refugees for rehabilitating them in West Bengal. Consequently, he suggested the refugees be rehabilitated according to the policy of the central government. But the refugees had been keenly interested to be rehabilitated in West Bengal so they were easily manipulated by the unfair politics of the communist leaders.

On the other hand, the Nehru government played an extreme anti-refugee role being indifferent against the attacks on refugees in Bangaon in 1964. For this P. R. Thakur resigned from the Congress Party and founded the Bangla Congress to contest in the Lok Sobha elections in 1967 from Nabadwip. At that time he supported the refugees' movement attending their meetings demanding rehabilitation of the refugees in the border areas of West Bengal. But he could not influence the Dandakaranya policy of the central government due to the disintegration of the refugee movement. The disintegrated and weak refugee movements failed to save them from the government's policy of rehabilitating them outside of West Bengal; consequently, they were exiled in infertile lands and unhealthy forest of Indian provinces far away from Bengal.

The fresh refugees, about 12 lakhs, mostly Namasudras, who came in the 1960s for the impact of the Indo-Pak war of 1964-65, were exiled forcefully in Dandakaranya with the camp refugees. They were directly dumped in this infertile land by train. Some special refugee trains were arranged to carry them from Sealdah to Jagaddalpur, the main town of Bastar districts. From there they were sent to Parulkot, Kondagaon, Pharasgaon and Jamori of Bastar district in Madhyapradesh and Malkangiri, Raigarh and Umerkot of Orissa, and then they were scattered in about 300 villages of Dandyakarany project.[51]

They were given, primarily, some minimum amount of rupees and food and a hut which had been made by the refugee himself. Plots of land were distributed through a lottery beside the road, made by the government. A committee namely AMPO was formed with the authority of Andhra Pradesh, Chhattisgarh and Orissa in November 1957. A.L Fletcher was appointed as the first chairman of the committee to organize the activities of the project. It was handed over to the Dandakaranya Development Authority (DDA) After July 23, 1958. All the responsibility for preparing irrigation, school, college, hospital, roads, bridge and electricity in the Project was given to the DDA. The land was not fertile so the authority decided to distribute seven acres of land to each of the families of the refugees but it would not be more than three acres which were not sufficient for the minimum requirement of the dwellers. The production was only 2.10 to 3.80 quintals of rice from the lands which had been provided out of the irrigation areas which was insufficient for the survival of a family. [52] In the irrigation areas, it was only up to 8.94 quintals per acre. The production of other crops like maize, pistachio and oilseeds was also very poor and thus the annual income per family reached only three thousand per year which discouraged the refugees from living in the place. In 1964, Saibal Gupta, the then chairman of the DDA ...pointed out that less than 10 percent of the soil of the land which the refugees had been provided was, in fact, arable, and by the most optimistic standards, the rest was simply uncultivable'.[53] Further, the responsible authority could not complete all the plans and prospects of the project within time. The irrigation project of Parulkot and Malkangiri which was scheduled to be completed within 1975, ended in 1989. In addition to this, there were problems of non-cooperation of the local people and aborigines of the forest, unbearable climate and lack of communication which led the Bengali refugees to leave the place.

Consequently, they began to return to West Bengal and went to different places in Indian provinces for survival. It was started in 1963 and continued up to 1979. About 1865 families in 1963, 1335 families in 1965, 3465 families in 1972 and 14388 families in 1978 deserted the places of the project. During their campaigning against the Congress, the Leftist leaders Jyoti Basu, Promod Dasgupta, Radhika Benerjee, Kironmoy Nanda, Tridib Chowdhury, Sibdas Mukherjee et.al promised to rehabilitate the refugees in West Bengal before 1977. They assured the refugees of Dandakaranya that they would arrange for rehabilitation in Marichjhapi in the Sundarbans and promised to fulfil all demands if they would come to power.[54] But after coming to power in 1977 the same leaders had taken opposite action against the refugees who returned to West Bengal expecting the support of the Leftist government.

The refugees could not understand the Communist leaders' use of rehabilitation issues as just a political agenda against Congress and resort to mouthing promises to get the support of the refugees in the election. The communist leaders discouraged the refugees from returning to West Bengal but they could not believe it. They knew that during the Congress regime, on 11 August 1959, the UCRC, submitting a statistical account regarding conditions of rehabilitation on the land of Marichjhapi, had appealed to the then Chief Minister Dr Bidhan Chandra Roy to rehabilitate them in that uninhabited island. Dr Roy was interested in rehabilitating them in Marichjhapi but the Nehru government was against it.[55] It was at the same time when the Communist leaders condemned the Nehru government and supported the demand of the UCRC. Even the spokesman of the Communist Party Jyoti Basu, in a meeting held on 25 January 1975 in Bhilai industrial area near Dandakaranya, declared before the refugee leaders 'if we get the power we must fulfil the demand of rehabilitation of the refugees in West Bengal'.[56] On the other hand, the refugee leaders, organizing several meetings in Dandakaranya, encouraged them to return and settle in Marichjhapi. Consequently, the refugees started to come back to settling in Marichjhapi immediately after winning the Left Front in the election of 1977.

A group of refugees about 30,000 out of 120,000 came back to West Bengal within 1978[57] and reached Marichjhapi through Hasnabad, crossing the Kumirmari Island by boat. They cleaned the jungle of the uninhabited island working hard and made all kinds of minimum necessary arrangements for survival. The land blossomed into a populous village within a short period by the effort of the refugees who arranged schools, roads, markets, bread factories and bidi factories without any help from the government. The Ramakrishna Mission, Bharat Sebasram Sangha and many other volunteer organizations helped them in many ways. The UCRC led the refugees to earn their living and to get help from various volunteer organizations. The refugees took various kinds of new occupations including fishing and collecting wood. They had no expectations from the government. Only they appealed to the government for permission to live there.

But the Jyoti Basu government and the Morarji government did not allow the lower caste refugees to live there. They ignored the humble appeal of the refugees rather made arrangements for removing them by any means from the island. The Communist leaders, dishonouring their previous promises, regarded the rehabilitation of the refugees in West Bengal as an extra problem. Jyoti Basu apprehended that it was not possible to rehabilitate the refugees but he requested the refugees to remain in Dandakaranya. He decided to finish the problem by arranging police action on the refugees of Mairichjhapi. He ordered the police force to clean Marichjhapi anyhow. At the first stage, the refugees had been given the warning to leave the island and pressure was brought upon them, closing all kinds of communication from outside and creating an economic block of settlement on 26 January 1979.[58] When the refugees did not want to go outside then the police force set fire to the huts and fired on the refugees who gathered to protest against police action on 24 January 1979.[59]

The island of Marichjhapi was depopulated by the betrayal action of the Jyoti Basu government[60]. The number of refugees killed was unknown to the general people. The refugees who were alive there again returned to Dandakaranya with great frustration leaving all the hopes of living in West Bengal. They again had to begin the struggle to survive in Dandakaranya with infertile land, unbearable weather and lack of minimum necessities. They realized that they had nothing to do either against the domination of the government or to get rehabilitation anywhere other than Dandakaranya.

The Bengali Refugees in Andaman, Nainital and Assam

The sufferings of Namasudra refugees who were rehabilitated in Andaman, Uttar Pradesh and Assam had been almost similar to the refugees of Dandakaranya. Rehabilitation in Andaman was started in 1949. The first phase of the rehabilitation was started in May 1949 shifting about 200 families by ship for settling there. They were selected from among the camp refugees who had occupational ability to be rehabilitated there.[61] Again on 17 March 1951, about 30 refugee families from west Bengal were sent to the Andaman by ship. Some areas were selected for refugee colonies in three main islands in the south, middle and northern part of the islands, cleaning the jungle and preparing the land for cultivation. The land was then almost without inhabitants. There was only a British colony in the southern part of the islands centring on Port Blair. Though some aborigines were already living in some areas of the islands they were entirely different from the main folk. They were living in forest areas without cultivation and with the aborigine lifestyle. They were the attraction of the tourists coming from outside. The place was used for exiling the accused persons of the Indian mainland during colonial times. But after independence, the system of exiling had been abolished.

The Bengali refugees who were mentally strong were rehabilitated there and had to be mentally strong to settle. The rehabilitating authority had made some necessary arrangements for perpetuating the rehabilitation there. The authority sent some fundamental requirements for them including hand instruments, shoes, baskets, spades, seeds of crops etc. for cultivating and provided some musical instruments such as mridanga, Danka(drum) Kartal, etc. for keeping mental health well. The cultivating families, mostly Namasudras, were able to survive there due to their cultivation success. They were distributed about ten acres of cultivating land for the survival of each family. Some lands were in hill areas and some were in low areas. Though the lands were of a different quality from Bengal it was better than the land of Dandakaranya. The natural weather was different from Dandakaranya because of its situation amid the sea.

Though it was situated near the equator the sea weather of the place was comfortable due to the presence of monsoon. But those refugees who were not habituated with cultivation and with the weather of the island could not survive. They had faced a lot of difficulties to earn their living due to the absence of industry and other scopes of earning bread. Further, there was a lack of educational and socio-cultural opportunities. Consequently, about 150 families returned to West Bengal. However, the cultivating families, mostly Namasudras, had survived on the island better than Dandakaranya.

Therefore, Dr Bidhan Chandra Roy, the then Chief Minister of West Bengal tried to rehabilitate more refugees in the Andaman Islands but the central government refused to take financial responsibility for the rehabilitation. So the state government could not take the necessary step for arranging available scopes for the rehabilitation in the Islands. But some of the Namasudra refugees settled there without any help from the central government for saving them from the inhuman weather in Dandakaranya with the help of the refugees who already settled in Andaman Island.[62]

Some refugees were rehabilitated at Nainital of Uttarakhand at the foot of the Himalayas far from Bengal. The land was full of the Jungle of the Terai zone. Some Jungle areas had been cleaned for preparation of the land for cultivation for the refugees who were skilled in cultivation. The place was suitable for jute cultivation due to available rainfall. About one thousand Bengali refugees were rehabilitated there. They were successful in cultivating jute and other necessary crops which were suitable to the weather and soil of the land. Though they had not been given SC status and could not avail of the socio-cultural opportunities as Bengal, yet they survived better than the refugees of Dandakaranya, forming a Bengali colony and society there.

The minorities, mostly Namasudras, who were uprooted from the northern and eastern part of East Pakistan, crossed the Assam border for surviving the tyranny of the Muslim hooligans. Their population reached eight lakhs in Assam in 1971.[63] Most of them rehabilitated themselves without the government's help. They made their settlement in Bijony, Bishnupur, Jokia, Beki, Panikheti and Manos in the Goalpara district; Bhatgaon, Bamundi, Baithabhanga, Neularbhita in Kamrup district; Tinsukia in Dibrugarh district, Laukhuan, Hojain, Lanka and Ambagan areas and 72 villages in Nagaon district, and almost all the villages in Cachar district on the bank of Brahmaputra River; Kathal Pudhari, Daluhat, Kalakhoa, Santipur, Bishnupur, Chilapathor, Majargaon, Panbari, Bhairavpur, Shibpur, Simenchapuri and many other places of Lakhimpur district.

They had to struggle against the local people who opposed them in rehabilitating due to fear of socio-economic crisis. But they succeeded in their struggle and improved their socio-economic status. Most of them have shifted their occupation from manual work to the high profession of doctor, lawyer and teacher despite their deprivation from many aspects of their rights. The local people had not allowed them to share the socio-cultural and economic resources in Assam, rather they had been trying to push them back to their homeland. The Muslims, both local and the immigrants, who had been trying to increase their population in Assam aiming at the creation of the Islamic majority, also opposed them.

On the other hand, the All Assam Student Union (AASU) organized a movement against the Bengali Hindu refugees for pushing back them for saving Assam from overcrowding and for eliminating the refugee factor from Assam politics. This organization led the Assam government to treat the Hindu refugees as doubtful voters and not to give citizenship to India. The AASU and the Assam government had jointly taken many steps for pushing back the Hindu refugees to Bangladesh but failed. Even the population of Bengali Hindu refugees increased due to the horrific activities of Islamic hooligans in Bangladesh.

These refugees knew that they would be killed if they returned to their homeland, so they tried to settle there. They were enthusiastic about developing themselves as a strong community. They set up schools, colleges, markets, roads and all other necessities through their own effort without government help in the barren lands of Assam. They organized themselves making several movements all over Assam to protest against their enemies. It was initiated with the effort of Ramratan Biswas of Gouripur in Goalpara district in 1968. Mahadev Das and Baliram Das under the leadership of Ramratan Biswas organized the Namasudras to move against their enemies. Sudhir Kumar Bagchi (doctor) organized an All Assam Conference at Baropeta road in Kamrup to protest against the anti-refugee activities in February 1968. He was the most influential organizer of the Conference. He organized the Namasudras and formed the 'All Assam Namasudra Samiti'(AANS) and its branches all over the districts of Assam targeting the fulfilment of their aims and objectives. Mr. Bagchi preached the ideology of Hari-Guruchand all over Assam and encouraged the Namasudras for the education of their children according to the guidance of Matuaism and for unification of the Namasudras all over Assam. Several schools were established in Namasudra concentrated areas under his leadership. Jopiapara M.I. High school in Goalpara district, Neular Bhita M.I. High school, Kahimari M. I. High school, Agram M.I. High school and Bamundi High school in Kamrup district were some of the important schools which were established within 1971. Some political leaders among Namasudras also played an important role in developing their community.

Kalachand Das of Srihatta district and Balaram Das of Kamrup district were able to be ministers under the Assam government. They had played an important role in moving the Namasudras against their enemies. Many political leaders among Namasudras were elected MLAs under eight SC legislative assemblies such as Sri Ayodharam Das, Sri Kandap Kumar Das, Khagendra Nath Samaddar, Mahadev Das and Rabin Choudhury who became a member of the Jogendra Hazarika ministry (1979).[64] They had played an important role in encouraging the Namasudras and to struggle against their enemies and to remain in Assam actively despite facing huge difficulties. The refugees never lost their mental strength to the threat of being de-voter and pushing back by the local people and AASU but they organized more strongly against their enemies for seeking a new path. Nevertheless, the NRC and CAA (December 12, 2019) of the BJP government led those refugees to be afraid of their survival in Assam. Protest movements broke out rapidly not only among the refugees of Assam but also across the country. The endeavour of their leaders encouraged them to survive and struggle against the difficulties they faced.

Conclusion

The hard-working nature of the Bengali refugees led them to struggle for survival in the inhospitable land of Dandakaranya and other places where they faced various difficulties and problems, in unbearable heat in the summer with lack of food, non-cooperation of the local people, financial crisis, the insufficient scope of earning bread, an inappropriate system of education and communication gap with their main folk, as the place was situated far away from Bengal. They became almost separated from the main folk in almost all ways in their lives.

In West Bengal, the Namasudra refugees had to struggle less than the refugees of other provinces. Having linguistic and cultural similarity they found more scopes to survive here than in other provinces. They were able to make a separate identity in West Bengal establishing a distinctive socio-cultural self-image through socio-educational and economic prosperity. P. R Thakur, grandson of Guruchand Thakur settled in West Bengal setting up a socio-religious centre of Matua Namasudras in Thakurnagar in north 24 Parganas where the Namasudras gathered every year on the occasion of Baruni Mela which was held originally at Orakandi in eastern Bengal. Focusing on their area of the Namasudras he also became successful in his political activities under the aegis of the Indian National Congress.

He mobilized the Namasudras separately with self-help spirit all over India reviving the Matua Mahasangha (MM) which was a non-political socio-religious organization of Matuas, the devotees of Hari-Guruchand. The MM was established at Orakandi in eastern Bengal during the time of Guruchand Thakur. The Namasudras, under this organization, arranged several movements against the central government demanding their rights of citizenship and rehabilitation. The members of the MM organized several protest movements against the anti-refugee policy and the Citizenship Amendment Bill of 2003. The main struggle of the Namasudras was for the citizenship and rehabilitation of refugees who crossed the Indian border after March 1971. This group of the Namasudras lost everything in their homeland due to the anti-Hindu policy of the Islamic leaders and got nothing in India due to the indifferent role of the central government. The government took a push policy but they did not go back due to the fear of being killed by the Islamic hooligans. The members of the MM have been struggling mainly for the rights of the refugees instead of preaching Matua Dharma, which was the main focus of the organization. It attached more importance to supporting the refugees who had been suffering from insecurity and uncertainty of settlement not only in West Bengal but also in other provinces. This non-political organization had its 6755 branches all over India up till 2008 for working on behalf of the followers of Matuaism.[65]

Besides their basic struggle for survival, the Namasudras had been trying to adjust socio-culturally in the new places. In Dandakaranya the local aborigine people could not influence the socio-cultural activities of the Namasudras. Rather the refugees succeeded in influencing the aborigines through their socio-cultural tradition.[66] The new generations detached from Bengali culture and were compelled to accept the socio-educational guidelines of the state government under which they had been residing. They have no scope to read and write the Bengali language. Their children were compelled to read and write in Oriya and Hindi. They neither read Bengali literature nor watched Bengali movies. Rather they derive pleasure by watching Hindi films. They rarely enjoyed the attractive and traditional folk and folk poetic songs of the famous folk poets and artists belonging to the Namasudras of Bengal. Even the various kinds of recorded Bengali songs are not available to the new generations of the Namasudras. The folk poets and the Jatra parties of Bengal did not desire to go far away due to difficulties of maintainability and less profit. They required high rates which the poor refugee residents outside of Bengal found difficult to pay. Thus their socio-cultural communication with their main folk almost stopped.

The Namasudras had been given the SC status in eastern states like Assam, Manipur, Mizoram, Meghalaya, Tripura, West Bengal and Orissa but in Madhyapradesh, Chhattisgarh, Uttarakhand and Uttarpradesh they have been deprived of the status for which they cannot be benefited from the opportunities of government jobs, education and politics. They cannot contest in the election as reserved candidates. According to an order of the Supreme Court, they should get SC status but the government authority of Madhya Pradesh, Chhattisgarh and Uttarakhand avoided this order arguing that the Namasudras who have been residing in their state do not have any economic and social backwardness.

Some of the Namasudra refugees in India have overcome economic backwardness by hard labour, cultivating skill and knowledge. Some among their new generations took the advanced profession of teaching, engineering, medicine and business. The literacy rate of the Namasudras in Dandakaranya reached 60 per cent in 1981. In West Bengal, it reached 71.93 per cent, in 2001, ahead of the provincial average of 68.64 per cent[67] which indicates the progressive trend of the community but still many of the Namasudras have not been given the right of citizenship and rehabilitation. They also suffer a lot due to the social ignorance of the upper castes that even in the twenty-first century treat the Namasudras as untouchable and keep them separate in socio-economic and cultural activities.

ENDNOTES AND REFERENCES

1. Joya Chatterjee: *The Spoils of Partition: Bengal and India, 1947-1967,* (New Delhi Cambridge University Press, 2007), p. 108.
2. Pafulla Kumer Chakraborty: *Prantik Manab: Paschim Bange Udbastu Jibaner Katha,* (Kolkata, Deep, Prakashan, 2013), p. 17.

3. Ramkrishna Bhattacharya: *Banga Bhanga: Swadeshi: Biplab Bad,* (Kolkata, K.P. Bagchi & Company, 2016), p. 150.
4. Hiranmoy Bandyopadhyay: *Udbastu,* (Kolkata, Deep Prakashan, 2013), p. 415.
5. Babul Kumer Pal: *Barishal Theke Dandyakaranya* (Kolkata, Mitram, 2010), p. 105.
6. Hiranmoy Bandyopadhyay: *op.cit.,* p. 416.
7. Madhav Godbole: *The Holocaust of Indian Partition: an Inquest,* (New Delhi, Rupa Publication, 2011), p. 34.
8. Joya Chatterjee, *op.cit.,* p. 111.
9. Madhav Godbole: *op.cit.,* p. 43.
10. S. Bandyopadhyay: *Caste, Protest and Identity in Colonial India; The Namasudras of Bengal, 1872-1947,* (New Delhi: Oxford University Press, 2011), p. 250.
11. Jaya Chatterjee: *op. cit.,* pp. 44-46.
12. Amalendu Dey: *Pakistan Prastab O Fajlul Huq* (Kolkata, Parul, 2014), p. 184.
13. Madhav Godbole, *op.cit.,* p. 4.
14. Pafulla Kumer Chakraborty: *op.cit.,* p. 31.
15. *Ibid.,* p. 86.
16. Hiranmoy Bandyopadhyay: *op.cit.,* p. 33.
17. Pafulla Kumer Chakraborty: *op.cit.,* p. 23.
18. Hiranmoy Bandyopadhyay: *op.cit.,* p. 421.
19. Prafulla Kumer Chakraborty: *op.cit.,* p. 15.
20. H iranmoyBandyopadhyay: *op.cit.,* p. 72.
21. Madhav Godbole: *The Holocaust of Indian Partition: an Inquest,* (New Delhi, Rupa Publication, 2011), p. 206.
22. Hiranmoy Bandyopadhyay: *op.cit.,* p. 87.
23. Census of 1951, 806 persons per square mile.
24. Hiranmoy Bandyopadhyay: *op.cit.,* p. 129.
25. Pafulla Kumer Chakraborty: *op.cit.,* p. 100.
26. S. Bandyopadhyay: *op.cit.,* p. 256.
27. Babul Kumer Pal: *op.cit.,* p. 74.
28. *Ibid.*

29. S. Bandyopadhyay: *op.cit.*, p. 257.
30. Hiranmoy Bandyopadhyay: *op.cit.*, p. 408.
31. Pafulla Kumer Chakraborty: *op.cit.*, p. 323.
32. Pafulla Kumer Chakraborty: *op.cit.*, pp. 94-95.
33. Bijay Majumdar, Ambika Chakrobrty and Naresh Benerjee.
34. Pafulla Kumer Chakraborty: *op.cit.*, p. 101.
35. Babul Kumer Pal: *op.cit.*, p. 79.
36. S Bandyopadhyay: *op.cit.*, p. 255.
37. Babul Kumer Pal: *op.cit.*, p. 82.
38. Hiranmoy Bandyopadhyay: *op.cit.*, p. 428.
39. Pafulla Kumer Chakraborty: Madhav Godbole, p. 99.
40. Manaranjan Byapari: *Itibritante Chandal Jiban*, (Kolkata, Kolkata Prakashan, 2012), p. 33.
41. Babul Kumer Pal: *op.cit.*, p. 92.
42. Pafulla Kumer Chakraborty: *op.cit.*, p. 87.
43. Joya Chatterjee: Madhav Godbole, p. 290.
44. S Bandyopadhyay: *op. cit.*, p. 254.
45. *Ibid.*, p. 255.
46. Babul Kumar Pal: *op.cit.*, p. 101.
47. *Ibid.*
48. S. Bandyopadhyay: *op.cit.*, p. 258.
49. *Ibid.*, pp. 260-61.
50. *Ibid.*, p. 264.
51. Manoranjan Byapari: *op.cit.*, p. 126.
52. Babul Kumar Pal: *op.cit.*, p. 115.
53. Joya Chatterjee: *op.cit.*, p. 137.
54. Sudhirranjan Haldar: *Itihaser Prekshapate Dandyakarany O Marichjhapi*, (Nadia, Kamala Publisher, 2008): p. 16.
55. Manoranjan Bepari: *Itibritantte Chandal Jiban*, Vol. I, (Kolkata, Kolkata Prakashan, 2012), p. 217.
56. *Ibid.*
57. S Bandyopadhyay, *op.cit.*, p. 261.

58. Gyanesh Kudaisya, Divided Landscape, Fragmented identities: East Bengal Refugees and Rehabilitation in India, 1947-79, in Howard D, A, Low & Brasted (ed.), *Northern India and Independence,* (New Delhi, Sage Publication), p. 122.
59. Babul Kumer Pal: *op.cit.,* p. 122.
60. Manoranjan Bepari: *Itibritte Chandal Jiban,* Vol. I, (Kolkata, Kolkata Prakashan, 2012), p. 216.
61. Hiranmoy Bandyopadhyay: *op.cit.,* p. 199.
62. *Ibid.,* p. 204.
63. Naresh Chandra Das: Namasudra Samproday o Bangladesh (Kolkata, Dipali Book House, 1997):, p. 213.
64. *Ibid.,* p. 216.
65. S. Bandyopadhyay: *op.cit.,* p. 267.
66. Babul Kumer Pal: *op.cit.,* p. 169.
67. S. Bandyopadhyay: *op.cit.,* p. 262.

Conclusion

The word 'Namasudra' is not found in any written ancient record. The Namasudras believe that their community's name has originated from their ancestor's name Namasa or Lomasa Muni and their *gotra*/ lineage came from the name of Kashyap Muni who was the father of Namasa Muni, and they observed all their social ceremonies uttering the name of Kasyap following Hindu social laws and orders. But it was not regarded as authentic by any Hindu social scientist; rather many of them treated the Namasudras as Chandal, which had been the lowest status in terms of Hindu caste hierarchy.

This community of Bengal did not belong to any exact socio-occupational caste. They were of various occupations including cultivation, carpentry, fishing and boat-making. Most of them had been in agricultural work since time immemorial, and they were anthropologically similar to the Brahman, Vaidya and Kayastha of Bengal. Hence, it is rational to call them a peasant community. The imposition of Chandal on them was nothing but the effect of the social conflicts that took place between the Buddhists and the Brahmans of Bengal in medieval times. For this social conflict, many social changes took place in the social history of Bengal.

Though the caste system was not so rigid in Bengal the Hindu social leaders and authorities of Bengal, since the reign of Sen Rule, had been trying to involve the Namasudras in the manual work. They applied the caste restrictions on them and made several social rules and regulations for domination. Hence, the caste restrictions and social injustice led the Namasudras to remain backward for centuries. The privileged castes of Bengal initiated such social laws and orders for safeguard of their privileges.

The privileged Hindus did not allow the underprivileged castes to receive advantages of education, cultural ceremonies and conventional occupations. The backward Hindus were exploited religiously, socio-economically and politically for centuries under the caste laws and orders. Consequently, the Namasudras could not be benefited from the process of modernization. They remained uneducated and unconscious for centuries for the social plan of the privileged castes. This plan deprived the Namasudras of sharing wealth and rights to society. They had no scope of using any weapons against the privileged castes or applying political power for social change. During the reigns of Sen, Sultanate, Mughal and British rule, the Brahman, Vaidya and Kayasthas of Bengal occupied the socio-economic opportunities. They influenced the anthropological and social survey of the British ruler for safeguarding the interests of the Hindu gentries.

According to the words of the Hindu gentries, the colonial census authority depicted the community's name of Namasudras as Chandal in 1872, instead of Namasudra. The Namasudras believed that the Hindu gentry intentionally provided such information to the British to keep them under social stigmas to serve their purpose of social domination over the backward Hindus. It was about the same time when Harichand Thakur, the popular socio-religious leader of the Namasudras initiated protest movements against social injustice in Bengal. Hence, the Namasudra leaders initiated a protest movement against the humiliating activities of the upper castes. They took an initiative to protest not only the dominative activities of the privileged Hindus but also all the social injustices in the society.

The British rulers opened the door of education through their missionaries for all social groups irrespective of caste and creed due to their purpose of getting educated Indian officials for their administrative and manual work. They unlocked not only the door of education but also initiated a liberal social system which led the deprived castes to participate in all kinds of socio-economic, occupational and political activities. In colonial times, they were encouraged to shift their occupation from agriculture, carpentry, fishing and boat making to the modern profession of teaching, medicine, business etc. with the effect of education which had been introduced by the colonial ruler and through their missionaries. A socio-cultural and educational revolution took place among the backward Hindus of Bengal after the arrival of the missionaries and the beginning of colonial rule. The Namasudras of Bengal were encouraged to break all the restrictions imposed on them. They began to violate the guru system of Brahmanism and protest against caste discrimination, prohibition of temple entry. Their social leaders initiated a new socio-cultural ideology according to the guidelines of their social leaders who followed the liberal social values launched by the missionaries avoiding the traditional orthodox social orders.

Harichand Thakur was the first social revolutionary leader among the Namasudras who, initiating Matuaism, led the Namasudras to move against social injustices, in the 1870s. It was a new socio-religious ideology followed by most of the Namasudras and some other backward Hindus of Bengal. He, for the first time, felt the necessity of a liberal religious ideology for the backward Hindus who were targeted to convert to Islam. Harichand saved them from the exploitation of the privileged castes and separated them from the discriminatory social system of Hinduism. He even avoided the liberal Vaishnavism due to its restrictive system of prayer and the injunction for the breaking of family ties to obtain personal salvation. Hence, he founded such a religious sect in Hinduism which could serve them both the spiritual salvation and socio-economic relief through a simplistic way of life in village society. He termed it as religion within the household where the devotees could carry on their ordinary activities in the family remembering and uttering god's name for spiritual aspiration.

All the Namasudras, before the arrival of this great social reformer, used to follow the Hindu social laws and orders. They abided by all the rules and regulations of the Hindu caste system. Though they observed Sasti Puja (birth rites), Annaprasan (initiation of rice meal), marriage ceremony and Shraddha (rites following the death) in the same way as the Brahman. But they were considered untouchables. Nevertheless, untouchability was not rigid in Bengal like the other states of India. So, the movement against untouchability was rarely seen in Bengal. Only there was a movement for social justice and equality. The Namasudras never considered themselves untouchable or socially backwards. Rather they avoided the foods and touch of Muslims, foreigners and castes other than their own due to presence of caste rule in the society before their religious movement took place.

After this movement, most of the Namasudras followed the socio-religious principles of Matuaism and the liberal values of missionaries overriding the social order of the caste system. They refused cooperation with the Hindu gentry, and protested against the process of social stigmatization, established schools for their children and reformed orthodox social laws and orders. They arranged several conferences and ceremonies for consciousness about social injustices. They successfully mobilized their people to accept the revolutionary reforms regarding child marriage, widow marriage, sati system, girl's education and the like.

Though their social leaders were able to move the backward Hindus, mostly Namasudras, against the orthodox social laws and order, they had to face several difficulties in the implementation of their reforms due to the lack of political power. So their leaders, like Guruchand Thakur, for the first time, encouraged participation in politics to share administrative power. They played an influential role in the nationalist movements to protest against social injustices. They disagreed with the Congress in the *Swadeshi* movement and supported the British for social protest. They decided to oppose those leaders who supported the caste restriction which was the main obstruction before the Namasudras to be uplifted. They appeared in politics for playing the role of the opponents of mainstream politics. They contested in elections not for sharing political power but for getting the right to live equally in society.

Though they could not make their mark in the elections of 1923 and 1937, but from 1946 they played an important role in creating consciousness of the backward Hindus by winning in some reserved seats in Bengal. This victory was very significant for the future and fortune of the backward Indians as without it Ambedkar could not have been able to become a member of the Constituent Assembly of India, and he would not have been able to inscribe his thoughts, for the backwards, in the Constitution which provided legal support to get the rights for the backwards.

But they could not influence the decision making on Partition of India. Being a marginal community they had to countenance the impact of partition as they had to segregate and disperse in different parts of Indian provinces. They faced not only the problem of segregation but also the loss of thousands of lives, wealth due to communal riots which took place for Partition. The privileged Hindus of eastern Bengal migrated to West Bengal during and immediately after the partition and received proper rehabilitation and opportunities with the help of their fellow castes but the backward and unconscious Namasudras were neither able to migrate immediately nor could they get the proper rehabilitation in West Bengal, due to the mismanagement and ignorance of the Hindu dominated Congress High command. The unconscious Namasudras crossed Indian border when they were forcefully uprooted by the Muslim hooligans. But the Congress High command neither allowed them in exchange for population nor permitted them to get rehabilitated in West Bengal.

The caste conflict between the Congress and deprived castes and difficulties of additional rehabilitation in West Bengal were two of the main reasons behind the policy of ignorance of the Congress high command. The Nehru government was sympathetic for the minorities of West Pakistan but indifferent for the minorities of East Pakistan due to the caste factors. The backward Hindu refugees were the supporters of the Communists which led the Congress high command to oppose the rehabilitation of the refugees in West Bengal. Consequently, the Namasudras and other backward Hindus who crossed the border late were dispersed outside of West Bengal. On the other hand, the leftist leaders, who were at the helm of political affairs in West Bengal in 1977, dishonoured their promises. They had promised to arrange for their rehabilitation. But once in power they went back on their promises and mercilessly directed the police force to stop the rehabilitation of the Namasudras in West Bengal.

The police force did not hesitate to fire in the huts of refugees and to conduct the massacre of Marichjhapi killing thousands of Namasudras who humbly requested the government only for allowing them to live in the vacant Islands beside Sundarban. They did not demand anything except permission but the then Jyoti Basu government was bent upon dispersing them to avoid further hazards regarding the rehabilitation of the backward Hindus. The island was forcibly evacuated of the refugees by the police. The Jyoti Basu government feared that more refugees from Dandakaranya would arrive in West Bengal demanding rehabilitation which would be an extra headache for the government. So the government did not hesitate to take action to force the backward Hindu refugees to evacuate the island of Marichjhapi.

The Namasudra refugees faced a lot of suffering due to the crisis of proper rehabilitation and the problem of citizenship in the divided country. They were neither able to live in their birth place due to the hooliganism of Muslims nor get proper rehabilitation in India. They had lost their social unity due to segregation of their population after partition so their protest movement against the social humiliation and injustices and anti-refugee policy suffered a decline after partition. Most of them were rehabilitated in the infertile land of Dandakaranya where they found little opportunity for survival.

The Namasudras refugees in Assam suffered from citizenship difficulties. The Namasudras in Andaman Island and in Nainital of Uttarakhand suffered from socio-cultural problems as they detached from their main folk. Thus they are deprived of various socio-cultural opportunities due to their dispersion to various places of the country. They were deprived of SC status in the State of Madhya Pradesh, Chhattisgarh, and Uttarakhand. They could not get opportunities of reservation in the government jobs and education and contest in elections as a reserved candidate.

The backward Hindu refugees who migrated after March 31, 1971, had not been given the right to citizenship and rehabilitation. The then central government attempted to push back these refugees denying their responsibility for the survival of the minority Hindus who were uprooted forcefully from Islamic Bangladesh. They never went back to their home as they knew that they would be killed if they went back home. So these refugees have been struggling to survive, living in uncertain conditions in a temporary shelter in unexpected places of West Bengal and other Indian provinces without proper identity and security. The then Indian government has hardly taken any step to solve the problem; rather a citizenship Amendment Bill was passed in 2003 to alert the refugees, who migrated after March 31, 1971, to go back. The BJP government has passed the CAA (December 11, 2019) for solving the citizenship problem but till now it has been under the debate and protest movement of the opposition.

On the other hand, many members of the Matua Mahasangha, with its 6755 branches all over India, have organized several movements for the right to citizenship and for a safeguard to the Hindu refugees who have been dispersed in different parts of India. The success of their movement depends on the mood of the political leaders who sought the support of the average voters in the country.

Select Bibliography

Primary Sources

(A) Printed Official Publications, Census Reports

Census of India, 1901, Volume V, Part-I, Bengal, Bihar, Orissa, (Calcutta, Central Publication Branch, 1932).

Census of India, 1911, Volume V, Part-I, Bengal.

Census of India, 1921, Volume V, Part-I, Bengal.

Census of India, 1931, Volume V, Part-I, Bengal.

Census of India, General, 1952.

Census of India, General, 1957.

Census of India, General, 1962.

Census of India, General 1967.

Census of India, General 1972.

Government of Bengal, *Assembly Proceedings,* Volume LXIV.

Legislative Department, *Records and Reforms Branch* Files.

Report on Administration of Bengal, 1924-1934, Calcutta.

(B) Bengal District Gazetteers

Bengal District Gazetteers, B, Volume for the District of Bakarganj (1891)

Bengal District Gazetteers, Khulna, by L.S.S. O'Malley (Calcutta, 1908)

Bengal District Gazetteers, Jessore, by L.S.S. O'Malley (Calcutta, 1912)

Bengal District Gazetteers, Bakarganj, by J. C. Jack (Calcutta, 1918)

(C) News Papers

Amrita Bazar Patrika

Ananda Bazar Patrika

Bartaman

Sanbad Pratidin

The Hindustan Times

The Statesman

The Telegraph

The Times of India

(D) Journals

Bengali

'Ananta Bijoy', 1940, Mahananda Halder (ed.): Bagerhat, Khulna

'Joydanka', 1979, Ramendranath Biswas (ed.): Ramnagar, Nadia

'Thakurnagar', 1947-1950, Nitai Chand Mandal(ed.): Thakurnagar, North 24 Parganas

'Matua Darpan', 2005-2015, Santosh Kumer Barui (ed.): Durgapur, Burdwan

'Matua', 1978, Akshay Kumar Mallick (ed.), Majhdiya, Nadia

'Namasudra Suhrid', 1907-1922, Aditya Choudhury (ed.): Orakandi, Faridpur

English

The Quarterly Review of Historical Studies, Volumes LV-No., 1, 2, 3, 4, (2015-2016) (Chittabrata Palit (ed): Kolkata

The Quarterly Review of Historical Studies, Volumes LII, No., 1,2,3,4, (2013-2014) (Dilip koomar Ghose (ed.): Kolkata

The Quarterly Review of Historical Studies, Volumes LIV, No. 1, 2, 3, 4, (2014-2015) (Nimai Chandra Saha(ed.): Kolkata)

The Economic and Political Weekly

(E) Reports and Survey Records

Hunter, W. W: *Annals of Rural Bengal,* (London, Smith, Elder and Co.1868). *Statistical Account of Bengal,* 20 Vols., (London, Trubner & Co., 1875-77), Reprinted in India, (New Delhi, Concept Publishing Company, 1984).

Wise James: *Notes on the Races, Castes and Trades of Eastern Bengal,* (London. Publisher not Known, 1883 *West Bengal District Gazetteers,* Government of West Bengal, Calcutta

Secondary Sources

(A) Books

English

Ajad, M.A.K.: *India Wins Freedom,* (New Delhi, Orient Longman, 1978).

Ambedkar, B.R.: *Annihilation of Caste: with an Introduction by Arundhuti Roy,* (Jaipur, Navayana Publishing Pvt. Ltd. 2014). *Annihilation of Caste,* (New Delhi: Critica Quest, 1937/ 2007)

Ahuja, Ram: *Indian Social System*. (Jaipur, Rawat Publication, 1993).

——, *Society in India: Concepts, Theories and Recent Trends*, (Jaipur, Rawat Publication, 1999/2015).

Bailey, F.G: *Tribe, Caste and Nation*. (Bombay, Oxford University Press 1960).

Bandyopadhyay, S. (ed.): *Bengal: Rethinking History; Essays in Historiography*. (New Delhi, Manohar, 2001).

Bandyopadhyay. *S: Caste, Politics and the Raj*, Bengal 1872-1937. (Kolkata, K. P. Bagchi & Company, 1990).

Bandyopadhyay, S.: *Caste, Protest and Identity in Colonial India; The Namasudras of Bengal, 1872-1947*, (New Delhi: Oxford University Press, 2011).

——, *Caste, Culture and Hegemony: Social Dominance in Colonial Bengal*, (New Delhi, Sage Publication, 2004).

Barman, Rup Kumar: *Partition and Its impact on Scheduled Castes of Bengal* (New Delhi, Abhijeet Publication, 2012),

——, *Contested Regionalism: A Look at the History, Cultural Change and Regionalism in North Bengal and Lower Assam*, (Delhi, Abhijeet Publication, 2012).

Bayly Susan: *Caste, Society and Politics in India*, (New York, Cambridge University Press, 1999).

Berreman Gerald D: *Hindus of Himalayas: Ethnography and Change* (Berkeley, University of California Press, 1963).

Beteille Andre: *Caste, Class and Power: Changing Pattern of Stratification in a Tanjore Village*, (Bombay and others: Oxford University Press 1996).

——, *Society and politics in India: Essays in a comparative perspective*, (New Delhi, Oxford University Press 1992).

——, *Castes: Old and New Essays in social structure and social stratification*, (Bombay: Asian Publication House, 1969).

Biswas, Ratan Kumar: *Namasudra Movement in Bengal* (Kolkata, Progress Book Forum)

Bose, N.K.: *The Structure of Hindu Society*. Translated with an introduction and notes by Andre Beteille (New Delhi, Orient Longman, 1975).

Channa, Subhadra Mitra: *Life as a Dalit*, (New Delhi, Sage Publications, 2013).

Chatterjee, Debi: *Ideas and Movements against Caste in India*, (Delhi, Abhijeet Publications, 1998).

Chatterjee, Joya: *The Spoils of Partition: Bengal and India, 1947-1967*, (New Delhi Cambridge University Press, 2007).

Chakraborty, Prafulla Kumar: *The Marginal Men* (Kolkata, Naya Udyag, 1999).

Chaudhury, Nirad C. and others: *The Hinduism Omnibus*, with an introduction by T.N. Madan. (New Delhi, Oxford University Press, 2003).

Despande, Satish (ed): The Problem of Caste, *Essays from Economic and Political Weekly* (New Delhi, Orient Black Swan. 2014).

Desai, A.R.: Social Background of Indian Nationalism. (Mumbai: Popular Prakashan, 1948/2000).

Despande, Satish (ed): The Problem of Caste, *Essays from Economic and Political Weekly*, (New Delhi, Orient Black Swan. 2014).

Dubois, Abbe J. A. and Beauchamp Henry K: *Hindu Manners, Customs and Ceremonies: General View of Society in India and general Remarks on the caste system*, 3rd edition, (Oxford University Press, 1906).

Dube, S.C: *The Indian Village*, (London, Routledge and Kegan Paul, 1955).

Dumont, Luis: *Homo Hierarchicus: The Caste System and Its Implications*, (Delhi, Oxford India, Paperbacks, 1970/1998).

Dutta, N.K.: Origin and Growth of Caste in India (Vol. II, *Castes in Bengal*) (Calcutta, Firma K.L Mukhopadhyay, 1931/1969).

Drinks, Nicholas B: *Caste of Mind: Colonialism and the Making of Modern India,* (Permanent Black, 2012).

Ghurye, G.S.: *Caste and Race in India,* 5th edition. (Bombay, Popular Prakashan, 1969).

Godbole, Madhav: *The Holocaust of Indian Partition: an Inquest,* (New Delhi, Rupa Publication, 2011).

Guha, Sumit: *Beyond Caste,* (New Delhi, Permanent Black, 2016).

Gupta Dipankar(ed.): *Social Stratification.* (New Delhi, Oxford University Press, 1991) Guha Ranajit (ed.): *Subaltern studies 1: Writings on South Asian History and Society.* (New York. Oxford University Press, 1982).

Gyanesh Kudaisya, Divided Landscape, Fragmented identities: East Bengal Refugees and Rehabilitation in India, 1947-79, in Howard D. A Low & Brasted (ed.): *Northern India and Independence,* (New Delhi, Sage Publication).

Howard D. A Low & Brasted (ed.): *Northern India and Independence,* (New Delhi, Sage Publication).

Halder Deep, *Blood Island: An Oral History of the Marichjhapi Massacre* (Noida, HarperCollins Publishers India, 2019).

Hutton J. H: *Caste in India,* 4th edition. (London, Oxford University Press, 1946/1963).

Jaiswal, Suvira: *Caste: Origin, Function and Dimensions of Change,* (New Delhi, Manohar Publishers 1998).

Jodhka, Surinder S.: *Caste: Oxford India Short Introduction,* (New Delhi, Oxford University Press, 2012).

Kothari, R.: *Caste in Indian Politics,* (New Delhi, Orient Black Swan, 1970).

Kumar, Raj: *Dalit Personal Narratives*, (New Delhi, Orient Black Swan 2010).

Karve, Irawati: *Kinship Organization in India*, (Bombay. Asia Publishing House, 1965).

Mitra, Hirendranath: *Banglar Loke- Utsav O Loke- Shilpa*, (Kolkata, Bangio Sahitya Parisad, 2007).

Mandal, Monika: *Settling the Unsettled: A Study of Partition Refugees in West Bengal*, (New Delhi, Manohar, 2001).

Majumdar, R.C. (ed): *The Vedic Age: The History and culture of Indian People* (Bombay, Bharatiya Vidya Bhavan, 1951).

Majumdar, R.C.: *History of Modern Bengal, 1905-1947*, (Calcutta, Tulsi Prakasoni, 2006).

Mukhopadhyay Apurba: *Postcolonial Democracy in India*, (Kolkata, Setu Prakashani 2013) Muir John: Original Sanskrit Text, Part 1: *Mythical and Legendary Account of the Origin of Caste, with an Enquiry into its Existence in the Vedic age*, (Delhi, Oriental Publisher, 1972).

O'Hanlon, Rosalind: *Caste, Conflict and Ideology*, (New Delhi, Cambridge University Press, 1985/2014).

O'Malley, L.S.S.: *India's Social Heritage*,(New Delhi, Bikash Publishing House Pvt. Ltd. 1934).

Omvedt, Gail: *Dalit and the Democratic Revolution: Dr Ambedkar and the Dalit Movement in Colonial India*, (New Delhi, Sage Publications 1994).

——, *Seeking Begampura: The Social Vision of Anti-caste Intellectuals*, (New Delhi, Navayana, 2008).

O'Leary Zina: The Essential Guide to Doing Your Research Project, (New Delhi Sage, 2010).

Pai, Sudha: *Revisiting 1956-B.R Ambedkar and state Reorganisation*, (New Delhi, Orient Black Swan, 2014).

Rao, Anupama: *The Caste Question, Dalit and The Politics of Modern India* (New Delhi, Permanent Black, 2009).

Rawat, Ramnarayan, S & K. Satyanarayan (ed): *Dalit Studies* (New Delhi, Permanent Black, 2016).

Ray, Niharranjan, *'Bangalir Itihas : adi parva'*, (Kolkata: Dey's Publishing, 1993).

Ray Niharranjan: *Bharater Itihas Jijnasa,* (Kolkata, Dey's Publishing, 2003).

Risley, H.H: *Tribes and Castes of Bengal,* vol. 1&II. (Kolkata: Firma KLM Private Ltd., 1891/2014).

Rice, Stanly: *Origin of Hindu Customs*. (New Delhi, Universal Voice, 1937).

Rodrigues, Valerian (ed.): *The Essential Writings of B.R Ambedkar,* (New Delhi, Oxford University Press).

Saha, Ghanashyam (ed.): *Caste and Democratic Politics in India*. (New Delhi, Permanent Black 2002).

Sanyal, Hitesh Ranjan: *Social Mobility in Bengal,* (Kolkata, Papyrus, 1981).

Sarkar, Sumit and Tanika Sarkar (ed): *Caste in Modern India,* (New Delhi: Permanent Black, 2014).

Shepherd, K.I., Karuppusamy, K.R. (eds): *The Shudras Vision for a New Path* (Haryana, Penguin Random House India, 2021).

Sen, Kshitimohan: *'Hindu Dharma'*. Translated by Soumendra Nath Bhattacharya. Calcutta: Pelican Books Ltd, 1961/2012).

Sen, Ranjit: *Caste, Class and the Raj: A Study of the Bengali society in transition in the Colonial Age,* (Calcutta: Progressive Publishers, 2000).

Sengupta, Sankar: *A Study of Women of Bengal,* (Calcutta, Indian Publication 1970).

——, *Folklore of Bengal: A Projected Study,* (Calcutta, Indian Publications, 1976)

Sengupta, Nitish: *History of Bengali Speaking People,* (Delhi, Rajkamal Electric Press, 2003).

Shah, Ghanshyam: *Social Movement of India, A Review of Literature,* (New Delhi, Sage Publication, 2004).

Singha, Sankar Prasad: *Towards Social Change,* (New Delhi, Orient Black Swan, 2014).

Srinivas, M.N.: *Social Change in Modern India,* (New Delhi, Orient Longman, 1966).

——, *On Living a Revolution and other Essays,* (Calcutta, Oxford University Press, 1992).

Srinivas, M.N.: *The Oxford Srinivas, With an Introduction by Ramchandra Guha,* (New Delhi, Oxford University Press, 2009).

Talbot, Ian: *Partition of India* (New Delhi: Cambridge University Press 2009).

Tripathi, Amales: *Indian National Congress and the Struggle for Freedom, 1885-1947.* Translated by Amitava Tripathi (New Delhi, Oxford University Press, 2014).

Wiser, William Hendricks: *The Hindu Jajmani System,* (Lucknow, Publication House, 1958).

Wiser. William & Charlotte: *Behind Mud Walls: 1930-1960.* (London, University of California Press, 1963).

Bengali

Bhadra, Goutam (ed.): *Nimnabarger Itihas,* (Calcutta, Ananda, 1998)

Bagchi, Jatin; *Jati Dharma O Samaj Bibartan,* (Kolkata, Sanjib Prakashan, 1990).

Bhattacharya, Ramkrishna: *Bangabhanga, Swadeshi, Biplabbad* (Kolkata, K.P. Bagchi and Co. 2016).

Banerjee, Sasanka S: *Bharat Mujibar Rahaman, Bangladesher Swadhinata o Pakistan,* (Sanchita, Bangladesh, 2013).

Bandyopadhyay, Atin: *Nilkantha Pakhir Khoje,* (Kolkata, Karuna Prakashani, 1971).

Bandyopadhyay, Sandip: *Desbhag,* (Kolkata, Progressive Publisher, 1999).

Bandyopadhyay, Hiranmoy: *Udbastu,* (Kolkata, Dip Prakashan, 1970/2013).

Bandyopadhyay, Nirmal(ed.): *Ramjanmabhumi- Babrimasjid Bitarka,* (Kolkata, Kristi, 2010).

Basu, Lokeswar: *Amader Padabir Itihas,* (Kolkata, Ananda, 1981).

Basu, Shamaprasad: *Jawaharlal Nehru,* (Kolkata, Dey's Publishing, 2012).

Basu Jogiraj: *Veder Parichay,* (Kolkata, Firma KLM Private Limited, 1983).

Basu, Asis Kumar: *Rabindranather Samaj o Rashtra Bhabna,* (Kolkata, Avenel Press, 2013).

Bepari, Manoranjan: *Itibritte Chandal Jiban,* Vol. I, (Kolkata, Kolkata Prakashan, 2012).

Bhattacharya, Ramkrishna: *Banga Bhanga: Swadeshi: Biplab Bad,* (Kolkata, KP Bagchi & Company, 2016).

Biswas, Kalipada: *Jukta Banglar Sesh Adhayay,* (Kolkata Naya Udyog, 2012).

Biswas, Manosanto: *Banglar Matua Andolan: Samaj Sanskriti Rajniti,* (Kolkata, Setu Prakashani, 2016).

Bose, N.K.: *Hindu Samajer Gadan,* (Kolkata, Loksiksha Granthamala, 1949).

Brahma, A.K.: *Bangalijatir Utsha sandhane,* (Kolkata, Gyanpith Publication, 2010).

Byapari, Manaranjan: *Itibrittante Chandal Jiban,* (Kolkata, Kolkata Prakashan, 2012).

Chattopadhyay, Bhabani Prashad: *Des Bibhag,* (Kolkata, Ananda, 1993/2013).

Chakraborty, Pafulla Kumer: *Prantik Manab: Paschim Bange Udbastu Jibaner Katha,* (Kolkata, Deep, Prakashan, 1997/ 2013).

Chakraborty, Soumen: *Udbastu Satway Bangali,* (Kolkata, Muktaman, 1912).

Chakraborty, Sourish: *Bharatiya Padabir Abhidhan,* (Kolkata, Ananda, 2012).

Chattopadhyay, *Saktinath: Rabindranather Visva Bhabna,* (Kolkata Manon Prakashan, 2012).

Chakraborty, Ashok Chandra: *Banglar Itihasher Bichitra Kahini,* (Kolkata, Manon Prakashan, 2012).

Choudhury Kamol: *Banglar Itihas,* (Kolkata, Dey's Publishing, 2006).

Choudhury Kamol: *Brihatara Bakherganjer Itihas,* (Kolkata, Dey's Publishing, 2002).

Choudhury, Nirad Chandra: *Atmaghati Bangali,* (Kolkata, Mitra o Ghosh, 1988).

Das, Naresh Chandra: *Namasudra Samproday o Bangladesh* (Kolkata, Dipali Book House, 1997).

Das, Narahari: *Jatitatta O Upadhimala,* (Kolkata, Nabapatra Prakashan, 2010).

Debnath Mrinal Kanti: *Jehad O Udbastu Chhele* (Kolkata, Book Bazar, 2008).

Dey, Amalendu: *Pakistan Prastab O Fajlul Huq* (Kolkata, Parul, 2014).

Dutta, Bhupendranath: *Banglar Itihas,* (Kolkata, Chirayata Prakashan, 2014).

Gangopadhyay, Sunil: *Purba Paschim,* (Kolkata, 1989).

Ghosh Semanti (ed): *Des Bhag Smriti ar Stabdhata* (Kolkata Gangchil, 2014).

Ghoshal Jayanta: *Rajnaitik Asahishnuta Ebang* (Kolkata Deep Prakashan, 2016).

Greenough, Paul: *Adhunik Bangla- Samriddhi O Daridra* (Kolkata K.P. Bagchi and Co., 1997).

Haldar, Acharya Mahananda: *Sri Sri Guruchand Charit*, (Thakurnagar: Resolution, 1943/2009)

Haldar Sudhir Ranjan: *Itihaser Prekshapate Dandyakarany O Marichjhapi*, (Nadia, Kamala Publisher, 2008).

Mandal, Jagadish Chandra: *Mahapran Jogendranath*, Vol. I&II. (Calcutta: Chaturtha Dunia, 1382 BS).

Murshid, Ghulam: *Hajar Bachharer Bangla Sanskriti*, (Dhaka, Abosar, 2006).

Mukhopadhyay, Subodh Kumar: *Prak Palasy Bangla* (Kolkata, K.P. Bagchi and Co. 1982).

Pal, Babul Kumer: *Barishal Theke Dandyakaranya*, (Kolkata, Mitram, 2010).

Ray, Niharranjan: *Bangalir Itihas: Adi Parva*, (Kolkata, Dey's Publishing, 1993).

Ray, Rasbehari: *Saral Namasudra Dvija Darpan*, (Khulna, Publisher not Known, BS 1321).

Roy, Debes: *Barishaler Jogen Mandal* (Kolkata, Dey's Publishing, 2010).

Roychoudhury, Tapan: Prabanda Sangraha, (Calcutta, Ananda, 2009).

Sarkar, Tarak Chandra: *Sri Sri Hari Lilamrta*, (Thakurnagar, Modern Press, 2010).

Sarkar, Probhatranjan: *Bangla o Bangali*, volume I & II, (Kolkata, Ananda Printers, 1988).

Sen, Dinesh Chandra: *Purbabanga Gitika*, volumes. III & IV combined, (Kolkata: Dey's Publishing, 2009).

——, *Brihat Banga*, in two volumes, (Calcutta: Dey's Publishing, 1935).

Sen, Kshitimohan: *'Hindu Dharma'*, Translated by Soumendra Nath Bhattacharya, (Calcutta: Pelican Books Ltd., 1961/2012).

Sen, Sukomol: *Bharoter Sobhyata O Samaj Bikase Dharma O Jatibhed*, (Kolkata, National Book Agency Pvt. Ltd., 1992).

Sen, Dinesh Chandra: *Purbabanga Gitika*, volumes. I & II, (Kolkata: Dey's publishing, 2009).

Sen, Sujit: *Jatpat o Sanrakshan, Bharatiya Prekshapat*, (Kolkata, Granthamitra, 2008).

Sen, Sujit (ed.): *Bisaya Sampradayikta, Phire Dekha*, (Kolkata, Mitram, 2008).

Sur, Atul: Bharater Nritattwik Parichay, (Kolkata, Sahityalok, 1988).

Sharma, Ramsaran: *Aryader Bharate Agaman*, (Kolkata, Orient Black Swan, 2008).

Thakur Sri Sri Promothranjan: *Atmacharitra ba Purbasmriti*, (Thakurnagar: Binapani Press, 1995).

Thakur Abanindranath: *Banglar Brata*, (Kolkata, Gangchil, 2013).

(B) Articles in Journals

Barman, R.K.: From ethnographic subject to 'Self– Respect' Movement: The Scheduled Caste of Colonial Bengal in Historiographical Perspective, in Saha Nimai Chandra(ed), *The Quarterly Review of Historical Studies*, (Kolkata, Institution of Historical Studies, October 2014-March 2015).

Mondal, R.: Gender Inequality and Attitude in Colonial Bengal: An overview on Namasudra Women, in S., Battacharya(ed), *Interdisciplinary Journal of Science and Humanity, Vol. 1*, pp. 54-60, ISSN: 2348-38222, (Burdwan: Dr B. N.S. Mahavidyalaya, 2014).

Mondal, R.: A Struggle for Mass Education: The Contribution of Hari-Guruchand in Colonial Bengal, in S, Bhattacharya (ed.), *Interdisciplinary Journal of science and Humanity*, Vol. 2, ISSN: 2348-38224 (Burdwan: Dr. B. N. S. Mahavidyalaya, 2015)

Mondal, R.: A Struggle for Religious Freedom: The Contribution of Hari-Guruchand in Colonial Bengal, in Dr. K.M. Mohasin and others (ed), *Itihas Prabandamala*, vol. 16. No. 15, pp. 383-390, ISSN: 2074-86634. (Dhaka, Itihas Academy, 2019).

Mondal, R.: The tradition of caste and social position of the Namasudras in Bengal, in Dr. N. Phukan (ed), *International Review of Social science and humanities*, vol. 9, No. 7, pp. 369-378, ISSN-2250-0715/2248-9010(O) (Assam July, 2019).

Mondal, R. Colonial impact on social belief system in backward Hindus: The Socio-religious Changes in Namasudra community in Bengal, in Dr. N. Phukan (ed), *International Review of Social science and Humanities*, vol. 9, No. 7, Assam, pp.337-345 ISSN: 2250-0715/ 2248-9010(O), (Assam, Aug., 2019).

Articles in Books

Mandal R.: "Matua Biswase Narir Obosthan", in Biwas Kapil Krishna (ed), *Sri Harichand Thakur O Matua Dharma Andalan* (Kolkata, Nikhil Bhara Prakashani, 2012).

Mondal, R.: "Casteism, Colonialism and Reformism: A Study of Namasudra Women Empowerment in Bengal", in P. K. Kuri, & S. T. Nasreen (eds), *Women, Society and Development*, Burdwan: UGC, ASC, B. U, 2013).

Mondal, R.: "Politics and Refugees Problems in India, in Ghosh Snehasis & Ghosh", Sampa (ed): *Bibhajita Banglay Udbastu Samasya O Bangla Sahite Tar Prabhab*, (Kolkata, Sribhumi Publishing House, 2014).

Mondal, R.: "Matua Movement and Women of Backward Classes: Bengal, 19th & 20th Century", in R.M. Azimbor (ed), *Women and Society in Colonial India*, (Burdwan, 2015).

Mondal, R.: "Ambedkar: Varna Baisamya O Asprisyatar Biruddhe Sangram", in D., Ghosh (ed) *Samaj Biplabi Ambedkar: Jiban O Sadhana*, (Kolkata: Parul, 2016).

Mondal, R.: "Rituals, Prejudice and Protest in Colonial Times: An Overview of the Namasudra- Movement in Bengal", in J Sarkhel & A. Banerjee (ed), *History Heritage and Religion: Problems and Perspectives*, (Kolkata, Book Syndicate (p) Ltd., 2020).

Mondal, R.: "Casteism and Indian National Integration", in Subhasis Chakroborty(ed), *The Spirit of Nationalism: Development of Modern India*, pp.147-155 (Rupali, Kolkata, 2020).

Mondal, R.: "Social Media on Dalit of India, in Dr. Abdul Matin and others" (eds) *Sociology of Social Media* (Delhi, ABS Books, 2021).

Palit Chittabrata: "Pangs of Partition: Dr B. C. Roy on the Refugee Problem in Bengal", in Ghosh Snehasis & Ghosh, Sampa (ed): *Bibhajita Banglay Udbastu Samasya O Bangla Sahit Tar Prabhab* (Kolkata, Sribhumi Publishing House, 2014).

Roy Prohlad: "Bipanna Jal, Bipanna Jati", in Roy Prohlad & Dutta Abhisek (ed), *Expression: Education, Literature and Society* (Solapur, Lakshmi Books Publication, 2013).

Appendices

Namasudra Population from 1872 to 1971

Year	*Namasudra population in united Bengal*	*Namasudra population in West Bengal*	*Namasudra population in East Bengal*	*Ratio of Namasudra population*	
				East Bengal	*West Bengal*
1872	1503518	201745	1301773	86.58	13.41
1881	1576076	168872	1407204	89.28	10.17
1891	1768119	195353	1572766	88.98	11.04
1901	1860914	174888	1686026	90.60	9.39
1911	1908718	1603304	1748424	91.60	8.39
1921	2006259	165027	1841232	91.77	8.23
1931	2094959	161804	1933155	92.27	7.72
1941	2150760	134748	2016012	93.73	6.27
1951		324723			
1961		729057			
1971		929075			

Source: J. H. E. Garrett I C S: Bengal District Gazetteers, Nadia,1910: Sarat Chandra Biwas, *Namasudra Samprodayer atmakotha*, Srimali Computers, kolkata p.191

Hindu and Muslim Population in United Bengal

Year	*Muslim population*	*Hindu population*	*Difference*	*Remarks*
1872	17609135	18100438	491303	Hindu population is more than Muslims
1881	18394426	18071296	491303	The Muslim population is more than Hindus
1891	20174832	18978300	1196532	"
1901	21954955	20155674	1799281	"
1911	24237228	20948357	3288871	"
1921	25486124	20812526	4673598	"
1931	27810100	22212069	5598031	"
1941	33005434	20059024	7946410	"

Source: Census of Bengal, 1872, p. xxxii-xxxiii, Census of India, 1931, vol. v, Report Part 1, 387, Data of 1941: V. B. Kulkarni: *Is Pakistan Necessary?*, Hind Kitab, Bombay 1944, p. 67.

Refugees in West Bengal (up to 1958)

District	*No. of camps and Homes*	*Population in Camps and homes*	*No. of govt. colonies*	*Population in Govt. colonies*	*Refugees outsides camps and colonies*	*Total Refugee population*
Burdwan	30	43127	8	6895	108481	158503
Birbhum	17	17400	6	1775	4375	23550
Bankura	7	11165	2	50	4796	16011
Midnapur	11	16838	38	4390	22654	43882
Hoogly	11	18013	38	21580	65017	104610
Howrah	7	7779	16	7575	75781	91135
24 Parganas	45	43284	209	105345	714161	862790
Calcutta	7	5059			571555	576614
Nadia	7	53160	32	61640	539730	664530
Murshidabad	8	12709	21	9945	54443	76097
Maldah	—		12	2939	69004	72924
West Dinajpur	1	989	111	3865	158095	162959
Jalpaiguri	—	—	9	7850	142306	150156
Darjeeling	—	—	2	3375	26668	30043
Cooch Behar	1	1159	12	6550	222118	227827
Purulia	—	—	—		1332	1332
Total	152	240682	389	243765	2778506	3262952

Source: Government of West Bengal: Relief and Rehabilitation of Displaced Persons in West Bengal (1958), Joya Chatterjee: *The Spoil of Partition,* New Delhi Cambridge University Press, 2008) p. 134.

PHOTOGRAPHS

Photo 1: Sri Sri Harichand Thakur and Santimata

Photo 2: Rajarshi Sri Sri Guruchand Thakur

Photo 3: Sri Pramoth Ranjan Thakur

Photo 4: Sri Jogendra Nath Mandal

Photo 5: Sri Shantanu Thakur at a Rally for right to citizenship

Photo 6: Protest Rally by members of the Matua Mahasangha against NRC and NPR

হিন্দু উদ্বাস্তুদের নাগরিকত্বের দাবি, আন্দোলনে মতুয়ারা

নিজস্ব প্রতিনিধি, কলকাতা, ১৪ জানুয়ারি: বাঙালি হিন্দু উদ্বাস্তুদের নাগরিকত্ব এবং অন্য ছয় দফা দাবিতে সম্প্রতি কলকাতার রানি রাসমণি রোডে এক সমাবেশ হয় সারা ভারত মতুয়া মহাসংঘের উদ্যোগে। এই সমাবেশে উপস্থিত ছিলেন মতুয়াদের বড় মা বীণাপাণি ঠাকুর এবং সংঘাধিপতি মমতা ঠাকুর। রাজ্যের বিভিন্ন জেলা থেকে ১০ হাজারেরও বেশি উদ্বাস্তু মানুষ এই সমাবেশে উপস্থিত হন। মতুয়া মহাসংঘের সহ সভাপতি ও মুখপাত্র সুকৃতিরঞ্জন বিশ্বাসের নেতৃত্বে এ দিন ৬ জনের এক প্রতিনিধি দল রাজভবনে গিয়ে রাজ্যপালের কাছে রাষ্ট্রপতি, প্রধানমন্ত্রী ও কেন্দ্রীয় স্বরাষ্ট্রমন্ত্রীর উদ্দেশে তিনটি আলাদা স্মারকলিপি দেন।

সূত্রের খবর অনুযায়ী, মতুয়াদের বড় মা অশীতিপর বীণাপাণি ঠাকুর ৯৫ বছর বয়সে অশক্ত শরীর নিয়ে প্রায় ৭৫ কিলোমিটার গাড়ি পাড়ি দিয়ে এসে উপস্থিত হন সমাবেশে। তিনি উপস্থিত জনতাকে উদ্দেশ্য আন্দোলন চালিয়ে যাওয়ার ডাক দেন। তিনি বলেন, যে মৃত্যুর আগে তিনি যেন দেখে যেতে পারেন মতুয়ারা ভারতের নাগরিকত্ব পেয়েছেন। এ প্রসঙ্গেই তিনি ভারতের আইনকে 'কালা আইন' বলে অভিহিত করে বলেন, জীবিত অবস্থায় তিনি দেখে যেতে চান ভারতের ওই আইন সংশোধন করা হয়েছে, যা মতুয়াদের দেশের নাগরিকত্ব পাওয়ার পথে অন্তরায় হয়ে দাঁড়িয়েছে। একই সঙ্গে মতুয়াদের সংঘাধিপতি, সাংসদ মমতা ঠাকুর এ দিন উদাত্ত কণ্ঠে মতুয়াদের নাগরিকত্বের দাবিতে আন্দোলন তীব্র থেকে তীব্রতর করে তোলার আহ্বান জানান। এরই সঙ্গে প্রতিশ্রুতি দেন যে, বিভিন্ন দলের বাঙালি সাংসদদের ঐক্যবদ্ধ করে তিনি মতুয়াদের নাগরিকত্বের দাবিতে লোকসভায় সরব হবেন। এই জনসভায় মতুয়াদের বিভিন্ন নেতৃবৃন্দ দাবি করেন, ২০০৪ সালের ৫ ডিসেম্বর রাষ্ট্রপতির স্বাক্ষর নিয়ে নাগরিকত্ব আইন কার্যকর হওয়ার মাত্র বারো দিন পর ২০০৪ সালের ১৫ ডিসেম্বর মতুয়া মহাসংঘ অনশন শুরু করে। কিন্তু তার পরেই তৎকালীন প্রধানমন্ত্রী মনমোহন সিং একজন সাংসদকে দূত হিসাবে পাঠান ও তাঁদের দিল্লি ডেকে নিয়ে বৈঠক করেন। তিনি অনশন তুলিয়েছেন। তৎকালীন প্রধানমন্ত্রী মনমোহন সিং তাঁদের সঙ্গে বৈঠকে বাঙালি উদ্বাস্তুদের নাগরিকত্বের সমস্যার সমাধানের জন্য প্রতিশ্রুতি দিয়েছিলেন। তারপরেও ৯ বছর মনমোহন প্রধানমন্ত্রীর পদে ছিলেন। কিন্তু সমস্যার সমাধান হয়নি। এ প্রসঙ্গে তাঁদের বক্তব্য, কেন্দ্র রাজ্য কোনও সরকারই তাঁদের এই সমস্যার সমাধান করেনি, হাজার প্রতিশ্রুতির পরেও।

এ দিনের সভায় তাঁরা ফের সেই দাবি তোলেন। তাঁদের দাবি মূলত স্থায়ী নাগরিকত্বের। এ ছাড়াও আরও ৬ দফা দাবিতেও সরব হয়েছেন তাঁরা। এ বিষয়ে ওই জনসভায় স্পষ্ট জানানো হয়েছে যে তা প্রয়োজনে চরম আন্দোলনের পথেও যেতে তাঁরা তৈরি।

Photo 7: Report of protest movement of Matuas for right to citizenship in Kolkata

Photo 8: Fast unto death by members of the Matua Mahasangha for right to citizenship

Index